# The quiet contemporary American novel

# Contemporary American And Canadian Writers

*Series Editors*
Nahem Yousaf and Sharon Monteith

*Also available*
**Making home: Orphanhood, kinship, and cultural memory in contemporary American novels** Maria Holmgren Troy, Elizabeth Kella, Helena Wahlstrom
**Thomas Pynchon** Simon Malpas and Andrew Taylor
**Jonathan Lethem** James Peacock
**Mark Z Danielewski** Edited by Joe Bray and Alison Gibbons
**Louise Erdrich** David Stirrup
**Passing into the present: contemporary American fiction of racial and gender passing** Sinéad Moynihan
**Paul Auster** Mark Brown
**Douglas Coupland** Andrew Tate
**Philip Roth** David Brauner

# The quiet contemporary American novel

Rachel Sykes

Manchester University Press

Copyright © Rachel Sykes 2018

The right of Rachel Sykes to be identified as the author of this work has been asserted by her in accordance with the Copyright, Designs and Patents Act 1988.

Published by Manchester University Press
Oxford Road, Manchester M13 9PL
www.manchesteruniversitypress.co.uk

*British Library Cataloguing-in-Publication Data is available*

ISBN 978 1 5261 0887 6 hardback
ISBN 978 1 5261 6361 5 paperback

First published by Manchester University Press in hardback 2018

This edition published 2022

The publisher has no responsibility for the persistence or accuracy of URLs for any external or third-party internet websites referred to in this book, and does not guarantee that any content on such websites is, or will remain, accurate or appropriate.

Typeset by Servis Filmsetting Ltd, Stockport, Cheshire

# Contents

| | |
|---|---|
| Series editors' foreword | vi |
| Acknowledgements | viii |
| Introduction | 1 |
| 1  The quiet novel | 14 |
| 2  '9/11' and the noise of contemporary fiction | 48 |
| 3  Quiet in time and narrative | 80 |
| 4  The quiet novel of cognition | 116 |
| 5  The novel of '(dis)quiet' | 151 |
| Conclusion | 190 |
| Bibliography | 196 |
| Index | 223 |

# Series editors' foreword

This innovative series reflects the breadth and diversity of writing over the last thirty years, and provides critical evaluations of established, emerging and critically neglected writers – mixing the canonical with the unexpected. It explores notions of the contemporary and analyses current and developing modes of representation with a focus on individual writers and their work. The series seeks to reflect both the growing body of academic research in the field, and the increasing prevalence of contemporary American and Canadian fiction on programmes of study in institutions of higher education around the world. Central to the series is a concern that each book should argue a stimulating thesis, rather than provide an introductory survey, and that each contemporary writer will be examined across the trajectory of their literary production. A variety of critical tools and literary and interdisciplinary approaches are encouraged to illuminate the ways in which a particular writer contributes to, and helps readers rethink, the North American literary and cultural landscape in a global context.

Central to debates about the field of contemporary fiction is its role in interrogating ideas of national exceptionalism and transnationalism. This series matches the multivocality of contemporary writing with wide-ranging and detailed analysis. Contributors examine the drama of the nation from the perspectives of writers who are members of established and new immigrant groups, writers who consider themselves on the nation's margins as well as those who chronicle middle America. National labels are the subject of vociferous debate and including American and Canadian writers in the same series is not to flatten the differences between them but to acknowledge that literary traditions and tensions are cross-cultural and that North American writers often explore and expose precisely these tensions.

The series recognises that situating a writer in a cultural context involves a multiplicity of influences, social and geo-political, artistic and theoretical, and that contemporary fiction defies easy categorisation. For example, it examines writers who invigorate the genres in which they have made their mark alongside writers whose aesthetic goal is to subvert the idea of genre altogether. The challenge of defining the roles of writers and assessing their reception by reading communities is central to the aims of the series.

Overall, *Contemporary American and Canadian Writers* aims to begin to represent something of the diversity of contemporary writing and seeks to engage students and scholars in stimulating debates about the contemporary and about fiction.

Nahem Yousaf<br>
Sharon Monteith

# Acknowledgements

This project was made possible by the Arts and Humanities Research Council who funded my research at the University of Nottingham. I would like to thank them and everyone at Nottingham's Arts Graduate Centre and the School of Cultures, Languages and Area Studies who provided invaluable training and support. The ideas in this book were shaped by the supervision and advice of Graham Thompson, who was always generous and encouraging, and Sharon Monteith, who has been my greatest critic and ally and without whom this book might not have been completed. My thanks, also, to Sarah Churchwell and Tony Hutchison for their thoughtful comments and to Nahem Yousaf for his support both of me and this project.

Many wonderful writers and editors have been kind enough to lend their advice and edits. Michael Wolfe and his colleagues at St. John's University published my first piece of academic work on '9/11', and Paul Harding, Emily St. John Mandel, Laura Stanhill and Andrew Ladd kindly answered my questions about quiet via email. Abridged versions of Chapter 2 and Chapter 3 appeared in *C21 Literature: journal of 21st-century writings* and *Critique: Studies in Contemporary Fiction* respectively; my thanks go to both editors. Finally, I must individually name the friends and colleagues who gave their time to long discussions and copy-edits: Katie McGettigan, Erin Greer, Maggie Deli, Jessica Lowry, Alice Lilly, Diletta De Cristofaro, Ben Pickford, Daniel King and Hannah Hawkins. To my family, James and David Link, Jenny Sykes, Rachel Elizabeth Williams and Rob Davy-Cripwell, and to Imogen and Heather who provide impetus and inspiration, always.

Eventlessness has no posts to drape duration on. From nothing to nothing is no time at all.

John Steinbeck, *East of Eden* (1952)

A much rarer gift – indeed, a most rare one – is the faculty of writing a *quiet* novel, whose interest does not depend upon these highly spiced and stimulating excitements. To write such a novel without lapsing into insipidity and tameness is one of the most difficult tests to which a writer of romance can be subjected, and to write one that will be successful with the public is a genuine triumph of art.

Henry Mills Alden, *Harper's New Monthly Magazine*<br>(November 1884)

# Introduction

Marilynne Robinson's epistolary novel *Gilead* (2004) opens in a moment of quiet. The text is a letter from the elderly Reverend John Ames to his six-year-old son, Robby, for whom Ames is writing a personal history and 'begats'.[1] Robinson's prose slows when Ames' final illness develops and it pauses when he pauses. Yet despite the primacy of the Reverend's voice, the novel begins with Ames' silence. 'You reached up', he writes at the end of the first page, addressing the young son sitting on his lap, 'and put your fingers on my lips and gave me that look [...] a kind of furious pride, very passionate and stern' (*G* 3). Robby's gesture may be small here, but it is rooted in a quiet that I argue is central to the development of *Gilead* and its partner novels *Home* (2008) and *Lila* (2014). By putting his fingers to his father's lips, Robby ends the need for speech and begins to communicate non-verbally, immersing father and son in a companionable and communicative quiet that lasts until the novel's final page. Their exchange is not silent, then, but quiet: a state better conceived as a mode of conversation than the complete absence of sound and an aesthetic of narrative that I argue Robinson develops in her fiction.

This book defines quiet as an aesthetic of narrative that is driven by reflective principles and places Robinson within a vibrant contemporary American trend. No definition yet exists of 'the quiet novel' and I use the term provocatively. At first appearance, 'quiet' is a contradictory description of any literary form. The novel, like all literature, facilitates discussion and the exchange of ideas to such an extent that any description of the form as quiet risks suggesting that the novelist has nothing to say or that the quiet of the text is representative of the author's failure to speak. However, as Rebecca Solnit suggests, 'Books are solitudes in which we meet' and although reading is best conducted in silence, the quiet of the novel is better conceived as a mode of conversation that occurs at a reduced volume rather than the complete absence of sound.[2] Philosopher Jean-Luc Nancy writes similarly about the act of listening: '[t]o be listening is always to be on the edge of meaning.'[3] For Nancy, the ways in which noise can 're-sound' within the individual reflects, if not the condition of being present, then the embodiment of presence as it arrives 'in waves on a swell' at the edges of conscious experience.[4] This book conceives of quiet in similar aesthetic terms. Just as Nancy believes that listening adds to the individual's sense of self in the present, and just as Solnit suggests that reading is a meeting of selves in solitude, so I suggest that quiet can be conceived philosophically: as an interior mode of discussion, a discrete articulation of selfhood and, perhaps most importantly, a resonant way of processing and paying attention in the present.

*The quiet contemporary American novel* makes two critical interventions. Chapter 1 maps the neglected history of quiet fictions and argues that from Hester Prynne to Clarissa Dalloway, from Bartleby to William Stoner, quiet characters fill the novel in the Western tradition. The introvert is a disruptive presence in many nineteenth-century texts, for example, including those by Nathaniel Hawthorne and Herman Melville where quiet is associated with a failure to speak or an absence of mind. In the early twentieth century, quiet protagonists were integral to the 'novel of consciousness' favoured by many writers including Virginia Woolf and Marcel Proust who equated quietness of character with a rich and dramatic internal life. As a phrase, this study also observes that 'the quiet novel' has a long and untraced history, dating back 150 years. The British journal, *London Society*, featured the first printed reference to the term in 1868; the first reference to the quiet novel in American periodicals was published in *Harper's New Monthly Magazine* in 1884.[5] These early reviewers hint at a quiet aesthetic and, perhaps understandably, leave the idea undeveloped. Yet throughout its long history, many critics have used 'the quiet novel' sometimes to denote praise but most often as a phrase that dismisses and derides the work of writers whose novels seem disengaged from the noise of their wider society. *The quiet contemporary American novel* finally takes up the long-referred-to idea of quiet fiction to ask what it means for a novel to be quiet and how we might specifically read for quiet in the American novel, which critics so often describe as noisy.[6]

My second point of intervention is to demonstrate how the novel's quiet undercurrent functions as an aesthetic in contemporary American fiction. Marilynne Robinson's *Gilead* and its partner novels, *Home* and *Lila*, Lynne Tillman's *American Genius; a comedy* (2006), Richard Powers' *The Echo Maker* (2006), Paul Harding's *Tinkers* (2010) and its partner novel, *Enon* (2013), Teju Cole's *Open City* (2011) and Ben Lerner's *Leaving the Atocha Station* (2011) are central to my analysis. While these novels are stylistically diverse, they are united, I argue, by a quiet that is central to the development of their prose style. The narrators of these novels enjoy quiet activities such as meditating, praying, writing, reading and studying, cultivating a rich internal life and entertaining a wide range of religious, political and social theories, ideas and philosophies. They are preachers (*Gilead*; *Home*; *Tinkers*), scholars (*American Genius*; *The Echo Maker*; *Tinkers*; *Open City*) and writers (*Leaving the Atocha Station*; *Open City*); in many cases, the quiet protagonist is a combination of all three. Each novel is also set in a quiet location: small towns (*Gilead*; *Home*; *The Echo Maker*; *Tinkers*; *Enon*), isolated communities (*American Genius*) and the art galleries and libraries of a city (*Open City*; *Leaving the Atocha Station*). Yet equally important is the idea that quiet novels are not restricted to remote locations so much as their protagonists seek out spaces for reflection in which they can contemplate and interpret the noise of the present from a distance.[7]

As later chapters in this study will demonstrate, the nine novels at the centre of this book are part of a far larger contemporary trend in which the interior lives of introverted, scholarly and often reclusive characters are prioritised. Geraldine Brooks' *March* (2005), Elizabeth Strout's *Olive Kitteridge: A Novel in Stories* (2008), Denis Johnson's *Train Dreams* (2012) and Alice Munro's *Dear Life* (2012) share a preoccupation with quiet people and quiet locations. Claire Messud's *The Woman Upstairs* (2013) and Rabih Alameddine's *An Unnecessary Woman* (2014) feature passionate and sometimes angry defences of antisocial female narrators whose lives have 'quieted' through old age.[8] Outside of North America, Austrian novelist Robert Seethaler's *A Whole Life* (2015) shares the quiet contemporary American novel's preoccupation with the rural lives of previous generations. Set in the Austrian Alps at the end of the First World War, Seethaler's protagonist prefers the ways in which everything works 'more slowly, even more quietly' in the seclusion of his location and the narrator continually highlights the protagonist's will to exist almost 'entirely without noise'.[9]

Fundamentally, and as Henry Mills Alden notes in the epigraph to this study, critics will most likely read a novel as quiet when it lacks narrative event. Caleb Crain's debut novel *Necessary Errors* (2013), for example, explores the 'quiet' aftermath of political activity through the story of a young novelist who arrives in Prague in the months following the Velvet Revolution of December 1989 and is 'comfortable with only one pleasure, reading'.[10] Similarly devoid of major incident and event, Sheila Heti's *How Should a Person Be?* (2012) and Tao Lin's *Taipei* (2013) play out the quiet implicit in explorations of interiority through unstable, closely focalised, metafictional narratives filled with quasi-autobiographical content. Even the 'cognitive turn' in the American novel, the subject of Chapter 4, that began with Jonathan Lethem's *Motherless Brooklyn* (1999) and continued through Powers' *The Echo Maker*, Rivka Galchen's *Atmospheric Disturbances* (2008) and John Wray's *Lowboy* (2009), privileges the quieter states of consciousness and, as I argue, might be read for its quieter qualities. Informed by developments in neuroscience made at the turn of the twenty-first century, these fictional dramatisations of cognitive operations attempt to subdue 'the full range of cultural noise' within the quiet of the mind.[11] Although these novels are then characterised by a feverish narrative instability that many quiet fictions lack, they share an essential eventlessness that is common to all quiet prose.

A burgeoning critical interest in these fictions is further reflected by the Pulitzer Prize committee's tendency to reward quieter narratives. Following *Gilead*'s victory in 2005, Brooks' *March* won in 2006, Strout's *Olive Kitteridge* in 2008, Harding's *Tinkers* in 2010 and Johnson's *Train Dreams* was nominated in 2012, a year when no prize was awarded. As much as a trend is apparent academics and reviewers seem increasingly receptive to quiet fictions. These novels are well reviewed, often become bestsellers and are sometimes saved from obscurity by a devoted readership. The 2006 republication of John Williams' neglected novel *Stoner* (1965), for instance, received widespread attention for the 'quietness' of its prose, while critics praise the English language translation of Karl Ove Knausgård's trilogy *My Struggle* (2009–11) for the author's ability to sustain a reader's attention through 3,600 pages in which 'nothing happens. Really: nothing happens at all.'[12] Central to my discussion of quiet fiction, therefore, is the idea that quiet is as much a method of engagement as a distinct trend in literature and a growing number of contemporary readers are reading for quiet as imaginative respite from a twenty-first-century culture that seems increasingly defined by its noise.

Indeed, I am interested in quiet's contemporary applications because the term remains so undefined. Reviews of Knausgård's *My Struggle* reveal a telling divide between readers who choose quiet texts and those who prefer noise: the author has been described both as 'Norway's Proust' and as a 'boring' and 'artless author-of-the-week', whose writing is an unfortunate consequence of Norway's movement for 'slow' activities.[13] Similarly, when Paul Harding's debut novel, *Tinkers* – which I analyse at length in Chapter 3 – received the Pulitzer in 2010, it was widely unknown and reviewed only fleetingly by major publications.[14] *Tinkers* had been rejected by many publishers before it was finally distributed by Bellevue Literary Press, with Harding receiving feedback that he was 'just another graduate' of the Iowa Writers' Workshop with a 'quiet little novel' he wanted to publish.[15] In certain circles, quiet remains a buzzword for unmarketable, unfashionable and unprofitable fiction. When Harding published *Enon* as a 'partner' novel to *Tinkers* in 2013, reviewers again read its quiet prose with suspicion. Harding's second novel is set in the same world as *Tinkers* and is named after the tiny village in which its precursor is based. Yet reviewers described *Enon* as a 'risky' follow-up, a novel that 'should be boring' but somehow manages to enthral through a profoundly 'unusual' narrative, which, like *Tinkers*, has very little narrative 'event'.[16]

Several contemporary novelists who share Harding's history of rejection have also felt forced to write in defence of their 'quiet' publications. Andrew Ladd, a novelist and editor for literary magazine *Ploughshares*, criticises the industry's 'schizophrenic' relationship with quiet novels, describing them as the 'quagmire' of literary publishing.[17] Canadian novelist Emily St. John Mandel published a similar complaint in August 2013 and, in a conversation conducted via email, notes that publishers often describe her fiction as 'too quiet'. Rather than reject the term entirely, Mandel suggests that the quiet novel is better characterised by its 'distilled' and 'unshowy' prose and 'a sense of grace' that values reflection over action.[18] Indeed, Mandel further observes that each quiet novel seems like a 'minor political act' that pushes against the prevailing norms of society. 'Quiet novels', she notes, stand 'in opposition to the unquiet contemporary world' and write a history of the contemporary through alternate means of communication.[19]

In 2012, Oregon-based novelist and editor Laura Stanfill went several steps further when she opened a regional press to publish the 'quiet' novels rejected by larger publishers in New York. Speaking again via email, Stanfill explained:

> I launched my press around this idea because many of my writer friends write quiet novels, and we all kept getting the same feedback from agents or editors – too quiet. If we all like to read and write quiet novels, then maybe we shouldn't be relying on New York to acknowledge and celebrate our tastes.[20]

As a direct result of criticism from corporate publishers, Forest Avenue Press distributes what Stanfill describes as '[q]uiet books for a noisy world' and accepts publications based on an appraisal of their opposition to 'the high-concept novel' popular with more mainstream companies. 'In quiet novels', Stanfill claims, 'the hero's journey is usually an interior one, where the character is changed by the world, rather than charging out to change the world.'[21] In different but arguably cognate ways, Ladd, Mandel and Stanfill contribute to a burgeoning literary conversation that is yet to account for the deeper motivations of writing a quiet text but that has begun to pay attention to the trend beyond its status as a marketing albatross.

Another reason to write about the quiet novel in its contemporary form is that after a century and a half of imprecise allusions, which I discuss at length in Chapter 1, 'the quiet novel' has entered the vocabulary of literary criticism. In his introduction to the 1990 translation of *Eugénie Grandet* (1833) by Honoré de Balzac, Christopher Prendergast, describes the text as a 'quiet novel of provincial life'.[22] Similarly, Hans Geppert describes *Der Stechlin* (1898), the final novel by German novelist Theordor Fontane, as a quiet novel 'full of conversation on the "old" and "new"'.[23] Indeed, the plot of *Der Stechlin* shares similarities with Robinson's *Gilead* and Harding's *Tinkers*; Fontane details the life of a widowed, elderly protagonist who lives modestly and in seclusion. Tellingly, of course, very little happens in *Der Stechlin* that might be described as action and Geppert, like many critics, uses 'quiet' to describe an outmoded, outdated way of life. For Virginia Brackett and Victoria Gaydosik, Anthony Trollope's *The Warden* (1855) is quiet because it tells the story of Reverend Harding and 'his struggle with conscience [...] without need for grandiose action.'[24] Notably, literary critics also reference quiet as a mode of reflection that might stage ethical debates in different contexts. James Gunn describes English writer H. G. Wells' *Star Begotten* (1937) as a 'quiet novel' about the complex relationship between religion and evolution, while Sharon Monteith describes Madison Jones' *A Cry of Absence* (1971) as 'quiet' for depicting white moderates' fear of racial change in 1950s Tennessee.[25] Edging closer to this book's conception of quiet, Joseph Ward describes the problem of speech in James Agee's *A Death in the Family* (1948) as a reflection on interior discord and suggests that the modern symphony of car engines and telephones 'are dramatic, symbolic, and melodic disruptions' that challenge the calm aesthetic of an otherwise 'quiet novel'.[26]

Any similarity between the novels listed above is fleeting: today, critics use 'the quiet novel' as a formal description for many reasons. Sometimes the phrase denotes a rural, domestic or old-fashioned setting; often the narrative will follow a conservative, elderly or religious protagonist. Indeed, by grouping these critics together, their use of the phrase seems more disparate than ever. Narrative quiet is referenced by reviewers and critics, maligned by publishers and addressed infrequently through blog posts and online essays. Although literary critics have singled out particular texts as quiet, as a phrase, 'the quiet novel' is rarely interrogated or defined and has no common usage.

Perhaps, then, the absent literary history of quiet and quiet narratives reveals the potentiality of a quiet aesthetic. Of greater relevance to this study and the aesthetic of quiet it proposes, Kevin Everod Quashie's *The Sovereignty of Quiet: Beyond Resistance in Black Culture* (2010) is the first study of its kind and the only work of criticism to conceive of 'quiet' in a way that is similar to my own. Focusing more specifically on mid- to late twentieth-century African American writers, Quashie argues that black culture 'is or is supposed to be loud' and suggests that quiet provides black authors with a potential site of resistance because of its marginalisation as a mode of expression.[27] Extending Quashie's notion of quiet's counter-cultural potential, *The quiet contemporary American novel* proceeds as follows. Chapter 1 maps the neglected history of quiet fictions and speculates about the potentiality of quiet as a literary aesthetic. Chapter 2 engages with the problem of 'event' as a noisy narrative device and discusses the opposition of quiet texts to narratives written in the aftermath of 11 September 2001 ('9/11'), an event that heralded to many the beginning of a noisy century. This study is concerned with how quiet manifests in an early twenty-first-century context, at a moment when globalisation, terrorism, and overseas military intervention began to merge with the phenomena of 24-hour news cycles, social media and the online 'noise' of the Internet to produce a kind of mental overstimulation and anxiety which many claim to be dissonant. This is not to state that the twenty-first century is noisier than any previous era, but to note the kinds of sounds that society deems to be noisy and to question how noise is then recreated in fiction.

Successive chapters of *The quiet contemporary American novel* conceive of quiet differently, applying a distinct lens to pairs of 'quiet' texts in order to account for the diversity of the term and its aesthetic applications. In Chapter 3, I move as far from the loud of '9/11' as a quiet narrative can travel to discuss the subjective depictions of temporality portrayed in the fiction of Marilynne Robinson and Paul Harding. Chapter 4 argues that cognitive fictions by Richard Powers and Lynne Tillman expand the focus of the quiet novel, uncovering the complex and often discordant recesses of human consciousness and challenging the traditional division between what is internally and externally felt. Finally, Chapter 5 brings together the varied strands of this monograph to discuss what happens to the quiet novel when Teju Cole and Ben Lerner set their quiet novels in the noisy environment of the city.

*The quiet contemporary American novel* is the first book to define 'the quiet novel' as a literary term. However, its summation is not prescriptive. Quiet can mean many things to one writer and an author's attention to quiet can vary both between novels and within one text. To accommodate and link a wide range of texts and themes, I therefore identify four common features that unite the quiet American novel in its contemporary form. First, the quiet novel represents the life of a quiet protagonist and an introvert. As protagonists, they privilege thought over action and spend most of their time in contemplation. Second, the protagonist will seek out quiet spaces in which to pursue quiet activities. The quiet novel is often set in rural towns but, if moved to the city, characters frequent art galleries, universities and bookshops. Third, consciousness will be a central character or a theme, providing a catalyst for narrative action that is independent of national or topical event. What has previously been referred to as the novel of consciousness, the psychological or confessional novel therefore finds new life through the perspectives of quiet characters who, in a culture trained to praise extroversion and spontaneity, are noticeably and notably quiet, if not dull. Fourth, and most important of all, is this central claim: the quiet novel is a novel where very little happens. It is a novel with 'no plot', as *The New York Times* claimed in 1898 because the narrative forsakes event and action for the interior exploration of consciousness.[28]

The fourth point I make here is the most important but also the most challenging to define. At first sight, these criteria appear unworthy of note because a dull protagonist in a fiction where very little happens is not devised to attract attention. The discussion of ideas, the recall of memory, reported speech and the minutiae of everyday routine fill the quiet narrative; it is therefore wrong to claim that entirely nothing happens. However, within a culture that privileges drama, noise and contingency, the cultivation and representation of reflective states distinguishes the quiet text. Very little happens in the quiet novel that is external to the protagonist's consciousness and quiet novels are driven by processes of reflection that retrieve a sense of self or what Virginia Woolf famously calls 'moments of being' from the rush of contemporary experience.[29] In this way, reading for quiet in contemporary fiction has the potential to question the social efficacy of action by shedding light on the intellectual processes which critics often deem too quiet to be political. That is not to say that quiet forms of expression are always successful as a form of protest, or that a quiet aesthetic is necessarily 'good'. Yet it is to argue that loud need not be the norm, reflection is an undervalued facet of and response to contemporaneity and reading for quiet can begin a nuanced discussion that contemporary discourse sometimes loudly shuts down.

## Notes

1  Marilynne Robinson, *Gilead* (London: Virago, 2006), p. 9.
2  Rebecca Solnit, *The Faraway Nearby* (New York: Penguin, 2013), p. 54.
3  Jean-Luc Nancy, *Listening*, trans. Charlotte Mandell (New York: Fordham University Press, 2007), p. 7.
4  Ibid., p. 13.
5  Henry Mills Alden, 'Miss Tommy', *Harper's New Monthly Magazine* 69.414 (November 1884), p. 141.
6  I refer to noisy and loud novels interchangeably, in part because critics do not use either with regularity. Although loud is perhaps more accurately the antonym of quiet, noise better expresses the perceived dissonance of contemporary existence and the kinds of sounds or, as I argue, ideas that fiction is expected to represent.

7   Another book might identify a parallel trend in British and Irish literature, though key examples only echo the discursive potential of any canon of 'quiet' fictions. John McGahern's *That They May Face the Rising Sun* (London: Faber & Faber, 2002) depicts one year in a rural, lakeside community and has been celebrated for a tone that is 'serene, often subdued, and frequently still', a novel where 'little happens', in which McGahern references only one dated event. Ray Ryan, 'John McGahern, *That They May Face the Rising Sun*', in *The Good of the Novel*, ed. Liam Mcllvanney and Ray Ryan (London: Continuum, 2011), p. 201. Jon McGregor's *If Nobody Speaks of Remarkable Things* (London: Bloomsbury, 2002) portrays a day in the life of a single street, moving between the inner worlds of each resident. Michael Cannon's *Lachlan's War* (London: Penguin, 2006) is set in a fictional Scottish village in 1941 where the events of the Second World War are just flickers at the edge of the central solitary life. Similarly, Simon Robson's *Catch* (London: Jonathan Cape, 2010) is a quiet novel about one day in the life of a married woman who has become fixated on that one day and the time she will spend away from her husband. Julian Barnes' award-winning novel, *The Sense of an Ending* (2011), is particularly quiet, constituted by one man's regrets following a lifetime of indecision and portrays 'the littleness of life that art exaggerates'. Julian Barnes, *The Sense of an Ending* (London: Vintage, 2011), p. 93.
8   Rabih Alameddine, *An Unnecessary Woman* (New York: Grove Press, 2013), p. 50. Strout's and Munro's books are short story collections; indeed, *Olive Kitteridge* is a story cycle. Another study could also be written about quiet in the short story, a form which might, in fact, be quieter than the novel because of its brevity, marginalisation in mainstream publishing and review culture and what Martin Scofield describes as a '"lightness" and mobility' that encourages impressionism, immediacy and a lack or at least a reduction of narrative event. See: 'Introduction', in *The Cambridge Introduction to the American Short Story*, ed. Martin Scofield (Cambridge: Cambridge University Press, 2002), p. 8.
9   Robert Seethaler, *A Whole Life*, trans. Charlotte Collins (London: Picador, 2015), pp. 3, 5.
10  Caleb Crain, *Necessary Errors* (New York: Penguin, 2013), p. 33.
11  Joseph Tabbi, *Cognitive Fictions* (Minneapolis: University of Minnesota Press, 2002), p. xv.
12  Arifa Akbar, 'John Williams' Stoner Enjoys Renaissance', *The Independent* (4 June 2013), http://www.independent.co.uk/arts-entertainment/books/features/john-williams-stoner-enjoys-renaissance-8642782.html; Emma Brockes, 'Welcome to the Summer of Nothingness: how one book made it hip to be bored', *The Guardian* (5 June 2014), http://www.theguardian.com/commentisfree/emma-brockes-column/2014/jun/05/summer-karl-ove-knausgard-book-hip-to-be-bored.

13 Hermione Hoby, 'Norway's Proust and a Life Laid Bare', *The Observer* (1 March 2014), 36; William Deresiewicz, 'Why has "'My Struggle" been anointed a literary masterpiece?' *The Nation* (2 June 2014), http://www.thenation.com/article/179853/why-has-my-struggle-been-anointed-literary-masterpiece.

14 Briefly noted in *The New Yorker* as outdated and 'adamantine', Harding garnered more attention from his inclusion on year-end lists for *NPR* and, again, in *The New Yorker*, through a blog appropriately titled 'Double Take'. 'Tinkers', *The New Yorker* (12 January 2009), http://www.newyorker.com/arts/reviews/brieflynoted/2009/01/12/090112crbn_brieflynoted2#ixzz1rSoOSryf. See also the apology printed in *The New York Times* which suggests that *Tinkers* was 'not on our radar' at the time of its publication. Gregory Cowles, *'Tinkers* by Paul Harding: The One That Got Away', *The New York Times* (12 April 2010), http://www.newyorker.com/arts/reviews/brieflynoted/2009/01/12/090112crbn_brieflynoted2.

15 Paul Harding, quoted in Motoko Rich, 'Mr. Cinderella: From Rejection Notes to the Pulitzer', *The New York Times* (18 April 2010), http://www.nytimes.com/2010/04/19/books/19harding.html?pagewanted=all.

16 Joseph M. Schuster, 'Post-40 Bloomers: The Risky Fiction of Paul Harding', *The Millions* (9 September 2013), http://www.themillions.com/2013/09/post-40-bloomers-the-risky-fiction-of-paul-harding.html; Kevin McFarland, 'Paul Harding: *Enon*', *The AV Club* (16 September 2013), http://www.avclub.com/review/paul-harding-ienoni-102847; John Barron, '*Enon* by Paul Harding', *Chicago Tribune* (15 September 2013), http://articles.chicago tribune.com/2013-09-15/features/ct-prj-0915-enon-paul-harding-20130915_1_paul-harding-printers-row-journal-enon.

17 Andrew Ladd, 'Blurbese: "Quiet"', *Ploughshares* (27 July 2012), http://blog.pshares.org/index.php/blurbese-quiet/. Via email, Ladd admitted many reservations and few positives about the term and was broadly disparaging about the reviewers who use it. Ladd, e-mail communication with the author (12 September 2013).

18 Mandel names *Open City* and *Gilead* as the only contemporary examples of quiet fictions and novels by Paul Yoon, Tove Jansson and Ruth Park to demonstrate the trend's international value. Mandel, 'On the Pleasures and Solitudes of Quiet Books', *The Millions* (27 August 2013), http://www.themillions.com/2013/08/on-the-pleasures-and-solitudes-of-quiet-books.html.

19 Mandel, e-mail communication with the author (1 September 2013). Our discussion took place before the publication of Mandel's fourth novel, *Station Eleven* (2014), which won the Arthur C. Clarke Award in 2015 and was nominated for the National Book Award, the PEN/Faulkner

Award and the Bailey's Prize for Fiction. Notably, *Station Eleven* was also described as 'a quiet novel' by *The New York Times* and other publications, which noted the text's rendition of a 'quiet apocalypse'. Alexandra Alter, 'The World is Ending', *The New York Times* (5 September 2014), http://www.nytimes.com/2014/09/06/books/station-eleven-joins-falls-crop-of-dystopian-novels.html.

20 Laura Stanfill, e-mail communication with the author (2 September 2013).
21 Stanfill, interviewed by Stefanie Freele, 'The Makings of a Regional Press: In Conversation with Laura Stanfill', *Late Night Library* (20 November 2013), http://latenightlibrary.org/the_makings_of_a_regional_press_laura_stanfill/.
22 Christopher Prendergast, 'Introduction', in his *Eugenie Grandet* (Oxford: Oxford University Press, 1990), p. xx.
23 Hans Vilmar Geppert, '"A Cluster of Signs": Semiotic Micrologies in Nineteenth-Century Realism: Madame Bovary, Middlemarch, Effi Briest', *The Germanic Review: Literature, Culture, Theory*, 73:3 (1998), p. 249. A footnote in Jay Clayton's *The Pleasures of Babel: Contemporary American Literature and Theory* (1993) also refers to Paule Marshall's *Praisesong for the Widow* (1983) as a quiet novel about a widow of sixty-four who moves to the suburbs after a lifetime in Harlem. Clayton, *The Pleasures of Babel: Contemporary American Literature and Theory* (Oxford: Oxford University Press, 1993), p. 166.
24 Virginia Brackett and Victoria Gaydosik (eds), 'The Warden', in their *The Eighteenth and Nineteenth Century British Novel* (New York: Facts on File, 2006), p. 468.
25 James Gunn, *Paratexts: Introductions to Science Fiction and Fantasy* (Plymouth: Scarecrow Press, 2013), p. 191; Sharon Monteith, 'Civil Rights Fictions', in *The Cambridge Companion to the Literature of the American South*, ed. Sharon Monteith (Cambridge: Cambridge University Press, 2013), p. 169.
26 Joseph Anthony Ward, *American Silences: The Realism of James Agee, Walker Evans, and Edward Hopper* (New York: Transaction Publishers, 2010), p. 106.
27 Kevin Everod Quashie, *The Sovereignty of Quiet: Beyond Resistance in Black Culture* (New Brunswick, NJ: Rutgers University Press, 2012), p. 11.
28 'Ada Cambridge's New Novel', *The New York Times*, Saturday Review of Books and Art (25 June 1898), p. 2.
29 Woolf first mentions 'moments of being' in her essay, 'A Sketch of the Past', which formed the basis of her posthumously published memoirs, *Moments of Being* (1985). Although Woolf never defines the phrase, she provides examples of these moments, defining them as flashes of

intense awareness that increase the individual's consciousness of their ongoing experience. Woolf, 'A Sketch of the Past', in *Moments of Being*, ed. Jeanne Schulkind (New York: Harcourt Brace & Company, 1985), pp. 61–138.

# 1

# The quiet novel

Quiet is a dynamic term. Whether constructed as a noun, adjective, adverb or verb, the word is older and more diverse than quietness or quietude and miscellaneous enough to remain applicable to many situations, states and, as this study argues, fictions. The third edition of the *OED* notes that the earliest use of 'quiet' as a noun appears in 1330, followed by 'quietness' in 1425, 'quietude' in 1598 and 'quietism' in 1687. 'Loud' is older and dates back to 800 with fewer listed meanings; 'noise' is only a century older than quiet and defined as an aggregate of sounds that somehow creates a 'disturbance'. The reason I focus on 'the quiet novel' rather than literary quietness, quietude or quietism is because of the relative instability embodied in the term. While quietness and quietude are often defined very simply as states or conditions of being quiet, quietism is primarily conceived as a form of religious mysticism that embraces internal contemplation and, in its contemporary form, has become an accusation of political inaction.[1]

To describe a novel as quiet, however, is first to personify it: to be quiet is to be calm, private or peaceful and to speak quietly is to be measured, patient and unobtrusive. Quiet has also been associated with a mode and method of being since antiquity. In the Bible, Jacob is described as a 'quiet man dwelling in tents' who makes little external noise, rarely raises his voice and is fond of quiet activities.[2] Compared with his brother, Esau, who is a man of action, 'a skilful hunter' and 'man of the field', Jacob creates little outward disturbance and leaves the world around him largely unchanged. Important to this study and the aesthetic of fiction it proposes, Jacob seems quieter when compared with the noise that Esau creates; in Genesis, he is praised for questioning the role that action plays in the outward expression of personality. When Jacob is renamed 'Israel', meaning one who wrestles inwardly with God, his renaming confirms that the essential and, indeed, worthy action of Jacob's life is and will be internal.

Quiet novels privilege the experience of men like Jacob and examine the relative value and variety of quiet states that philosophy has valued for centuries. In Ancient Greece, for example, quiet was famously associated with inner tranquillity, characterised as an idyllic condition, free from mental or emotional agitation and undisturbed by external influence, action or event. Plato described the Greek concept of *sophrosyne*, denoting soundness of character and mind, as 'a certain quietness'; Aristotle believed the quiet life to be a necessary condition for independent thought and the creation of art; Euripides proclaimed that only 'the genial, quiet life, / Ruddered by right-thinking, / Knows calm security'.[3] For Euripides, in particular, society's activity and noise seemed distracting to the individual but personal quietude restores composure by reclaiming the mental space that reflection requires in the present. To be quiet is to be private and peaceful but most importantly quiet can be a philosophically active state, an 'energy and essence' as Aristotle suggests in *Metaphysics* (350 BC) that strengthens the individual's ability to exist and participate in society.[4]

Historically, reviewers have used the term similarly, yet when references to 'the quiet novel' first appeared in the book review sections of British and American newspapers and periodicals in the 1860s, these early reviews contained little precision as to what 'the quiet novel' might be and shared no common authors. In 1868, the periodical *London Society* compared the quiet novel to 'the very fast novel' and described the experience of reading the two 'like turning aside from the heat and glare and dust of a crowded street into some chapel, very still and quiet'.[5] Notably, the unnamed reviewer hints that reading a quiet novel both requires and encourages a different faculty of mind, comparing the experience with that of entering a sacred space in search of tranquillity.[6] A year later, in 1869, another unnamed reviewer described the quiet novel as any 'successful attempt at characterisation' in which incidents are 'neither extravagant nor slow'.[7] This reviewer emphasised how a lack of narrative action facilitates quiet prose, an association that trails 'the quiet novel' throughout its history. In 1884, Henry Mills Alden took up this idea in his review of Dinah Mulock's *Miss Tommy* for *Harper's Monthly Magazine*:

> A much rarer gift – indeed, a most rare one – is the faculty of writing a *quiet* novel, whose interest does not depend upon these highly spiced and stimulating excitements. To write such a novel without lapsing into insipidity and tameness is one of the most difficult tests to which a writer of romance can be subjected, and to write one that will be successful with the public is a genuine triumph of art.[8]

Here, Alden refers to the quiet novel as the marginalia of a noisy culture and defines its quietness only by the absence of action: a lack of 'highly spiced and stimulating excitements'.[9] He claims that it is wildly popular for authors to write 'dramatic scenes and incidents' but uncommon for them to write quietly. Its implied rarity therefore leads Alden to praise the form as a 'genuine triumph of art' without further definition of its formal properties. Similarly, although *The New York Times* did not refer to 'the quiet novel' until 1929, its writers used 'quiet' as a description of the novel's aesthetics as early as 1898 when an unnamed reviewer described Ada Cambridge's *Materfamilias* (1898) as a novel with 'no plot' and a 'quiet and unassuming' style.[10] To write quietly, these nineteenth-century reviewers suggest, is a worthy enterprise that requires the reader to reflect more slowly on the text and the ideas it introduces. However, the same reviewers also acknowledge that the quiet novel could be dismissed as trivial when it is not seen to compete with the overwhelming noise of the surrounding culture and that it risks going unheard when competing authors depict 'stimulating excitements' that could lure the reader's attention elsewhere.

Throughout the phrase's 150-year history, and as this chapter demonstrates, one idea is common to all discussions of quiet fiction: if society is noisy, then quiet becomes a much rarer commodity. Indeed, although quiet remains a necessary state for both reading and writing, many critics suggest that quiet prose risks going 'unheard' because quiet states seem so antithetical to the perceived noise of civilisation. The study of the quiet novel therefore has something important to say about the production and distribution of literary fiction. As Amelia DeFalco suggests, '[i]nterpreting contemplation, being, even resting or sleeping as meaningful, morally valuable states goes against the grain of teleological, capitalist-inflected discourses of activation that associate inactivity with weakness and diminished work.'[11] The life of 'quiet observation' that DeFalco attributes to Ames in Marilynne Robinson's *Gilead* lacks drama, excitement and event in the same way that Henry Mills Alden observes of the quiet novel in 1884.[12] That is, without 'dramatic scenes and incidents', both Robinson and Dinah Mulock represent an existence in which action is not the primary experiential framework and ideas are encountered within the text at a rate of 'extreme deceleration' that is out of step with the accelerated pace of a capitalist society.[13]

It is this feature of narrative that I believe reviewers refer to when they describe a novel as quiet; a slow, contemplative prose style that denies the teleological drive to conclusion by largely eschewing narrative event. It is also in this way that I argue the four conditions for quiet outlined in my Introduction, from the depiction of quiet people and locations, to a focus on interior life and the absence of narrative event, facilitate an aesthetic of narrative that has not yet been defined despite consistent references throughout twentieth- and twenty-first-century literary criticism.

## The quiet American novel

A major contention of *The quiet contemporary American novel* is that the quiet novel has a long history in Anglophone literature and is often positioned against an opposing norm of loudness and noise. The quiet contemporary American novel therefore joins a centuries-old tradition. Still, there is something peculiarly un-American about the idea of a quiet novel, which often focuses on the depiction of bookish, antisocial, solitary protagonists who set out to achieve 'nothing'. In thinking about the relationship between quiet and the American nation-state, Graham Greene's *The Quiet American* (1955) most immediately comes to mind. Greene's anti-war novel is not a quiet novel, per se, nor is it written by an American author. However, it does imagine the implications of describing an American citizen as quiet. Alden Pyle, a CIA agent working undercover in Vietnam, is the quiet American of the title and Greene describes his quiet as antithetical to his nationality: '"He's a good chap in his way. Serious. Not one of those noisy bastards at the Continental. A quiet American."'[14] Greene's narrator, a British foreign correspondent called Thomas Fowler, intends his description to be an insult, not only against Pyle but also against all Americans; he compares the phenomenon of a 'quiet American' to '"a blue lizard [...] a white elephant"', animals of equal unlikeliness. As the novel develops, the significance of Pyle's quiet changes from a calm enigmatic façade into a wider failure to speak against an American government that charges him with increasingly dubious tasks.[15] He is a quiet American, then, because his demeanour hides even quieter, morally questionable actions, which ultimately lead to Pyle's death.

Notably, Fowler finds the idea of a 'quiet American' ironic because he believes Americans and, by extension, America to be noisy. Part of America's perceived loudness comes from its association with action, read historically in everything from the nation's violent inception and aggressive foreign policies to the wide-reaching noise of US consumerism and media cultures, symbolised by the cacophonous Hollywood blockbuster.[16] Colloquially, Americans are also often referred to as 'noisy people' who assert their needs and desires above those of others, prioritising sounds necessary to the completion of their own aims that are more likely to be deemed unwanted by non-American citizens. For instance, in a 1957 article for *Life* magazine, called 'How We Appear to Others', journalist Robert Coughlan notes that fundamentally:

> [T]he American is noisy. In a public place his talk and his laughter are too loud and draw attention. He drinks too much, and when he drinks he becomes louder. A Turkish girl touches several sore points: 'The Turk admires and yearns for the freedom of America, but he hates the way the Americans come here and act as if this country were a dominion of America.'[17]

Articles like this, playing off several xenophobic stereotypes, illustrate how popular perception of American noise exceeds the mere production of sound. Indeed, accusations of American loudness seem more related to the *kinds* of noise associated with the country and its citizens rather than a specific volume. When viewed from abroad, the noise of America seems like confidence granted by at least a century of relative prosperity and security, which attracts negative attention when that noise appears to claim what Coughlan calls 'dominion' over quieter nations.

Among American writers, a mixture of pride and frustration has also marked cultural responses to noise. Historian Emily Thompson notes that earlier twentieth-century Americans, like F. Scott Fitzgerald, saw the 'pervasive din' of the American city as 'the keynote of modern civilization'.[18] While some, like Fitzgerald, celebrated noise, others campaigned to eliminate it. However, as Thompson argues, '[a]ll perceived that they lived in an era uniquely and unprecedentedly loud'.[19] This attitude persists in contemporary American writing. Tired of what he perceives to be an increasingly noisy New York, George Prochnik's *In Pursuit of Silence: Listening for Meaning in a World of Noise* (2010) documents the author's thwarted search for a kind of peace that he concludes no longer exists in America.[20] The same year, *Harper's* columnist Garret Keizer published *The Unwanted Sound of Everything We Want* (2010). In a chapter entitled 'Loud America', Keizer suggests that American politicians and advertisers encourage the production of noise to such an extent that 'America means exceeding the limits, cranking it up, letting her rip [...] You have to be willing to stick your prerogatives in somebody else's ears or face.'[21]

What music writer Brandon LaBelle calls the 'intense relationality' of all sound is important here.[22] For LaBelle, to make noise is 'to live in more than one head, beyond an individual mind' so that listening becomes 'a form of participation in the sharing of a sound event, however banal'.[23] In this way, it is easy to see how America's size, as well as its cultural and global military presence creates a sonic footprint that is both real and metaphorical, making America seem louder, first, because the noise produced there is so widely imposed and, second, because these sounds are present in the fabric of many more people's experience of the everyday.

Noise is also important to cultural notions of the contemporary. If, for instance, as this study argues, each generation believes that society is getting louder, what does it mean for the novel to embody an aesthetic of quiet in its representation of the present? To the nineteenth-century reviewers surveyed in this chapter thus far, the quiet novelist's endeavour to write largely without event and adventure already seemed old-fashioned. This meant that both British and American critics described only English novelists as quiet and never associated the term, 'the quiet novel', with the search for an original American voice. Not only that, but the idea of 'quiet' was only attributed to novels and novelists who wrote about the past, a time that seemed much quieter in comparison to what many assumed to be the increasing and totalising noise of the present.

Contrarily, however, American literature contains a long history of representing quiet people, places and states. These characters largely observe rather than participate in the world and seem somehow 'un-American' in their search for solitude, peace and quiet. The narrator of Edgar Allan Poe's 'The Man of the Crowd' (1840), for example, watches life through a café window and is obsessed with an elderly man who wanders aimlessly through the streets and 'refuses to be alone', just as the narrator cannot imagine anything but solitude.[24] Twenty-eight years later, the first review of the quiet novel would suggest that reading a quiet text was like escaping 'the heat and glare and dust of a crowded street' and in 1840, Poe wrote that noise constantly stifled the modern citizen amidst the 'very denseness of the company' in the American city,[25] in much the same way, the quiet protagonist of the nineteenth century was often an outcast from society or an object of suspicion because they chose to spend the majority of their time alone. In the romances of Nathaniel Hawthorne, quiet characters are both intentionally and unintentionally cut off from society.[26] *The Scarlet Letter* (1850) depicts Hester Prynne's enforced seclusion as 'quiet, sad, delicious happiness' that results from the questionable decision to keep her silence.[27] Miles Coverdale, the protagonist of *The Blithedale Romance* (1852), abandons the utopian community of Blithedale to be alone and, like 'The Man of the Crowd', to watch people through windows, associating with people who are unfit for communal living because of their 'quiet countenance' or 'quiet moods'.[28] The quiet protagonists of Poe and Hawthorne are therefore antisocial and often quite strange. If their seclusion is a choice, the decision represents an inability or unwillingness to cope with the noise of society and often demonstrates fragility rather than a quiet independence or strength. Most importantly, their inner life is often anxious, indicating a disturbance of mind rather than a measured state of reflection that could be therapeutic to the individual.

The portrayal of the 'introvert' as a volatile and problematic character reflects a societal preference for 'extroversion' that grew throughout the nineteenth century and was closely associated with capitalism. Adopting terms first developed by cultural historian Warren Susman, Susan Cain suggests that the nineteenth century saw a shift from the 'Culture of Character' that values the cultivation of the inner self to a 'Culture of Personality' that values extroversion as a display of charisma in the pursuit of success.[29] Without subscribing here to binary definitions of extro- and introverted personality types, as Cain undoubtedly does, Poe's and Hawthorne's 'introverts' pose a challenge to narratives of progress because they lack qualities such as charisma and outspokenness that broker success in a capitalist economy and proclaim the individual's value to potential employers.

In contrast, the introvert becomes a source of disruption and distrust. Bartleby, the eponymous 'quiet man' of Herman Melville's 1853 magazine story, typifies the suspicion attached to quiet characters.[30] Specifically, his quiet disrupts the productivity of the workplace; Bartleby's famous retort 'I would prefer not to' denies the requests of his employer, co-workers and ruling officers by questioning the efficacy of action and articulating the wish to remain inactive. At first, Melville's narrator, Bartleby's pitiful employer, believes quiet to be a favourable quality and Bartleby, 'a man so singularly sedate in aspect', appears to be the ideal employee until, that is, his employer begins to equate his denial of action with a troubled internal environment.[31] Bartleby's failure to act finally divorces him from what Clark Davis calls 'the sense-making world' by impeding the social and economic order of the lawyer's office and disturbing conventional ideas of progress in denying the capitalist logic of action.[32] Significantly, Bartleby does not reject the usefulness of action so much as he articulates a preference not to participate in it.[33] Rather than characterising a desire for inaction, per se, Bartleby actually exhibits a state of attention that could turn to action at any moment. He is self-reliant in other words and the narrator waits for an inward prompt to action that never occurs.

Of course, Ralph Waldo Emerson provides the most famous contemplation of action and inaction which speaks to any discussion of quiet characters and states. In many ways, Emerson was himself a quiet man: Laurence Buell describes the philosopher as 'more of a thinker than a joiner or doer' and throughout his work Emerson discusses the influence of action on the formation of a distinctly American cultural identity.[34] In 'The American Scholar' (1837), Emerson argues that action is a subordinate concern for the American thinker but because the transcendentalist tradition conceived of the world as an expression of subjectivity, he also states that action is the thinker's natural duty. The American scholar would have a composite identity which, according to Emerson, would be able to withstand hard work, tedium and solitude, celebrating the role of reflection in the creation of national character without rejecting action as a form of social engagement:

> In silence, in steadiness, in severe abstraction, let him hold by himself; add observation, patient of neglect, patient of reproach, and bide his own time [...] For the instinct is sure, that prompts him to tell

his brother what he thinks. He then learns that in going down into the secrets of his own mind he has descended into the secrets of all minds.[35]

In this passage, Emerson suggests that patience develops when the individual engages with quiet and reflective states. Not only that, but in solitude the scholar locates their autonomy and moves closer to achieving independent thought. In keeping with nineteenth century references to 'the quiet novel', Emerson believes that the noise of society permeates everything and the competing opinions of others prove an especially noisy threat to the individual. In moments of quiet reflection, 'in severe abstraction', truths are revealed to be more complex and fully formed than those garnered in society and as a result Emerson valorises quiet as a condition of philosophical inquiry.

Four years later, in 1841, Emerson famously addressed the relationship between the solitary self and social action in his essay, 'Self Reliance', further defining the act dramatised in Bartleby's disruptive state as a call to action that falls outside any theory of historical progress. The stillness of reflection is not passive in Emerson's formulation; it signals attentiveness, a state of listening and a form of quiet that may or may not turn to action at any time. Self-reliance, that is, is a site of activity and contemplation that is never fully divorced from the external world. The quiet aesthetic developed here follows Emerson in this respect; it, too, aims to complicate notions of progress and the individual's 'usefulness' as defined by demonstrations of noise and activity, disturbing the idea that effort is only meaningful if it leads to action while also appropriating the Emersonian idea that action begins with the subjectivity of the individual and not in the social world. As Emerson writes, 'Men imagine that they communicate their virtue or vice only by overt actions, and do not see that virtue or vice emit a breath every moment.'[36] A quiet aesthetic communicates in much the same way. It is a representation of life between events that shifts focus from noisier instances or actions and reprioritises the subjective as a locus for experience.

A fellow transcendentalist and quiet contemporary of Emerson's, Henry David Thoreau, also sought a wider understanding of society through exercises in personal reflection. Thoreau praised the introversion of others, tested how quiet could be personally cultivated, and in *Walden* (1854) famously detailed his experiences over two years, two months and two days spent in a cabin constructed on Emerson's woodland near Concord, Massachusetts. The book further defines active and passive forms of quiet, noting how in the cities of the 1850s man has 'no time to be any thing but a machine' and suggesting that the lack of self-reliance that modern living entails, demonstrated primarily by the lack of both time and reflection, leads the masses to 'lives of quiet desperation'.[37] For Thoreau, the worker's expression of quiet is a depressing contradiction that belies the inner cry of his subjectivity. However, he also believes that the individual can enjoy a quiet existence through a relationship with nature. When a 'simple and natural man' calls at his cabin, Thoreau describes his visitor as inherently quiet: 'he interested me because he was so quiet and solitary and so happy withal; a well of good humor and contentment which overflowed at his eyes.'[38] Of course, Thoreau has no real idea of the man's inner life, nor does he attempt to guess it. Instead, he presumes the man's outward calm reflects a state of contentment obtained through his affinity for the 'natural' world, which is represented by the surrounding woods.

Famously, Thoreau's conception of quiet is also full of contradictions. As Martin Bickman suggests, two competing drives compel *Walden*: the first, 'a responsiveness to a continually changing world', is often countered by a second more conservative drive 'to rescue and preserve from that world something of permanent shape and beauty.'[39] Quiet is useful for Thoreau because the term can be diversely constructed; among the masses, a quiet countenance can imply desperation, the suppression of dissent and a manifestation of conformity but, in solitude, quiet represents a contentment developed through a personal affinity with an idealised version of nature. Most importantly, Thoreau believes that quiet is only possible as the result of a complete retreat from society and its associated noise, an act that he aspires to by building his cabin 'far from noise and disturbance' where he can enact the principles of self-reliance 'in undisturbed solitude and stillness'.[40] But while the author portrays his stay in the cabin as a monastic retreat, it is widely known that Thoreau deliberately excluded the noisier and more social elements of his life from the narrative: he would often walk into the nearby town to talk with friends and to receive payment for the completion of odd jobs.[41] *Walden*'s portrayal of seclusion could not subsume these events and so Thoreau excludes the noise of people, society and commerce in order to sustain a quieter aesthetic, revealing a cultivation of contemplative quiet that would be available to few.

## Noise and modernity

Acknowledging the extent to which Thoreau fabricates details of his seclusion helps us to understand what a precious commodity quiet seemed in modernity, at least for those who sought it. Although quiet remained essential to the completion of creative and intellectual acts, by the beginning of the twentieth century it was seen as a privilege that few could experience. According to historian Karin Bijsterveld, throughout the nineteenth century the sounds of new technologies were 'considered to cut through the existing social order' to such an extent that intellectuals discussed urban noise pollution as a kind of barbarism that threatened the integrity of civilisation.[42] In 1851, Arthur Schopenhauer criticised newly established traffic systems because the whip-cracking of drivers 'puts an end to all quiet thought'; in 1864, Charles Babbage launched a campaign against London street music that specifically targeted the lower classes.[43] Indeed, as Bijsterveld states, discussions about noise pollution often disparage sounds that do 'not fit into the lifestyle of a growing professional urban class longing for peaceful reading and studying' and the end of the nineteenth century saw both technological and street noise conceived as profoundly unintellectual forces.[44]

These discussions continued long into the twentieth century. In 1933, Albert Einstein suggested that all scientific minds should seek 'the monotony of a quiet life' to stimulate creativity in a time of 'world crisis'.[45] A similarly quiet undercurrent continued throughout many political discussions of the period. Virginia Woolf's famous speech on a woman's right to 'luxury and privacy and space' in *A Room of One's Own* (1929) also highlights the scarcity of quiet environments. Woolf pictures the 'quiet rooms' in the 'quiet quadrangles' of Oxford and notes that the value of privacy is in actuality the privileged space for reflection.[46] The loud noises of public spaces worked against creativity. In Woolf's formulation, '[d]ogs will bark; people will interrupt' in the spaces usually ascribed to women but 'to have a room of her own, let alone a quiet room or a sound-proof room' frees the subject from the disturbance of external noise.[47] It is interesting to note that although literary scholars reference and parody the title of Woolf's essay, her stipulation that a room of one's own should also be quiet is rarely considered. A room in which to read and write is of little use, for instance, if it is noisy and Einstein and Woolf both argue that denying the individual privacy and solitude also denies their right to quiet spaces.

A middle-class and intellectual privileging of quiet is similarly inextricable from the idea of progress in a capitalist economy. The monotony of the production line and the tyranny of mechanical time, which many modernist writers railed against, are broadly symptomatic of an industrial society that conflates the act of reflection with a lack of productivity. By comparison, quiet contemplation is anti-utilitarian, using thought as a therapeutic exercise and emphasises the need to wait, to pause, to consider, with no expectation of a profitable end or product. With society increasingly geared towards production and profit, quiet began to seem less available to the individual. Moreover, if for Euripides society was loud through the chatter of 'unruly tongues', the noise of the twentieth century seemed increasingly inhuman, symbolised by the roar of industry, the rattle of machine guns and the din of progress. Even if society was not getting louder, it often appeared to be, precisely because the root cause of society's noises seemed both more remote and harder to control.

Despite this, the early years of the twentieth century saw noise become a favoured literary aesthetic. Modernism, as Marshall Berman suggests, 'nourished itself on the real trouble in the modern streets, and transformed their noise and dissonance into beauty and truth.'[48] In response to the increasing noise of the culture, art developed a vocabulary of radical political, cultural and aesthetic forms to articulate the new sounds of modernity. Futurist art was composed of a 'jabber of lines, planes, light, and noise' that refused to compress experience into a smaller picture, seeking louder and broader, frames for experience.[49] Similarly, Vorticism claimed to represent the 'crude energy' of the world through 'vivid and violent ideas', as declared in the manifesto for *Blast* in 1914.[50] *Blast*'s editor, Wyndham Lewis, claimed the journal's title referred to Vorticism's militant aesthetic, 'the blowing away of dead ideas and worn-out notions' that would be realised in an explosion of noise and colour.[51] Importantly, Lewis believed that art should account for noise as a symptom of modernity and the avant-garde increasingly criticised artists who neglected or ignored society's volume, diagnosing quiet as a failure to meet the radical, modernising, terrifying but often exciting changes that were happening in the culture of the time.

The proliferation of manifestos written during this period further reflects early twentieth-century ideas about the position of the artist in relation to society. The manifesto, as a public declaration or proclamation, articulates, justifies and defends a particular position by outlining a set of aesthetic decisions. By their nature, manifestos blur the distinction between politics and art, with many defining their position in relation to the failures of another movement. The Dadaist Manifesto of Berlin written in 1918 accused expressionism of political quietism and characterised expressionists as 'people who prefer their armchair to the noise of the street'.[52] The Dadaist Manifesto further insinuated that to be quiet was to be politically passive, to ignore the activity of the world outside of the comfort of your home and to obscure the essential dynamism of existence:

> Life appears as a simultaneous muddle of noises, colours and spiritual rhythms, which is taken unmodified, with all the sensational screams and fevers of its reckless everyday psyche and with all its brutal reality.[53]

Dadaists therefore emphasised what many modernist schools suggested. Accepting that noise suffused modern society, the Futurists, Vorticists and Dadaists believed that the artist had to represent the noise of society in order to fully engage with their contemporary moment. Although this noise could be 'brutal' for an artist and would sacrifice the comfort of repose, an aesthetic of noise was deemed the only way in which to engage with the 'reality' of the historical moment.

Many novelists writing in the first half of the twentieth century also explored the ubiquity of noise in contemporary urban life. In *Ulysses* (1922), James Joyce wrote a portrait of Dublin full of sounds: keys that 'jingled', barrels 'dullthudding' and 'wild newsboys' who cried out; a place where God is conceived as 'a shout in the street'.[54] Attempting to produce 'the fullest account ever given of the city in which he lived', Joyce regards the bustle of the streets with curiosity, joy and inevitability.[55] The citizens of Joyce's imagined Dublin consider the benefits of quiet with irony: a housewife who claims to do '[a]nything for a quiet life' admits that quiet states are an idealised respite from the working day and not a realistic alternative for a woman of her position.[56] Even Leopold Bloom, who loves the noise of the city, shaves at night time so that he may enjoy 'quiet reflections' he would not otherwise have time for.[57] On occasion, Bloom travels to the 'quiet parts of the city': in the 'Hades' episode, he attends Paddy Dignam's funeral and spends time alone in the cemetery where he reflects on his mortality.[58] However, this moment of contemplation ends with a rejection of death's ultimate silence in favour of the 'warm fullblooded life' of the city filled with 'the loud throbs of cranks'.[59] Sounds fascinate Bloom. He is a citizen of the modern age who thrives by identifying the varied noises of the streets and whose name is even misspelt as 'L. Boom' when it appears in the newspaper, a mistake that further links his identity to the noise of the city. The noises of Dublin are, then, a kind of symphony, a vital part of Bloom's experience and celebration of the everyday. Correspondingly, quiet exists as a minor element of *Ulysses'* portrayal of experience, found only in cemeteries or at night when the work of the day is over.

Joyce was perhaps exceptionally enthused by the noise of his contemporary world. Many more modernist writers invoked an aesthetic of noise to express its intellectual threat. On the other side of the Atlantic, John Dos Passos wrote negatively about the sickening volume of New York City in *Manhattan Transfer* (1925). In the novel, the residents of Manhattan often find themselves 'reluctant to go back into the noise and fume'; they are besieged by air that 'smells of crowds, is full of noise and sunlight.'[60] Indeed, the crowds that Poe and Hawthorne identified as a source of disturbance to the quiet individual of the nineteenth century seem toxic and deafening in the volume of twentieth-century New York. Dos Passos is particularly critical of the ways in which the flow of the working day denies the city dweller time in which to pause and reflect. *Manhattan Transfer* opens with workers being fed into the city as if on a production line, 'crushed and jostling like apples fed down a chute into a press', suggesting that while the pressures of capitalism sicken the citizen with noise, the relentless pace of modernity also denies the individual the mental and physical space in which to recover.[61] In *Manhattan Transfer*, the noise of society is increasingly inhuman and the human subject increasingly dehumanised by their part in a much louder machine.

By comparison, and when positioned against the noise of the twentieth century, the quiet novel seemed old-fashioned and troublingly out of touch. Literary critics aimed accusations of quietism at women writers whose fiction did not seem to reflect society's advancements. In 1900, Charles Frederick Johnson retrospectively defined Jane Austen as a quiet novelist in his survey of British and American literature. Austen, he claims, was 'an English girl [who] set the model for the quiet novel of contemporary society.'[62] In 1905, an unnamed reviewer for *The Spectator* called German novelist Mrs Alfred Sidgwick a writer 'of a quiet kind' whose novels lack the capacity to 'harrow or perplex' that male novelists exhibit.[63] As the noise of society seemed to increase, these reviewers associated quiet with a retreat to the home, domesticity and conservatism. In 1921, American critic Maurice Francis Egan proclaimed 'The Return of the Quiet Novel' in London journal *The Bookman* and argued that the quiet novel provides refuge from the present when the political climate becomes too exciting. Victorian novelists of 'comfortable quietness' provided Egan with refuge from the events of the First World War, at a time when citizens became 'bored', he claimed, by the overtly 'sociological problems' of wartime.[64] However, rather than the return of the quiet novel, Egan suggests a rereading of novels that centre on quieter lives and his nostalgic analysis equates the quiet prose of his age with primarily women authors whom he reads as disengaged from national and political culture.

Egan's reading of quiet fiction reflects the critical attitudes of his time: the soundscape of modernity was so characterised by noise that intellectuals only occasionally reclaimed the necessity of reflection, solitude and quiet in the present. In *The Conquest of Happiness* (1930), Bertrand Russell created a guide for everyday living that might also cultivate quiet. Recalling classical and transcendentalist philosophers before him, Russell criticises noise for degrading the quality of independent thought and offers quiet as an alternate means of joy and resistance: 'A happy life must be to a great extent a quiet life, for it is only in an atmosphere of quiet that joy dare live.'[65] Importantly, and as I argue in Chapter 2, Russell connects the noise of a capitalist society to a culture that privileges the event as a temporal construct. The citizens of a post-industrial society are prone to boredom, Russell suggests, and the idea of event becomes increasingly attractive to their unused minds because it distinguishes one day from the next. When the choices offered by modernity threaten to cripple the individual, a quiet life turns away from prescriptive ideals and by rejecting the common markers of success, quiet restores the time for independent thought to the present moment. Like Emerson and Thoreau a century before him, Russell then extends the idea that reflection can be an alternative form of personal and social action, if the individual takes the time to cultivate a quiet environment around them.

At the height of modernity's engagement with noise, psychoanalysis formed a parallel and often competing discourse that borrowed heavily from literature's central problems. This developing field both influenced and challenged the exploration of subjectivity – a primary object of the modernist novel – while sharing its fascination with human origins, dreams and fantasies, sexuality and 'the primitive'. Freud's theory of the unconscious famously proposed new ways in which suppressed desires rose to interrupt consciousness and was hugely influential to many modernist writers who depicted interiority as a tapestry of known and unknown desires.[66] In Virginia Woolf's final novel, *Between the Acts* (1941), desire speaks loudly beyond the reserve that society imprints onto her characters: '[t]he whole world was filled with dumb yearning [...] It was the primeval voice sounding loud in the ear of the present moment.'[67] Indeed, as Woolf indicates, psychoanalysis proposed that desire undercut the civilised exterior of society and many writers represented consciousness as a series of internal shouts that disrupted the logic of the external world.

At the same time, Western – and specifically American – culture compounded a preference for 'extroversion' following the publication of a major psychoanalytic work. In *Psychological Types* (1921), Carl Jung popularised the use of introvert and extrovert as oppositional elements of personality, arguing that the difference between the two originates from the outside stimulation that each requires to function. An extroverted personality is gratified by activities outside of the self, while introverts share none of the former's interest in the logical order of outward reality. Importantly, the introvert problematises the role of action in their daily existence and, Jung admits, looks 'useless' from a rationalistic standpoint. However, Jung counters that:

> [V]iewed from a higher standpoint, [introverts] are living evidence that this rich and varied world with its overflowing and intoxicating life is not purely external, but also exists within ... their lives teach the other possibility, the interior life which is so painfully wanting in our civilisation.[68]

Jung claims here that introverted personalities lead a 'rich and varied' existence through quiet practices that distance them from society. Their love of quiet teaches 'the other possibility', a way of living that is predicated by reflection rather than external action and event.

Most important to the quiet aesthetic developed here, while extroverts project an articulate outer life that reassures the wider world of a peaceful and efficient interiority, introverts avoid confrontation, are often reluctant to draw attention to themselves and rarely make demands on the attention of others. So, as psychoanalysis associated quiet with the suppression of desire, and despite Jung's praise for both ends of his introvert/extrovert spectrum, by and large Western capitalism continued to distrust quiet people and equated their cultivation of internal life with a nervous withdrawal from civilisation and the noise of modern life.

## The quiet modernist novel

Against a cultural suspicion of quiet people, and alongside the widespread assumption that quiet environments were under threat, writers and artists continued to elevate quiet characters, states and spaces. Indeed, many modernist fictions used characterisation to elaborate interior environments, emptying out the idea of narrative so that the action of the 'story' dissolved to what David Shields calls the 'mental architecture of time'.[69] As Saikat Majumdar argues, particularly in a colonial and postcolonial context, many modernist writers believed that 'the banality of eventlessness' and the 'quiet folds of the everyday' crystallised the experience of living in modernity better than the comparatively rare experiences of spectacle and drama.[70] Yet by saturating their novels in portrayals of subjectivity and prioritising the presentation of consciousness over topical event many modernist writers were also accused of political quietism.

Initially conceived as a form of religious mysticism that embraces internal contemplation, quietism is most commonly used in the context created by the French Revolution when it became associated with inactivity and used as an expression of political abuse.[71] Of particular relevance to this book and the aesthetic of fiction it proposes, literary critics often use the term to accuse older schools of apathy. In 1998, Vincent B. Leitch described New Criticism as the inclination to combine 'quietism and asceticism'; in the same year, narratologist Mark Currie linked deconstruction to a form of 'political quietism' in his influential survey of postmodern narrative theory.[72] For many critics, strands of radicalism that have lost their edge also stand accused. Feminist critic Martha Nussbaum describes Judith Butler's move away from 'old-style feminist politics and material realities' as a brand of 'hip quietism' that sacrifices integrity to enforce the status quo.[73]

# The quiet novel

Similarly, postcolonial theorist Edward Said criticised the late work of Michel Foucault for justifying 'political quietism with sophisticated intellectualism'.[74] Notably, critics rarely define what quietism means and, like quiet, its use as a term of accusation rests almost entirely on residual associations with inaction and passivity.

Yet the persistence of a quiet aesthetic, as I define it, throughout the twentieth century seems directly connected to the ways in which artists imagine their relationship with society. As later chapters in this study will argue, noise has the potential to reaffirm our relationality to others and to stress our ongoing relevance to the contemporary world. To some, representing noise also provides evidence of the artist's total immersion in society, invoking solidarity with the masses that face its day-to-day threat. Many strands of modernism were therefore attracted to noise as a representation of life's breadth and an indication of the artist's function in modernity. Yet reading, writing and contemplation remained fundamentally 'quiet' activities and although many strands of modernism were noisy, the modernist novel continued to provide a home for reflective processes. Virginia Woolf, for example, received particular criticism for her portrayal of the interior lives of quiet characters, specifically those of women.[75] Many of Woolf's characters find it difficult to process the noise of society and, if read for quiet, her novels often preach the benefits of reflection. The character of Mrs Ramsey, in *To the Lighthouse* (1927) lives so much for others that she fiercely defends her moments of solitude:

> [I]t was a relief when they went to bed. For now she need not think about anybody. She could be herself, by herself. And that was what now she often felt the need of – to think; well, not even to think. To be silent; to be alone. All the being and the doing, expansive, glittering, vocal, evaporated; and one shrunk, with a sense of solemnity, to being oneself, a wedge-shaped core of darkness, something invisible to others.[76]

Rather than entirely retreating from the world, Mrs Ramsey seeks the quiet as respite from the action of the day and as a necessary part of family life. In solitude, the ability to 'be silent; to be alone' returns her to an elemental form of being where social need or collective value does not predicate her desires. It is, in other words, a space of liberation in which '[a]ll the being and doing' resolves into a calm and restorative solitude.

Accusations of quietism are similarly quashed when we consider Woolf's characters in light of her essay, 'Modern Fiction' (1921). In it, Woolf contends that the fiction of Edwardian novelists like Arnold Bennett and John Galsworthy do not represent the modern citizen's experience; that 'an ordinary mind on an ordinary day' looks nothing 'like' the life presented in popular works of high realism.[77] 'Modern Fiction' further affirms Woolf's commitment to representing society as it is commonly, if quietly, experienced and suggests that her depictions of moments of stillness and reflection are in fact acts of social engagement. In Mrs Dalloway (1925), maintaining a complex web of social relationships consumes Clarissa, thus demonstrating her continued engagement with the world. An introvert with an extrovert's social circle, she is defined by her relationship to others even in the novel's title.[78] Yet Mrs Dalloway ultimately wants to escape her party, a highly anticipated 'event', and claims to prefer moments of quiet. The noise of the party frightens Clarissa, '"But the noise!" she said. "The noise"', and although her guests reassure her that its loud tenor is a 'sign of success', the party's volume continues to upset her.[79] Clarissa is, then, unlike her friends who seem to be at ease with noise; she prefers the late evening of the party as it begins to slow down, when 'one found old friends; quiet nooks and corners; and the loveliest views.'[80] Indeed, Woolf contrasts Clarissa's discomfort in noise with the pleasure of the people around her and the eponymous Mrs Dalloway expresses a preference for quiet that goes beyond a personal aversion to people.

In delineating the practitioners of a quiet aesthetic, we might also think of Marcel Proust whose À la recherche du temps perdu (1913) is premised on the action of inaction. Samuel Beckett located Proust's originality in the 'conflict between intervention and quietism' that complicates the relationship between action and repose and, fittingly, the opening of volume one, Du côté de chez Swann, is a description of both falling asleep and of coming into being, highlighting the individual's 'sense of existence as it may quiver in the depths of an animal'.[81] There is something elemental to this kind of writing, in Proust's words an 'original simplicity' that is particularly difficult to describe narratologically.[82] Indeed, I would argue that the unnarratability of Proust's fiction embodies the alternate drive of all quiet fictions that are notably free from the external progression of event. Proust's protagonist, Marcel, is an introverted man who seeks out quiet locations. He cultivates quiet spaces, retreating to a room at the top of the house and valuing the unobtrusive nature of his pastimes: 'all of those occupations of mine that demanded an inviolable solitude: reading, reveries, tears and sensuous pleasure.'[83] Tellingly, Marcel also reads quiet novels. He recommends the works of George Sand first because of her focus on ordinary events and second because Sand does not attempt to paint a broad social picture. In line with the terms defined in my Introduction, À la recherche du temps perdu meets the conditions of a quiet aesthetic: Proust's protagonist Marcel is quiet in countenance, seeks out quiet locations and, as a narrator, focuses on the internal movement of thought to tell the novel's 'story'.

Most significantly, and key to my discussion of the quiet novel in its contemporary form, very little happens in À la recherche du temps perdu that might outwardly be perceived as action. Proust relies on the reader's interest in the process of reflection and the reveries he depicts to carry their attention to the novel's end. The narrative of all four volumes is driven by the premise that experience only becomes meaningful through reflection, progressing narratologically through the complex relationship of past and present rather than following a series of events. Reflection is therefore the central engine of Proust's fiction. As Marcel reflects on his childhood, he acknowledges that the passing of time has changed his feelings, his pleasures and his pains. However, a quiet environment allows these feelings to return to him more clearly. In a quiet place, in the attic, in seclusion, in Combray, Marcel feels his pain anew:

> [I]f I take care to listen, the sobs I was strong enough to contain in front of my father and that did not burst out until I found myself alone again with Mama. They have never really stopped and it is only because life is quieting down around me more and more now that I can hear them again, like those convent bells covered so well by the clamour of the town during the day that one would think they had ceased altogether but which begin sounding again in the silence of the evening.[84]

When Marcel is undisturbed by the events of his present, the past returns to him and quiet is here linked to a lack of narrative event as Marcel inhabits an inactive 'now' through which he is able to draw lessons from the past. Although life is 'quieting down' around Marcel, it is not because the volume of his experience is diminishing but because less and less happens around him. It is only in quiet, moreover, that Marcel is able to notice the ways in which the present cannot be divorced from the past and, as I foreground in my discussion of '9/11' in Chapter 2, it is only in quiet that he is able to understand his present moment in terms of its continuities rather than its traumatic ruptures.

Beckett's reference to quietism in his description of Proust reveals yet another way of exploring the ideological tension between performances of action and inaction that I argue quiet fictions elaborate. As a strand of philosophy, and when differentiated from its use as a term of accusation, quietism shares several traits with quiet prose: both have therapeutic goals (i.e. they seek no narrative or philosophical resolution), emphasise narratives of continuity over rupture and seek a vocabulary for experience that is not based on the teleological force of action. Amy M. King's theory of narrative stillness is particularly interesting in this respect. King seeks a vocabulary for forms of duration that tends to dynamism and attention beyond the progression of event, reading passages of narrative description for the practice of reverence that is animated by a will to 'be at peace and pay attention' rather than the reader's desire to reach the end of the story.[85] As noted in my Introduction, Kevin Everod Quashie's *The Sovereignty of Quiet: Beyond Resistance in Black Culture* (2010) is the only work of criticism to conceive of a quiet aesthetic similar to my own; he argues that black culture 'is or is supposed to be loud, literally as well as metaphorically, since such loudness is the expressiveness that articulates its resistance.'[86] For Quashie, quiet has the potential to express black subjectivity in a way that is 'expansive, voluptuous, creative; impulsive and dangerous'.[87] Yet quiet's expressiveness is hard to read. Its patience is often mistaken for passivity and its lack of external movement often hides internal motion. *The Sovereignty of Quiet* therefore constructs a quiet aesthetic that is colloquial and discursive, conceiving quiet's expressiveness as 'a quality or a sensibility of being' that prioritises the communication of subjectivity over the progression of narrative action.[88]

The discussions staged by King and Quashie also confirm why the 'eventless' prose of quiet fiction is the hardest aspect to delineate. Action is the traditional engine of fiction, the drive that moves a narrative forward and, historically, theories of narrative tend to centre on episodes as devices that advance the plot.[89] To write a novel where very little happens would seem to conflict with a primary object of narrative which is to tell a story from beginning to end. However, in the quiet novel 'contemplation is an activity – intense, intellectual, and often physical', as Gérard Genette once wrote of the work of Proust.⁹⁰ Quiet narratives are propelled by thought-processes, the present recall of memory and the configurations of conscious experience. While the absence of plot and topical content leaves them open to accusations of disengagement, the quiet narrative is composed, as Michael Sayeau also claims of modernist narratives, by 'a rhythm defined by banal continuity rather than accentuated series of revolutionary shocks'.⁹¹ As such, the reader must work to connect a quiet text with its political and historical contexts because the cultivation and representation of reflective states will often appear to be apolitical.

After modernism, postmodernism's preoccupation with the failure of novelty and innovation sidelined quiet and widespread concern for the breakdown of language frequently conflated the term with silence. Under this system of analysis, quiet became associated with an enforced passivity, the absence of discussion and the failure to object.⁹² Yet the quiet novel did not cease to exist entirely. A key precursor of today's quiet narratives is John Williams' 1965 novel *Stoner*, republished to great acclaim in 2006. The novel's eponymous protagonist is an unassuming professor of literature at the University of Missouri who is Proustian in his mannerisms and introverted in his habits, retreating into scholarly seclusion both because he finds it comforting and because his seclusion shields him from the noise of society. Stoner enjoys a moderately successful career but remains a paragon of inaction, a trait that is encouraged by his position in the academy.

When the First World War breaks out, Stoner's reaction is 'a vast reserve of indifference'.⁹³ He is mildly upset at the prospect of disruption in his life but otherwise unmoved and the novel is quiet, here, because Williams largely excludes historical events from the narrative. On campus in Missouri, the professor burrows further away from the outside world, choosing to remain at the university rather than to participate in the war:

> He stayed in his small room, struggling with his decision. His books and the quiet of his room surrounded him; only rarely was he aware of the world outside his room, of the far murmur of shouting students, of the swift clatter of a buggy on the brick streets.⁹⁴

Stoner is a quietist, then, not simply because he objects to the war but because he questions the logic of direct action. Most telling of the novel's quiet aesthetic, although Stoner's life is not without personal hardship,[95] he is not punished for his lack of political engagement and even benefits from his avoidance of the war when he obtains a teaching contract due to a shortage of candidates. As a novel, *Stoner* also differs from the quiet aesthetic defined here in both its modernist and its contemporary forms in one significant respect: Williams' protagonist is declaratively averse to interiority and never develops 'the habit of introspection' because he finds it 'distasteful'.[96] As a result, the narrative is more inclined to realism than the interior narratives examined in later chapters of this study and the novel is quiet in its measured observances rather than its inherent subjectivity.

*Stoner* is also of interest to *The quiet contemporary American novel* because its publication shares parallels with the experience of many quiet contemporary novelists. In 1965, the novel received little critical attention: newspapers did not widely print reviews, *The New Yorker* only briefly noted its publication and consequently *Stoner* sold just 2,000 copies. However, Williams had the right readers. Irving Howe wrote favourably of the novel in *The New Republic* and *Stoner* was an underground favourite by the time Williams received the National Book Award for his fourth novel *Augustus* in 1972.[97] Reviews of *Stoner's* 2006 republication largely agree that the book is old-fashioned but novelist Steve Almond, an MFA student in the 1960s, claims that *Stoner* was 'audacious' at the time for its negation of the vogue to 'make it new'.[98] By the time of its republication, the novel's ideas had finally 'come of age', he claims, for a different generation of MFA programmes who value slowly unfolding narratives. Consequently, the reprint of Williams' text attracted rave reviews and became a worldwide bestseller.[99] When it was finally reviewed by *The New York Times* in 2007, Morris Dickstein, best known for his work on the fiction of the 1960s, called *Stoner* 'a perfect novel' because of the 'quality of attention' found in its prose.[100] The success of *Stoner's* contemporary revival was celebrated for its 'perfect' singularity; Williams was not linked to a body of quiet writers and nor was comparison drawn to the multiplicity of quiet characters that proliferate in American fiction.

Contrasting literary and philosophical oppositions of quiet and loud continued throughout the postmodern era and into the early twenty-first century. Chapter 2 will explore this dynamic at greater length, by arguing that noise is often favoured in situations that seem to be unprecedented, with the terrorist attacks of 11 September 2001 as representative. The residual association of quiet with silence is an important factor in the former's continued association with inaction. Toni Morrison provides a notable use of the colloquial phrase '*Quiet as it's kept*' to begin the narrative of nine-year-old narrator Claudia MacTeer in her debut novel *The Bluest Eye* (1970): 'Quiet as it's kept, there were no marigolds in the fall of 1941. We thought, at the time, that it was because Pecola was having her father's baby that the marigolds did not grow.'[101] The phrase here is conspiratorial and intimate as Claudia overhears her parents using it.[102] However, as the '*kept*' secret is quickly revealed to be the sexual abuse that Pecola suffers at the hands of her father, the phrase is also associated with the suppression of harmful information. Claudia's quiet is not communicative and, in this instance, threatens to incur further harm because it hides an act of oppression. Trapped within a 'cocoon' that she has not chosen for herself, Pecola retreats, becoming subdued as a person because she feels unable to participate in or compete with the noise of society.[103] Morrison therefore invokes quiet as a form of silence that suppresses the vulnerable and covers a history of abuse, marginalising its victims as an expression of trauma.

Morrison's use of 'quiet' in *The Bluest Eye* also points to the difficulty of defining the term absolutely. Expansive for some and a survival strategy or imposition for others, the value of quiet is ultimately subjective, embodying different qualities in different contexts. For women, especially LGBTQ women and women of colour, keeping quiet has been essential to avoid social chastisement. 'I look quiet and consistent', Anaïs Nin wrote in her early diaries, 'but few know how many women there are in me.'[104] Nin's use of quiet here implies that her outwardly 'quiet' countenance protects noisier multitudes that society would deem inappropriate. Her diary is full of references to keeping or being 'kept quiet' because, she writes, it is 'the best thing I can do'.[105]

Ultimately, while keeping Morrison's and Nin's use of the term in mind, this study conceives of quiet as a dynamic term, one that is neither wholly negative nor positive, but one that critics often neglect as an aesthetic of contemporaneity because of its residual associations with passivity and inaction. Rather than claiming our contemporary moment to be unique in its volume, or to frame quiet as a uniquely positive state, which might extend the exceptionalism this study interrogates, I argue that the quiet novel prioritises a mode of reflection and meditation that has always existed at the margins of American culture. This book seeks a vocabulary for writing about prose that divorces narrative meaning from the noise of the contemporary world and examines how and why quiet has so often been dismissed as unfashionable, even as un-American, because of its association with inaction. In this, I do not wish to dismiss the importance of evental narratives so much as to decentre them while also problematising the necessity of noise and narrative action as a marker of any text's contemporaneity. It is this idea, then, and the noisy aesthetic of contemporary American fiction, that I deconstruct in the next chapter.

## Notes

1 Religious quietism began as a movement in Spain and France in the seventeenth and eighteenth centuries to promote the abandonment of individual determination to the higher notion of God's will. Quietism therefore originally instructed the abandonment of subjectivity and, to an extent, the acceptance of passivity by eschewing all spiritual and moral struggles in order to entertain God's will. See: Stephen R. Munzer, 'Self-Abandonment and Self-Denial: Quietism, Calvinism, and the Prospect of Hell', *The Journal of Religious Ethics* 33: 4 (December 2005), pp. 747–781.
2 Genesis 25:27, *New International Version*, p. 27. In Gen. 32, Jacob wrestles with a physical manifestation of God who then names him Israel. So, while Israel, as a name, is centred on the act of internal wrestling, a more literal, physical episode of wrestling occurs later in the same book.
3 Plato, 'Charmides', quoted by L. A. Kosman, 'Charmides' First Definition: Sophrosyne as Quietness', in *Essays in Ancient Greek Philosophy II*, ed. John Peter Anton and Anthony Preus (New York: State University of New York Press, 1983), p. 204; Euripides, *The Bakkhai*, *The Essential Euripides*, trans. Robert Emmet Meagher (Amherst: University of Massachusetts Press, 1995), p. 478.
4 Aristotle, *Metaphysics*, trans. Thomas Taylor (London: Davis, Wilks, & Taylor, 1801), p. 192.
5 A Peripatetic, 'The Piccadilly Papers: The Confessions of Novelists', *London Society* XIII (London: William Clowes and Sons, February 1868), p. 155.
6 Such religious imagery does not continue through reviews of quiet novels, although the novels of Marilynne Robinson and Paul Harding are examined in depth in Chapter 3 and both explore the regional history of Christianity in Iowa and Massachusetts. See: Anne Thurston, 'Marilynne Robinson and the Fate of Faith', *Studies: An Irish Quarterly*

*Review*, 99:396 (winter 2010), pp. 449–454; Paul Harding, interviewed by Alexander Benaim, 'Q&A', *Intelligent Life*, http://moreintelligentlife.com/blog/alexander-benaim/qa-paul-harding-author-pulitzer-prize-winner.

7   The unnamed and uncited review is quoted in the back cover of Zachary Edwards, *Primitae* (London: Provost and Co., 1869), p. 203.
8   Alden, 'Miss Tommy', p. 141.
9   Ibid.
10  'Ada Cambridge's New Novel', p. 2.
11  Amelia DeFalco, 'In Praise of Idleness: Aging and the Morality of Inactivity', *Cultural Critique*, 92 (winter 2012), p. 98.
12  Ibid., p. 103.
13  Ibid., p. 100.
14  Graham Greene, *The Quiet American* (London: Vintage, 2004), p. 9.
15  This 'failure to speak' is common to a lot of Greene's protagonists: the 'whiskey priest' in *The Power and the Glory* (1940), Henry Scobie in *The Heart of the Matter* (1948) and Sarah Miles in *The End of the Affair* (1951). Even if Greene sees quiet as an odd characteristic for an American, he is interested in its relation to humanity in a more general sense. Interestingly, and although I do not agree, journalist and war correspondent Gloria Emerson described *The Quiet American* as a 'quiet novel' in her 1978 profile of Greene for *Rolling Stone*, stating that it is a 'small and quiet novel [that] told us nearly everything'. Emerson, 'Our Man in Antibes: Graham Greene', in *Conversations with Graham Greene*, ed. Henry J. Donaghy (Jackson: University Press of Mississippi, 1992), p. 123.
16  For historical studies of American noise, see: Eric Schmidt, *Hearing Things: Religion, Illusion, and the American Enlightenment* (Cambridge, MA: Harvard University Press, 2002); Richard Rath, *How Early America Sounded* (Ithaca, NY: Cornell University Press, 2003); Emily Thompson, *The Soundscape of Modernity: Architectural Acoustics and the Culture of Listening in America, 1900-1933* (Cambridge, MA: Massachusetts Institute of Technology University Press, 2004); Kara Keeling and Josh Kun (eds), *Sound Clash: Listening to American Studies* (Baltimore, MD: Johns Hopkins University Press, 2012).
17  Robert Coughlan, 'How We Appear to Others', *Life* (23 December 1957), p. 151.
18  Thompson, *The Soundscape of Modernity*, p. 115.
19  Ibid.
20  Prochnik delineates a 'war' between quiet and loud environments, suggesting that '[i]n the United States alone the cost of noise is upward of $4 billion a year'. George Prochnik, *In Pursuit of Silence: Listening for Meaning in a World of Noise* (New York: Random House, 2010), p. 200.

21  Garret Keizer, *The Unwanted Sound of Everything We Want: A Book About Noise* (New York: Public Affairs, 2010), p. 165.
22  Brandon LaBelle, *Background Noise: Perspectives on Sound Art* (London: Bloomsbury, 2006), p. xi.
23  Ibid., p. xi.
24  Edgar Allan Poe, 'The Man of the Crowd', *The Collected Works of Edgar Allan Poe* (Chatham: Wordsworth Editions, 2004), p. 212. Poe begins 'The Man of the Crowd' with this ambiguous quote from Jean de la Bruyère: '*Ce grand malheur, de ne pouvoir être seul*' (Such a great misfortune, not to be able to be alone). The line could be taken two ways, the misfortune being either to be always surrounded by others, or to lack the capacity to survive by oneself, leaving the narrator's obsession with the eponymous crowd equally ambiguous. Poe's 'The Murders in the Rue Morgue' (1841) also depicts an unnamed narrator who locks himself away to avoid human contact and only ventures into the city at night, 'amid the wild lights and shadows of the populous city, that infinity of mental excitement which quiet observation can afford.' Poe, 'The Murder in the Rue Morgue', *The Collected Works of Edgar Allan Poe*, p. 5.
25  Poe, 'The Man of the Crowd', p. 207.
26  Hawthorne was also a notorious recluse and provided a lengthy descriptions of a quiet life in 'The Custom House', his famous introduction to *The Scarlet Letter* (1850). The author describes the narrator's life as a government official in small town Massachusetts and laments 'the tedious lapse of official life' where he is doomed to repeat menial tasks amongst a retinue of aging colleagues. The narrator's quiet nature means that he is suited to this life, but also sentences him to its continuation. As the narrator points out, 'it would never be a measure of policy to turn out so quiet an individual as myself.' Hawthorne's quietness, then, commits him to a life of tasks for minor government but, surrounded by similarly uninspiring men, he finds himself unable to write, the industrial nature of his boredom eventually defeating any creative impulse. See: Hawthorne, *The Scarlet Letter* (New York: Penguin, 1983), p. 36.
27  Hawthorne, *The Scarlet Letter*, p. 77.
28  Nathaniel Hawthorne, *The Blithedale Romance* (New York: Tark Classic Fiction, 2008), pp. 183, 15.
29  Susan Cain, *Quiet: The Power of Introverts in a World That Can't Stop Talking* (London: Penguin, 2012), p. 12. Although Cain's book was extremely successful, spawning a million think pieces on the 'quiet revolution', its usefulness to this study is limited by the author's over simplification of the introvert/extrovert binary and her role as a business analyst specialising in maximising the employment potential

of introverts. See also: Sophia Dembling, *The Introvert's Way: Living a Quiet Life in a Noisy World* (London: Penguin, 2012); Jennifer B. Kahnweiler, *Quiet Influence: The Introvert's Guide to Making a Difference* (San Francisco, CA: Berrett-Koehler Publishers, 2013).

30  Herman Melville, 'Bartleby, The Scrivener: A Story of Wall Street', in his *Billy Budd and Other Stories* (Ware: Wordsworth Classics, 1998), p. 23. In 1989, Dan McCall praised the 'quiet mysteries' of Melville's story, arguing that decades of elaborate methodological readings had divorced the work from its quietly affective content. McCall, *The Silence of Bartleby* (New York: Cornell University Press, 1989), p. 177. Interestingly, McCall's book was widely neglected on publication but, in 2008, became the subject of a critical reappraisal that hoped to rescue the 'quietly'-received work from 'the bibliographic depths'. See: Douglas Anderson, 'Re-Reading *The Silence of Bartleby*', *American Literary History*, 20:3 (fall 2008), p. 479.

31  Melville, 'Bartleby', p. 26.

32  Clark Davis, '"Not Like Any Form of Activity": Waiting in Emerson, Melville, and Weil', *Common Knowledge*, 15:1 (winter 2009), p. 48. Notably, by narrating 'Bartleby' from the perspective of the employer, Melville also denies the reader access to Bartleby's inner monologue. The reader can only wonder if the sedateness of his aspect reflects the mental instability the narrator suspects he possesses.

33  Contrarily, Walter Benn Michaels suggests that Bartleby's refusal conforms to rather than rebels against capitalism. In a contract society, Michaels writes, the individual has the freedom not to make a contract and so refusal, as per my suggestion, is always and in itself a form of action. Michaels, *Gold Standard and the Logic of Naturalism* (Berkeley: University of California Press, 1987), pp. 18–19. Bartleby's influence on the Occupy Wall Street movement further demonstrates his embodiment of a 'very passive resistance': see Regina Dilgen, 'The Original Occupy Wall Street: Melville's "Bartleby, the Scrivener"', *Radical Teacher*, 93 (spring 2012), p. 54; Jac Asher, '"Preferring Not To" in the Age of Occupy', *Periscope* (28 March 2013), http://socialtextjournal.org/periscope_article/preferring-not-to-in-the-age-of-occupy/.

34  Lawrence Buell, *Emerson* (Cambridge, MA: Harvard University Press, 2003), p. 243.

35  Ralph Waldo Emerson, 'The American Scholar', in *The Essential Writings of Ralph Waldo Emerson*, ed. Brooks Atkinson (New York: Random House, 2000), p. 53.

36  Emerson, 'Self Reliance', in *The Essential Writings of Ralph Waldo Emerson*, p. 139.

37  Henry David Thoreau, *Walden* (Princeton, NJ: Princeton University Press, 2004), pp. 6, 8.

38  Ibid., p. 146.
39  Martin Bickman, *Walden: Volatile Truths* (New York: Twayne Publishers, 1992), p. 47.
40  Thoreau, *Walden*, pp. 88, 111.
41  Rebecca Solnit, 'Introduction: Prisons and Paradises', in her *Storming the Gates of Paradise: Landscapes for Politics* (Los Angeles: University of California Press, 2007), p. 4. See also Robert Ray's essay 'Distance' that defends Thoreau's 'distance problem' as a '*genre* issue' in his *Walden x 40: Essays on Thoreau* (Bloomington: University of Indiana Press, 2012), p. 37.
42  Karin Bijsterveld, *Mechanical Sound: Technology, Culture, and Public Problems of Noise in the Twentieth Century* (Cambridge, MA: MIT Press, 2008), p. 92.
43  Quoted in Bijsterveld, *Mechanical Sound*, p. 94.
44  Ibid.
45  Albert Einstein, 'Civilisation and Science', lecture at the Royal Albert Hall, London (4 October 1933), published as 'Personal Liberty' in *The New York Herald Tribune* (4 February 1934), pp. 14, 12.
46  Virginia Woolf, *A Room of One's Own* (New York: Harvest Books, 1989), p. 23.
47  Ibid., pp. 51, 52.
48  Marshall Berman, *All that is Solid Melts into Air: The Experience of Modernity* (New York: Simon and Schuster, 1982), p. 31.
49  Robert Hughes, *The Shock of the New* (London: Faber & Faber, 1991), p. 44.
50  Wyndham Lewis (ed.), *Blast: Review of the Great English Vortex*, 1 (20 June 1914), p. 7.
51  Lewis, 'Rebel Art in Modern Life', *Daily News* (7 April 1914), p. 14.
52  Richard Huelsenbeck, 'First German Dada Manifesto', in *Art in Theory 1900–1990: An Anthology of Changing Ideas*, ed. C. Harrison and P. Wood (Oxford: Blackwell, 1992), p. 254.
53  Ibid.
54  James Joyce, *Ulysses* (Oxford: Oxford University Press, 2008), pp. 116, 104, 130.
55  Declan Kiberd, *Ulysses and Us: The Art of Everyday Living* (London: Faber & Faber, 2010), p. 5.
56  Joyce, *Ulysses*, p. 525.
57  Although Bloom realises that shaving by daylight would be more efficient, and less dangerous, he continues to shave at night because 'absence of light [will] disturb him less than presence of noise'. Joyce, *Ulysses*, p. 558.
58  Ibid., p. 103.
59  Ibid., p. 108.

60  John Dos Passos, *Manhattan Transfer* (New York: Houghton Mifflin Company, 2000), pp. 196, 16.
61  Dos Passos, *Manhattan Transfer*, p. 3.
62  Charles Frederick Johnson, *Outline History of English and American Literature* (New York: American Book Company, 1900), p. 358.
63  'In Other Days', *The Spectator* (26 June 1915), p. 22.
64  Maurice Francis Egan, 'The Return of the Quiet Novel', *The Bookman* (September 1921), p. 18.
65  Bertrand Russell, *The Conquest of Happiness* (Oxford: Routledge Classics, 2006), p. 43.
66  In *The Unconscious* (1927), Freud writes of unconscious desire as 'the real motive force behind the advances that have brought the nervous system, with its infinite capabilities, to its present height of development.' Sigmund Freud, *The Unconscious*, trans. Graham Frankland (London: Penguin, 2005), p. 16. We might say, then, that psychoanalysis equated quietness with the concealment of louder instinctual desires that might lead the individual to a more decisive and more satisfying action.
67  Virginia Woolf, *Between the Acts* (New York: Harcourt, 1969), p. 40.
68  Carl Gustav Jung, *Psychological Types*, trans. H. G. Baynes (Princeton, NJ: Princeton University Press, 1990), p. 404.
69  David Shields, *Reality Hunger: A Manifesto* (New York: Hamish Hamilton, 2010), p. 19.
70  Saikat Majumdar, *Prose of the World: Modernism and the Banality of Empire* (New York: Columbia University Press, 2015), pp. 7, 107.
71  Recent scholarship has sought to define political and philosophical quietism beyond its origins in religious thought and to imagine, briefly, quietism's potential in literary criticism. There are few comprehensive surveys but in 2008 six special issues of the interdisciplinary journal *Common Knowledge* were dedicated to exploring the breadth of quietism. See: Jeffrey M. Perl, 'Introduction: More Trouble than They Are Worth', *Common Knowledge*, 15:1 (winter 2009), pp. 1–15; Perl 'Introduction: *Meza Voce* Quietism?' *Common Knowledge*, 16:1 (winter 2010), pp. 22–23. Today, quietism also exists as a minor strand of contemporary philosophy that has primarily therapeutic aims and stands against the formation of positive theses, locating the value of philosophy in revealing the flawed logic of existing concepts. See: Richard Rorty, 'Naturalism and Quietism', *Philosophy as Cultural Politics*, Vol. 4 of *Philosophical Papers* (Cambridge: Cambridge University Press, 2005), pp. 147–159; Stelios Virvidakis, 'Varieties of Quietism', *Philosophical Inquiry*, 20:1–2 (2006), pp. 157–175; Philip Pettit, 'Existentialism, Quietism, and Philosophy', in *The Future of Philosophy*, ed. Brian Leiter (Oxford: Oxford University Press, 2006), pp. 304–328; David

Macarthur, 'Pragmatism, Metaphysical Quietism and the Problem of Normativity', *Philosophical Topics*, 36 (2009), pp. 1–30.

72  Vincent B. Leitch, 'Poststructuralist Cultural Critique', in his *Cultural Criticism, Literary Theory, Poststructuralism* in *Literature: An Introduction to Fiction, Poetry, and Drama* (New York: Columbia University Press, 1992), p. 9; Mark Currie, *Postmodern Narrative Theory* (London: Palgrave Macmillan, 1998), p. 4. Leitch later broadened his complaint to identify 'quietism' in much of contemporary literary criticism due, he claims, to widespread institutionalisation in the humanities. Leitch, *Theory Matters* (London: Routledge, 2003), p. 71.

73  Martha Nussbaum, 'The Professor of Parody', *The New Republic* (22 February 1999), http://www.tnr.com/archive/0299/022299/nussbaum022299.html.

74  Edward Said, *The World, the Text, and the Critic* (Cambridge, MA: Harvard University Press, 1983), p. 245.

75  See: Rebecca L. Walkowitz, 'Virginia Woolf's Evasion: Critical Cosmopolitanism and British Modernism', in *Bad Modernisms*, ed. Douglas Mao and Rebecca L. Walkowitz (Durham, NC: Duke University Press, 2006), pp. 119–144. David Bradshaw also defends Woolf against charges of quietism and counters that her fiction is filled with references, often brief and unsustained, that indicate Woolf's political engagement. Bradshaw, 'Woolf's London, London's Woolf', in *Virginia Woolf in Context*, ed. Jane Goldman and Bryony Randall (Cambridge: Cambridge University Press, 2012), pp. 229–242.

76  Virginia Woolf, *To the Lighthouse* (Oxford: Wordsworth Classics, 1994), p. 45.

77  Woolf, 'Modern Fiction', in *Selected Essays*, ed. David Bradshaw (Oxford: Oxford University Press, 2008), p. 9.

78  Here, I read Clarissa as the quiet protagonist of the novel, although many of the same claims can be made of Septimus Smith, who Woolf describes as Clarissa's double in her Introduction to the 1928 edition of *Mrs Dalloway*. The structural oppressions of society trouble both characters and an inability to communicate leaves both feeling isolated. However, Septimus' experience of shell shock leaves his mind so troubled that he is unable to locate a quiet retreat, ultimately choosing the silence of death as his act of 'defiance', his 'attempt to communicate' in a manner that evades the noise associated with his war trauma, but that he now finds overwhelming in society. Woolf, *Mrs Dalloway* (London: Wordsworth Editions, 2003), p. 134.

79  Woolf, *Mrs Dalloway*, p. 128.

80  Ibid., p. 139.

81  Samuel Beckett, 'Proust in Pieces', *The Spectator* (23 June 1934), p. 63; Marcel Proust, *The Way by Swann's*, trans. Lydia Davis (London:

Penguin Books, 2003), p. 9. Beckett also developed an interest in quietism while living in Berlin through his readings of Thomas à Kempis, Arthur Schopenhauer and Proust. He titled his review of the Irish modernist poet Thomas MacGreevy 'Humanistic Quietism' and wanted to introduce quietism into the writing of *Murphy* (1938). See: Mark Nixon, 'Psychoanalysis, Quietism and Literary Waste', *Samuel Beckett's German Diaries 1936–1937* (New York: Continuum Books, 2011), pp. 37–59; Seán Kennedy, 'Beckett Reviewing MacGreevy: A Reconsideration', *Irish University Review*, 35:2 (winter 2005), pp. 273–287.

82   Swann even remarks on his dissatisfaction with the event as a mark of contemporaneity: 'What I fault the newspapers for is that day after day they draw our attention to insignificant things whereas only three or four times in our lives do we read a book in which there is something really essential.' Proust, *The Way by Swann's*, p. 29.

83   Ibid., p. 16.

84   Ibid., p. 40.

85   Amy M. King, 'Quietism and Narrative Stillness', *Common Knowledge*, 16:3 (fall 2010), p. 534. King explains that her essay is an account of '[t]he closest thing I know to quietism narrativized' but suggests that without the call for papers issued by the symposium 'quietistic' narratives would not have formed a part of her schema for stillness. See also: King, 'Stillness: Alternative Temporalities in Nineteenth-Century Narrative', *English Language Notes*, 46:1 (spring/summer 2008), pp. 95–103.

86   Kevin Everod Quashie, *The Sovereignty of Quiet: Beyond Resistance in Black Culture* (New Brunswick, NJ: Rutgers University Press, 2012), p. 11.

87   Ibid., p. 21.

88   Ibid., p. 334.

89   Canonical theories of narrative rely upon a language of progression that is based on the desire for conclusion. See, for example: Fredric Jameson, *The Political Unconscious: Narrative as a Socially Symbolic Act* (Ithaca, NY: Cornell University Press, 1981); Gérard Genette, *Narrative Discourse: An Essay in Method*, trans. Jane E. Lewin (1980; Ithaca, NY: Cornell University Press, 1983); Peter Brooks, *Reading for the Plot: Design and Intention in Narrative* (Cambridge, MA: Harvard University Press, 1984); Roland Barthes, *The Rustle of Language*, trans. Richard Howard (Berkeley: University of California Press, 1986).

90   Genette, *Narrative Discourse*, p. 105.

91   Michael Sayeau, *Against the Event: The Everyday and the Evolution of the Modernist Narrative* (Oxford: Oxford University Press, 2013), p. 5.

92   Silence, for instance, is a key trope of postmodernism: to literary theorist Ihab Hassan, the 'invocation of complex, articulate silences' is a particularly postmodern form of discussion, while to cultural

critic Susan Sontag postmodern art is 'noisy with appeals to silence'. Hassan, *The Postmodern Turn: Essays in Postmodern Theory and Culture* (Columbus: Ohio State University Press, 1987), p. 94; Susan Sontag, 'The Aesthetics of Silence', in her *Styles of Radical Will* (New York: Picador, 2002), p. 12. Silence is therefore conceived as a mode of communication or an absence that invites language, but, most importantly, silence is always impossible. To the artist John Cage, '[t]here is no such thing as silence. Something is always happening that makes a sound' and, with this impossibility in mind, my discussion of quiet is distinct from postmodern ideas of silence. Cage, '45' for a Speaker', *Silence: Lectures and Writings* (Middletown, CT: Wesleyan University Press, 2001), p. 191.
93  John Williams, *Stoner* (London: Vintage Classics, 2012), p. 39.
94  Ibid., p. 42.
95  His marriage fails, his wife is cartoonishly cruel and punishing and, despite his inoffensiveness, he acquires a professional enemy. Reading for quiet in Williams' depiction of women, Edith is portrayed as hysterical and withholding with no internal life of her own. Particularly concerning sex, Stoner's 'desire' for Edith is rarely consensual and their intercourse becomes a silent endeavour in which she makes 'no sound' and he tells her 'in the quietness of his love'. Critics have not yet noted these unsettling undertones. Williams, *Stoner*, p. 69.
96  Ibid., p. 42.
97  Several online articles have addressed the popularity of *Stoner*'s reissue. See: Claire Cameron 'A Forgotten Bestseller: The Saga of John William's *Stoner*', *The Millions* (6 June 2013), http://www.themillions.com/2013/06/a-forgotten-bestseller-the-saga-of-john-williamss-stoner.html; Dominic Preziosi, 'Quiet Novel Goes Global', *Commonweal* (13 June 2013), http://www.commonwealmagazine.org/blog/quiet-novel-goes-global; Tess Malone and Marisa Weiher, 'John Williams' Obscure *Stoner* Gets a Successful second chance', *Vox* (1 August 2013), http://www.voxmagazine.com/stories/2013/08/01/how-john-williams-obscure-stoner-went-jesse-hall-w/.
98  Steve Almond, 'Lost and Found', *The Rumpus* (26 January 2009), http://therumpus.net/2009/01/lost-and-found-by-steve-almond/.
99  *Stoner* was a bestseller in the Netherlands for two months and 85,000 copies were in print by April 2013. Gabe Habash, '*Stoner* Finds Overseas Success', *Publisher's Weekly* (20 April 2013), http://www.publishersweekly.com/pw/by-topic/international/international-book-news/article/56913-stoner-finds-overseas-success.html.
100 Morris Dickstein, 'The Inner Lives of Men', *The New York Times* (17 June 2007), http://www.nytimes.com/2007/06/17/books/review/Dickstein-t.html?pagewanted=1&_r=2&.

101  Toni Morrison, *The Bluest Eye* (London: Vintage, 1999), p. 4. Excepting the prologue, that Morrison writes as a pastiche of the Dick and Jane reading primer, 'quiet' is the first word of the novel.
102  Morrison explains her attraction to the phrase in the Afterword to *The Bluest Eye*, stating that it was familiar to her as a phrase used at home between women sharing confidences and that it also intimated solidarity within the black community by suggesting that withholding information from outsiders might return a sense of agency to them. Another book might consider Morrison's aesthetic of quiet, especially if we consider the phrases opening parts 1 and 2 of *Beloved*: '124 was loud' and '124 was quiet'. Morrison, *Beloved* (London: Vintage, 2007), pp. 169, 239. For further exploration of Morrison's conception of quiet in a traumatic context, see: J. Brooks Bouson, *Quiet as It's Kept: Shame, Trauma, and Race in the Novels of Toni Morrison* (New York: State University of New York Press, 1999).
103  Morrison, *The Bluest Eye*, p. 86.
104  Anaïs Nin, *Linotte: The Early Diaries, Volume 1: 1927–1931*, trans. Jean L. Sherman (New York: Harcourt Brace & Company, 1978), p. 71.
105  Ibid., p. 218.

2

# '9/11' and the noise of contemporary fiction

In November 2013, Manhattan resident Kenny Cummings sent an email of inquiry to his local newspaper. 'Have you ever heard from neighbors about the wailing World Trade Center?', he wrote, claiming that an 'eerie sound' could be heard a couple of blocks away from the newly constructed building of One World Trade Center.¹ When the email was published, many Tribeca residents confirmed that the sound was real by posting comments and uploading videos of the tower's 'wailing' to YouTube. 'It's all the screams of those that died', one commentator suggested, while others replied that the flute-like moaning sounded more like the opening of 'a portal to heaven'. In reality, the building's acoustics created the sound and as wind rushed past the so-called 'Freedom Tower', its metal bars vibrated, creating similar sound waves to those of an Aeolian harp.² Still, many New Yorkers believed that the building was haunted or, worse, screaming and the sound of the wind's natural vibrations against One World Trade Center reminded the public of the cacophonous noise of '9/11' long after 'Ground Zero' had been cleared and the site rebuilt.³

The 'wailing' of One World Trade Center provides us with a literal example of the sonic afterlife of '9/11'. The sound was the result of the tower's design; first noticed by residents during Hurricane Sandy in October 2012, it had ceased entirely by the time the building was completed in January 2014. Beyond its literal noise, however, this chapter conceives of the coordinated terrorist attacks on the World Trade Center and the Pentagon on the morning of 11 September 2001 as culturally dissonant in both a real and metaphorical sense. I want to suggest not only that the events of that day were noisy but that the terrorist attacks produced and inspired noise in their representation so that the cultural resonance of '9/11' far outlasted the scenes of destruction at 'Ground Zero'. In the weeks, months and years that followed, many American writers and critics inherited and mimicked the apocalyptic and 'postlapsarian' discourse of the Bush administration, often capitalising on pre-existing ideas of American exceptionalism and adding to the cacophony that surrounded them.[4] In the immediate aftermath, it was easier to conceive of 11 September 2001 as a moment that loudly divorced this century from the last than to track its continuities with the world as it was on 10 September. It was also easier, I argue, to conceive of '9/11' as an epochal event that would noisily and profoundly influence contemporary American fiction than it was to claim the time for reflection and quietly consider what Lauren Berlant describes as the 'becoming-event' in which both the crisis and contemporary fiction were situated.[5]

This chapter stands apart within *The quiet contemporary American novel* because it sets out everything that the quiet novel is not. If the novel is quiet when it embodies an aesthetic that is calm, private and peaceful, then the novel is noisy when it is anxious, public and obtrusive. Consumed by the sounds of the present, driven by the desire to speak loudly and convinced of the importance of traumatic 'event' both to the present moment and to the lives of future generations, novels of the political 'now' are often afflicted by what Jacques Derrida refers to as 'archive fever', a phenomenon characterised by an eagerness to dispose of the present into the past and to imagine how the contemporary world will be remembered by future generations.[6] It is in this way that I suggest the most famous 9/11 novels written by Don DeLillo, John Updike, Jonathan Safran Foer, Jess Walter and Amy Waldman are better understood as ideologically inflected narratives that emphasise the noise of contemporary culture, associating the present with the singularity of '9/11' and limiting how novelists write a history of their contemporary moment. Particularly after the terrorist attacks in New York and Pennsylvania, many novelists felt compelled to represent the noise of terrorism because, as Berlant writes, the 'intimate experience' of a disaster appears 'exemplary of a shared historical time'.[7] This chapter therefore argues for a reappraisal of '9/11' fiction within a longer history of noise in the American novel to question the agenda of those critics and novelists who assumed a literary response to the attacks was in some way inevitable and anticipated a body of '9/11' fiction before any of their texts were published.

## Fiction 'post-9/11'

In the weeks that followed 11 September 2001, fiction writers eager to explore the disruption of a 'post-9/11' world published a deluge of articles, mostly autobiographical in nature. Ian McEwan wrote one of the earliest responses, lamenting the new frailty of 'Our civilisation' and suggesting that after the attacks 'the world would never be the same': in fact, 'it would be worse.'[8] By 20 September, *The New York Times* had published essays by Joan Didion, Tim O'Brien and Joyce Carol Oates and by 30 September, Martin Amis, Peter Carey, David Grossman and Jeanette Winterson had all published personal responses, reflecting on the future of authorship after the event. In a noteworthy gesture, *The New Yorker* devoted the entirety of its 'The Talk of the Town' section to nine 700-word vignettes by contemporary writers to 'reflect on the tragedy and its consequences.'[9] Taking these vignettes as representative, it is clear how quickly the rhetoric surrounding the events defined them as singular and exceptional. Just one week after, Jonathan Franzen observed that 'the new world' was already 'a different world', its newness generated by the shock of tragedy on US soil.[10] Susan Sontag saw the alleviation of common ignorance in what she called the 'monstrous dose of reality' dealt to Americans on that day.[11] However, Sontag also acknowledged the transitory nature of collective trauma. The public, she felt sure, had not been 'asked to bear much of the burden of reality' and would soon return to their former more comfortable existence. John Updike elaborated on the problem of representation by asserting that after the attacks reality appeared to be reflexive. The lines between fact and fiction were irrevocably blurred, he wrote: 'there persisted the notion that, as on television, this was not quite real; it could be adjusted; the technocracy the towers symbolized would find a way to put out the fire and reverse the damage.'[12] In the days after, Updike and many others struggled to interpret their role, caught between two impulses: should the artist respond rapidly to the event, in an attempt to make meaning for the confused public, or should they take time to look beyond the initial spectacle, projecting the event's importance into an equally uncertain future?

The irony has already been widely noted that many of the novelists who lamented the impossibility of authorship in the days and weeks after would write novels depicting the aftermath of '9/11'.[13] McEwan, who published one of the earliest responses, was also among the first to publish a work of fiction with the release of *Saturday* in 2005. Then between 2005 and 2008 a number of prominent writers of fiction published novels based around the events in New York in particular.[14] These included McEwan's *Saturday*, Safran Foer's *Extremely Loud and Incredibly Close* (2005), Updike's *Terrorist* (2006) and DeLillo's *Falling Man* (2007), novels that are now studied as key examples of '9/11 fiction' because they recreate either the events of that day or the year that followed. More established authors would also reference the attacks as an epochal shift in the consciousness of the Western world. Paul Auster's *The Brooklyn Follies* (2005) used '9/11' as shorthand for presidential change and to signal the end of the protagonist's nostalgic remembrance of late Clinton-era America. In Philip Roth's *Everyman* (2006), the events of 11 September 2001 coincide with the protagonist's move to a retirement village and take on a further poignancy as Roth's lonely 'everyman' sees the events as 'the origin of his exile'.[15] Jonathan Franzen, who did not depict the attacks directly, recreated what he calls the 'post-9/11 slump' of the United States in his 2010 novel *Freedom*, which broadly articulated the personal, economic and political repercussions of the time.[16] A number of lesser-known but critically acclaimed novelists also published fictional accounts of the attacks within the same two-year period: Jess Walter's *The Zero* (2006), Ken Kalfus' *A Disorder Peculiar to the Country* (2006), Claire Messud's *The Emperor's Children* (2006), Jay McInerney's *The Good Life* (2006), Mohsin Hamid's *The Reluctant Fundamentalist* (2007) and Joseph O'Neill's *Netherland* (2008). Just four years after the attacks on the World Trade Center and the Pentagon, a trend was becoming evident: novelists were not only incorporating '9/11' into their novels but attempting to depict and represent the attacks or their aftermath in sustained ways.

The novels listed above have become key texts in an assumed body of '9/11' fiction.[17] However, it remains difficult to assess whether the above examples of '9/11 fiction' reflect a period, genre or trend. If '9/11 fiction' constitutes a genre, then its generic features should be clearer. According to Fredric Jameson, genres 'are literary *institutions*, which like the other institutions of social life are based on tacit agreements or contracts', yet if we are to apply these terms to the inclusion of 11 September 2001 in fiction what 'agreements' have DeLillo, Updike and Foer reached?[18] Similarly, if the '9/11' moniker refers to a period, when does that period end? As Jeremy Green suggests, declaring anything 'post' is a negative device that freezes historical process as 'a gesture of disavowal and repression' and while periodisation is often a tool that Peter Tookey argues attributed order to a period of confusion, critics began discussing the existence of a '9/11' novel before a trend could be established.[19] Indeed, critics created the category even as they asserted its future necessity. Controversial *New York Times* reviewer Michiko Kakutani first introduced the term 'post-9/11 fiction' in 2005 when she described McEwan's *Saturday* as 'one of the most powerful pieces of post-9/11 fiction yet published'.[20] In her review, Kakutani suggests that McEwan 'fulfilled that very primal mission of the novel: to show how we – a privileged few of us, anyway – live today'. Tellingly, however, she groups *Saturday* within a body of 'post-9/11 fiction', despite there being only a dozen fictional representations of the event in existence.

By grouping these novels as a trend, period or genre, it also becomes clear that they are not 'about' the events of 11 September 2001 in any cohesive way. DeLillo, Kalfus and Walter produced fictional accounts of the survivors and their families, imagining the experiences of those who escaped from the towers. Of these, DeLillo depicts the psychological consequences of surviving the attacks while Kalfus and Walter undercut similar narratives with a satirical portrayal of corporate life under the Bush administration. McInerney and Messud depict the experience of the wealthier residents of New York as they watch the events unfold and, in *Extremely Loud and Incredibly Close*, Safran Foer adopts the perspective of a nine-year-old boy who grieves for the father he loses on that day. McEwan's novel, *Saturday*, engages more indirectly with the attacks. Set against the London demonstrations that preceded American and British intervention in Iraq, McEwan describes '9/11' briefly, as an 'induction into international affairs' for citizens of the West or Global North.[21] Unique among these examples, in *Terrorist*, Updike chronicles the thoughts of an American-born Muslim who attempts to blow up the Lincoln Tunnel between New Jersey and New York City. Finally, Hamid, with considerably more nuance than Updike, explores the motivations of a Pakistani-born American resident who comes to embrace a militant version of Islam after becoming exiled from the 'growing and self-righteous rage in those weeks in September'.[22]

Novels that take 11 September 2001 as their direct subject inevitably share some common themes: a white middle-class context predominates and symbols of futurity, including children, the elderly and the fall from innocence implied by the attacks preoccupy the protagonists. However, the most common theme of any '9/11' novel is the novelist's fear that fiction may be culturally irrelevant at a time of crisis. Oskar Schell, the nine-year-old protagonist of *Extremely Loud and Incredibly Close*, is an 'inventor' of narrative, continually creating scenarios of his father's death that he 'can't stop inventing'.[23] Through Oskar, Foer suggests that the creative impulse in the wake of tragedy is a necessary part of healing and, in doing so, validates his own position as novelist. Similarly, in *Terrorist*, Updike writes a parallel version of the attacks, representing the mindset of a young extremist as he becomes disillusioned with America and plans his own act of terrorism to coincide with the September anniversary. Writing a version of the attacks in which the bomber repents and tragedy is avoided, Updike links the existence of terrorism to the amplifying dissonance of America's screens. His protagonist Ahmad searches for 'traces of God in this infidel society' but finds only noise and disruption. While searching for spaces of peace and interiority, Ahmad encounters the 'jabber' of news teams and the 'electronic chatter' of the Internet, the noisy harbingers of the modern age that were equally integral to the spectacle of 11 September 2001.[24] To Updike's horror, and as reflected in his piece for *The New Yorker*, television mediated the public's experience of '9/11', representing and interpreting the attacks in ways that the novelist could not.[25] Rather than adapting, reinventing or accepting the position of the novelist at a time of crisis, Updike, Foer and many of their contemporaries embraced the portrayal of noise in the hope that the novel could capture the dissonance of '9/11' and preserve a record of the events for posterity.

The first wave of book-length studies to address the burgeoning group of novels also appeared quickly: both *Literature After 9/11* (2008) edited by Ann Keniston and Jeanne Follansbee Quinn and Kristiaan Versluys' *Out of the Blue: September 11 and the Novel* (2009) survey a range of texts in the attempt to establish a literary trend. In both volumes, the prioritisation of DeLillo and Foer as the 'hypercanonical' forerunners of a '9/11' canon is already in evidence. Subsequent scholarship has favoured a severely narrow range of texts, broadly accepting these limited representations of 11 September 2001 as 'constitutive of a new collective American identity'.[26] Revealingly, critics largely fail to ask *why* the event should be a necessary inclusion in fictional representations of the twenty-first century or exactly *who* demands its inclusion. Versluys, in particular, characterises 2001 as a time of 'quiet apocalypse' and describes '9/11' as both 'unpossessable' and of the utmost importance to the continued innovation of realist fiction.[27] Using the term by which I define an oppositional aesthetic, Versluys' use of 'quiet' is purposefully paradoxical, perpetuating the idea of the event's importance without analysing or surfacing any of its muted undertones.

Inevitably, and as the decade progressed, the field of '9/11' studies began to widen, with the publication of Mohsin Hamid's *The Reluctant Fundamentalist* and Joseph O'Neill's *Netherland* essential to an expanded field. Both novels met with critical acclaim for their transnational reimaginings of the terrorist attacks and their reception fed into a critical evolution that imagined the event's global and postcolonial implications.[28] In 2010, Elleke Boehmer and Stephen Morton contextualised the phenomenon of terror as 'the ground upon which sovereignty is in many cases defined in the colonial present', expanding the previously limited understanding of 11 September as an American tragedy and calling for a reflective approach to global politics in which 'foreignness is not conflated with noise'.[29] Likewise, Richard Gray's essay, 'Open Door, Closed Minds: American Prose Writing at a Time of Crisis' (2009), was one of the first works of criticism to diagnose a failure of imagination in the work of DeLillo and his contemporaries.[30] For Gray, the events of 11 September 2001 still emerge as a defining force in the future of literature. His essay is interspersed with exclamations of disbelief at the 'cataclysmic', 'radical', 'terrible' and 'obscene' events of '9/11'; throughout the essay collective pronouns, 'we' and 'our', reinforce the necessity of a public response.[31] Yet, just two years later, Gray's book-length study *After the Fall* (2011) became the first detailed work to bridge the gap between US-centred and postcolonial critiques. In it, Gray presents twenty-first-century America as 'a transcultural space in which different cultures reflect and refract, confront and bleed into one another' and by explaining the position of the US in a global era defined by economic and political crisis, *After the Fall* questions the enduring relevance of '9/11' to our ongoing history of the contemporary.[32]

Arguably, however, the more that '9/11' is understood as a transnational and transcultural event, the more dissonant the literary response to the attacks is likely to become. Understanding the critical evolution of a '9/11' literature is vital to the project of *The quiet contemporary American novel* because it demonstrates how many novelists believe that topical event crystallises the reality of the moment in which they are writing. For novelist Zadie Smith, *Netherland* is indicative of a broader crisis in a 'breed of lyrical Realism' that has been culturally dominant for too long. She writes that *Netherland* is 'so precisely the image of what we have been taught to value in fiction that it throws that image into a kind of existential crisis, as the photograph gifts a nervous breakdown to the painted portrait.'[33] If, as Lilian R. Furst suggests, contemporary forms of realism can be diagnosed by the central problem of 'how to translate an allegedly true (but necessarily subjective) vision into words', in the aftermath of 11 September 2001 the novelist turned from translation to depiction in order to compete with the visual records of the attacks that captured both sight and sound.[34] For novelist and critic Andrew O'Hagan, on 11 September '[a]ctuality showed its own naked art' and non-fiction gained primacy over the 'dead' metaphors of fiction.[35] Yet so strict a definition of what reality might be, or of what authors can and must represent, radically diminishes the imaginative possibilities for fiction.

The '9/11' novel thus marks a departure from, and arguably a reduction of, the mimetic function of the postmodern novel, that which Brian McHale suggests reflects 'the pluralistic and anarchistic ontological landscapes of advanced industrial cultures.'[36] The problem of representing '9/11' in fiction is that it seemed the 'most real of all real events', proving hypnotic to many practitioners of fiction at the turn of the century.[37] Yet the events of 2001 articulated what had been present in American life for decades. Pankaj Mishra reasons that '[t]he shock of the attacks was probably greater for writers who had been ensconced deep in [...] the extraordinarily complacent mood of the decade after the end of the cold war.'[38] In 1996, Franzen had also reconsidered the future of the novel in his essay, 'Perchance to Dream', arguing that the importance of the novel in 'the age of images' was to 'Address the Culture and Bring News to the Mainstream'.[39] In order to do this, Franzen suggests that fiction must bridge the gap between the personal and the social in a 'broad-canvas novel' that would facilitate 'maximum diversity and contrast' and turn away from a 'retreat into the Self'.[40] That '9/11' might present such an opportunity was the underlying assumption that drew together and, I argue, noisily reasserted existing anxieties about the novel's waning dominance as a cultural form, causing a select group of authors to then take '9/11' as evidence of fiction's renewed social worth.

## Noise and the contemporary American novel

In my formulation, the '9/11' novel embodies an aesthetic of anxiety and noise, what Kathy Knapp describes as an 'aesthetic of contingency', that denies the time for reflection in the present and reveals a sometimes crippling fear of change in the literary establishment.[41] This narrative discontent and disquiet pre-dates the attacks. Jeremy Green identifies a 'free-floating anxiety' in many pre-millennial forms of realist fiction; James Wood famously diagnosed the encyclopaedic novels of DeLillo, Thomas Pynchon, Zadie Smith and David Foster Wallace as 'hysterical realism' for what he saw as the authors' obsession with the totalising 'noise' of the topical and their avoidance of silence, subjectivity and reflection.[42]

Debates about the death of the novel are as old as the form itself, but questions of the novel's social worth often coincide with claims that society has become 'too noisy' to represent. In Chapter 1, I argued that throughout the twentieth century, as the noise of society became increasingly associated with inhuman sounds, the roar of industry and the mechanical noise of 'progress', literary modernism, to quote Marshall Berman, often 'nourished itself' on 'noise and dissonance'.[43] When postmodernist experimentation turned fiction away from 'the noise of the street', however, the novelist invoked increasingly metafictional techniques to defend the novel from the threat of technological advance and tackle the burden of history. Significantly, novelists and critics continued to express postmodern debates about the usefulness of fiction in terms of noise, conflating creativity with the need to speak loudly through increasingly experimental and expansionist frameworks. In 1984, Salman Rushdie argued that 'in this world without quiet corners' fiction could not afford to turn away from noise because history, in essence, is a 'terrible, unquiet fuss'.[44] Indeed, many novelists suggested that the only way to write fiction was to write bigger, bolder and noisier texts. In 'Stalking the Billion-footed Beast' (1989), Tom Wolfe criticised writers from Samuel Beckett and Vladimir Nabokov to John Barth and Robert Coover for turning to absurdist and minimalist fictions that displaced the novel's social function. Wolfe wanted to read novels of the cultural moment that were filled with contemporary noise: 'the big novels of the racial clashes, the hippie movement, the New Left, the Wall Street boom, the sexual revolution, the war in Vietnam.'[45] His adjectives for fiction are as brash as they are loud, claiming that the form should be 'confrontational', 'radical', capable of representing 'the American century, the century in which we had become the mightiest military power in all history'.[46]

Other prominent American novelists would reiterate Wolfe's view as the century reached its end. Directly responding to Wolfe, Franzen entreated the novelist to 'Address the Culture and Bring News to the Mainstream' and Don DeLillo defined the writer as 'the man or woman who automatically takes a stance against his or her government'.[47] Even Philip Roth stated that the novelist should reject the 'inroad into consciousness' in order to serve a public function.[48] Elsewhere, calls for what DeLillo described as 'the big social novel' or what James Wood referred to as 'the Great American Social Novel' promised to halt the death of the form by loudly affirming its social necessity.[49] We might think particularly of DeLillo's 1985 novel, *White Noise*, praised for its descriptions of a rampant American consumerism 'awash with noise' and the 'dull and locatable roar' of industry.[50] Similarly, Jonathan Franzen's *The Corrections* (2001) was published just days after '9/11' and opens with an 'alarm bell of anxiety' that rings so loudly it creates a 'kind of metasound whose rise and fall was not the beating of compression waves but the much, much slower waxing and waning of [the] *consciousness* of the sound.'[51] Both Franzen and DeLillo link the noise of contemporary culture to a system of late capitalism in which teleological narratives of consumption and progress invade all conscious experience. In *The Corrections*, the alarm bell is triggered by '[t]he anxiety of coupons', 'expiration dates' and 'sixty cents off' while the 'white noise' of DeLillo's title is 'the intermittent stir of factories' and the ways in which noise contributes to the 'extrasensory material' of modern life.[52] As the French economist Jacques Attali wrote in 1985, the year *White Noise* was published, '[noise] is unavoidable, as if, in a world now devoid of meaning, a background noise were increasingly necessary to give people a sense of security.'[53]

In the twenty-first century, many scholars also write from a defensive position, riled by the suspicion that since the 1990s the rate of technological advancement signals literature's impending irrelevance when '[t]he rate and magnitude of change [has] outstripped the integrating powers of the psyche.'[54] The global expansion of the Internet and its continued evolution through handheld computers, social media, mobile phones, e-books and hypertext further provides what Jeremy Green describes as 'a foretaste of a future without books' and debates about the death of the novel have gained traction since it has been forced to compete with cultural forms capable of making noise.[55] The insistent beeps, flashing lights and bright screens characteristic of modern technologies pose a threat to formerly quiet environments. To think again of Virginia Woolf's discussion of the conditions required for creativity, the sounds produced by barking dogs and noisy people now compete with the constant and low-level noise pollution of traffic, mobile phones and handheld devices. It is not that there is more noise, per se, but that it seems more pervasive; in the same way that media theorist Douglas Rushkoff describes 'digital omniscience' as evoking a 'schizophrenic cacophony of divided attention and temporal disconnection'.[56] Among the 'schizophrenic' noises of digitised cultures, reflection seems not only rarefied but also mentally impossible. If the quiet novel has always existed as a rare and undervalued commodity, then it becomes even rarer and, I argue, riskier to produce fiction that is aesthetically quiet within a culture increasingly defined by its sources of overstimulation.

I am particularly interested in how the idea of quiet has been explored by American novelists at the beginning of the twenty-first century as we enter a period defined by Jeremy Green as 'late' postmodernism. According to Green, American fiction today is often forced to 'encompass and distil' the 'strange and myriad forms' of the contemporary United States.[57] If, with post structuralism, literary theory moved from the assumed transparency of narratological analysis to the idea that structure was a projection, narrative also became an unstable entity and post-structuralists emphasised its heterogeneity. In an essay entitled 'What Is American Literature?', Elizabeth Renker argues that in order to survive in the twenty-first century, American literature must do all it can to meet '[t]he post-American exceptionalist, postcanonical, transatlantic, transnational, subnational, prenational, hemispheric, global, oceanic, planetary, world moment.'[58] Literary criticism continues to ask how the novel can become bigger, noisier and more diverse in order to maintain its dominance as a cultural form, working against any suggestion that acts of reflection might access a broader understanding of any contemporary moment. Citing Mikhail Bakhtin's concept of literary polyphony, Ted Gioia argues that twenty-first-century fiction is characterised by a 'new fragmented novel' that 'resists disunity, even as it appears to embody it.'[59] Mark Greif identifies the same trend as the 'big, ambitious novel' in turn-of-the-century works by Franzen, DeLillo, Pynchon, Foster Wallace and William Vollman. These works 'feel stuffed', Greif claims, either 'overfull, or total; they feel longer than their straightforward story would require, and bigger than other books of similar length or complexity of plot.'[60] These are novels, in other words, of ever-greater ambition that seek to survey American experience in its breadth, totality and volume, but paradoxically limit the remit of contemporary fiction by overshadowing any text that does not fit their expansionist paradigm.

## '9/11' and the aesthetic of noise

Into the projected tumult of contemporary experience, the events of 11 September 2001 seemed like the most 'real of all real' events, a revelation of uncomfortable truths about America's relationship with the world, and a presentation of '[a]ctuality' that could not be ignored.[61] At least part of its importance seems related to its invocation of noises, both real and metaphorical, that had long been associated with America but that its citizens rarely heard.

If, for example, noise is a key theme in the first flush of '9/11' fictions, then it cannot be coincidental that one of the most studied examples is Jonathan Safran Foer's *Extremely Loud and Incredibly Close*. The event, the explosions, the screams of observers, the sound of bodies hitting the sidewalk, all contributed to a terrible and cacophonous volume that held the public's attention for weeks and months after. Foer's title alludes to the anxiety that afflicted the citizens of New York City and *Extremely Loud and Incredibly Close* examines the barrage of sounds associated with a trauma that was thought to be unique to US soil. In the novel, Oskar, Foer's nine-year-old narrator, both rejects and invites noise, wistfully imagining a future in which a siren warns people of imminent disasters. This warning would sound above the din of any catastrophic event and allow people time to prepare for the process of grieving that follows. '[W]hen something *really* terrible happened', he suggests, '– like a nuclear bomb, or at least a biological weapons attack – an extremely loud siren would go off.'[62] Although the siren is a fantasy, the extreme loudness of Foer's novel is continually associated with terrible occurrences and Oskar's wish for a warning system is an attempt to rid noise of its disruptive potential. Noise, Oskar notes, keeps an event at the forefront of the mind. When he arrives at his grandmother's house to find her mysteriously absent, Oskar imagines possible scenarios and notes how 'extremely loud' his most pessimistic thoughts become.[63] A terrible event is noisiest, Foer seems to suggest, because of its negative affect and in *Extremely Loud and Incredibly Close* he depicts citizens meeting the noise of '9/11' with the production of more noise.

Foer was not alone in aestheticising the louder elements of the attacks. Jess Walter's *The Zero* tells the story of New York City's recovery from the perspective of a 'hero cop', Brian Remy, as he pieces together his memories in the days after the attacks. Searching through the wreckage of the World Trade Center, Remy believes that the site is 'humming'; the rubble produces a constant noise occasionally punctuated by 'the shriek of shifting steel' or by the hope 'that someone was calling his name'.[64] Notably, the wreckage of the World Trade Center emits a low rumble that is accented by both real and imaginary noises and Walter's description here anticipates the real-life 'wailing' of One World Trade Center, where the 'shrieks' of the building reminded local residents of the 'screams of those that died'.[65] Remy's desire that the dead should speak also hints at a discomfort about the state of quiet after a disaster. His longing to hear cries among the silence of the rubble speaks of a desire for human contact and a wish to hear shouts above the noise of destruction that had silenced so many voices. This is perhaps also why for many novelists, quiet represented a collective loss for words. Amitav Ghosh traces silence to the moment the first tower collapsed: 'everything went absolutely quiet', he writes, from that moment on, 'like the onset of a nuclear winter'.[66] Martin Amis alleges that by 12 September many writers considered changing profession because they lost the confidence to speak with authority: 'the voices coming from their rooms', he suggested, 'were very quiet.'[67] In the aftermath of tragedy, Amis believes that this quiet indicates a loss of nerve and he admits a hope that a collective, creative confidence will return so that authors might process the event for the public.

Perhaps the most striking expression of authorial quiet appeared two years later. Toni Morrison published a poem, 'The Dead of September', in 2003, suggesting that the event might continue to defy representation. 'I have nothing to say', Morrison writes, 'no words / stronger than the steel that pressed you into itself.'[68] In the years after 2001, poetry took a different path to fiction, one that embellished the sense of continuity the event evoked. As Ann

Keniston argues, the majority of 'post-9/11' poetry avoids the novel's dilemma of originality by focusing on the connections between pre- and 'post-9/11' writing projects, self-consciously including the event as part of a longer discussion about the 'public' function of poetry in American life.[69] Similarly, of the responses previously noted only Morrison's suggests that silence might be the best method of engagement or that reflection over a longer period might be preferable to rapid responses.[70] The final line of Morrison's poem is a plea to the dead that the author might 'understand, as you have done, the wit / of eternity: its gift of unhinged release tearing through / the darkness of its knell.' To Morrison, the 'release' of death can only be comprehended by accepting the limitations of language, a medium that is only partially capable of explaining death's final 'knell'. Referencing 'eternity', the novelist imagines an afterlife undefined by the present reality of 'Ground Zero', releasing the poem from prescriptive markers of time and event. Morrison is unusual in recognising the 'gift' of reflection at a time of crisis, rearticulating the opening tautology of the poem and an idea first articulated by John Cage in his 'Lecture on Nothing' (1949): 'I have nothing to say / and I am saying it / and that is poetry / as I need it.'[71] In comparison, the feature articles and novels discussed in this chapter mention quiet only as an enforced state, a loss of nerve and a failure of conviction in the wake of terrorism.

Just as Morrison's poem echoes earlier expressions of postmodernism in confronting the impossibilities of representation, discussion of the insufficiency of language at a time of crisis was not new. In the Western tradition one parallel can be found in the responses of the New York Intellectuals to the role of literature after the Holocaust. In 1955, reflecting on the relationship between society and cultural criticism, Theodor Adorno famously suggested that '[t]o write poetry after Auschwitz is barbaric',[72] echoing what Lionel Trilling had argued two years previously: 'There is no possible way of responding to Belsen and Buchenwald.'[73] What is demonstrated by biographical and fictional responses to the events of 11 September 2001 is that fiction writers, particularly those based in New York, felt what Adorno described as 'the drastic guilt of him who was spared'.[74] Revisiting his statement on Auschwitz in 1966, Adorno identified a cultural form of survivor's guilt made manifest in the artist who is caught between capturing an event's singularity and negotiating it into the past. Burdened by a sense of duty to those who have died and an accountability to those who remain, Adorno claimed that '[b]y way of atonement [the artist] will be plagued by dreams such as that he is no longer living at all'.[75] Any event presented as a rupture in the teleological narrative of the nation-state draws the artist into a temporal loop where they are unable to relegate the event's significance to the past and project its legitimacy into the future. Caught in a stasis, then, art is unable to evolve because the artist thinks in terms of ruptures instead of progression. In other words, 'he is no longer living at all' and the event looms larger and, I argue, louder, provocatively extending throughout the past, present and future, while simultaneously limiting the artist's innovative and transgressive capacity to write.

Indeed, I argue that any focus on a singular event is noisy as a narrative conceit. In the case of '9/11', the problem of event began with the terminology of 'Ground Zero' and the symbolism invoked by the digits 911. The act of defining the day and month without any indication of the year symbolised its future orientation and entered the event into what W. J. T. Mitchell foresaw as a temporal loop in October 2001. 'It is Day One of an event whose days are unnumbered, indefinite, an emergency in which the emergent order has yet to make itself clear.'[76] As '9/11', 11 September 2001 became part of the future, endowed with the weight of history but removed from a sense of historical continuity and context.

Yet, again, I would state that any narrative focus on event is, or at least seems to be, noisy. For postcolonial theorist Homi K. Bhaba, the 'linear equivalence' of event had always been an exclusionary structure and signifies 'a holistic cultural identity' that suppresses the diversity of a culture.[77] By the end of the twentieth century, as Bhaba argues, Western society had entered a 'beyond' time when experience could no longer be conceived by its singularities and national event no longer symbolised the collective experience of the present.[78] Seven months prior to the attacks, in February 2001, Derrida had also published *Dire l'évènement, est-ce possible?*, a volume that discussed the ongoing difficulties of articulating the event as a temporal structure. Here, the philosopher turned the idea of event on its head, suggesting that it was not the event, per se, but the contemplation of it that revealed a 'certain impossibility' of representation.[79] Unlike Bhaba, Derrida contends that event is never singular: 'as a structure of language, it is bound to a measure of generality, iterability, and repeatability.'[80] However, Derrida suggests that the 'iterability' of event also leads to the homogeneity that Bhaba identifies, similarly restricting the potentiality of the present as a performative space.

In the wake of the terrorist attacks, Derrida extended this argument to comment on the language of '9/11' directly:

> When you say 'September 11' you are already citing ... You are inviting me to speak here by recalling, as if in quotation marks, a date or a daring that has taken over our public space and our private lives ... The very impact of what is at least *felt*, in an apparently immediate way, to be an event that truly marks, that truly makes its mark, a singular and, as they say here, 'unprecedented' event.[81]

Here, Derrida makes an important distinction between what is '*felt*' to be singular and what is really 'unprecedented'. Commentators presented 11 September 2001 as an immediate rupture in time so that the event '*felt*' like a turning point before any time had passed. The event was noisy, that is, in the very idea of its exceptionalism. As Derrida points out, the danger in referring to 9/11 without quotation is that the speaker or writer will forget that they are citing, accepting the event as an objective reality and not as a temporal construct that homogenises the wider moment in which the crisis is situated. To Derrida, the event is therefore a fascinating contradiction but only full of possibility in its linguistic *im*possibility.

## *Falling Man* and *The Submission*

In the weeks following '9/11', as this chapter demonstrates, fiction writers and critics remained attracted to the idea of the event's singularity, unable to escape the catastrophic images they had seen but equally unable to articulate what was unique about the tragedy. The notion of the event as a temporal rupture is no more apparent than in the most studied example of '9/11' literature: Don DeLillo's 2007 novel *Falling Man*. In the novel's opening pages, DeLillo introduces the reader to the city of New York in the minutes after the collapse of the World Trade Center when 'The roar was still in the air, the buckling rumble of the fall.'[82] New York City is later described as historically 'loud and blunt' (*FM* 69) but in the moments after the attacks the loudness of the city extends, becoming terrifying and inescapable.

'The noise lay everywhere', DeLillo writes, 'they ran, stratified sound collecting around them, and he walked away from it and into it at the same time' (*FM* 4). Moving away from the towers and down the street, the noise of the event follows DeLillo's protagonist, Keith Neudecker, reaching him through 'the trembling air' (*FM* 5) as the second tower falls and 'a soft awe of voices' rises in the distance. Tellingly, the noise of the attacks echoes around New York, showing no sign of stopping and as Keith emerges from the wreckage of the North Tower time itself seems to have stopped.

DeLillo's prose therefore reflects the notion of temporal rupture as perpetuated in 'post-9/11' discourse through the cacophony of the attacks. 'These are the days after', DeLillo mourns, 'Everything now is measured in after' (*FM* 138). As crisis is often conceived in terms of the post-apocalyptic, in *Falling Man* the moment in which the towers fall is the moment in which the world ends. Keith fatalistically decides '[n]othing is next. There is no next. This was next' (*FM* 10), consigning the events of 11 September to a unique bubble, frozen in the present and with no real future. As Donald Pease suggests, the Bush administration immediately invoked the attacks as 'one sociopolitical compact' and the event was conceived as a crime committed against the American people that 'exonerated any and every wrong (past, present, or future) for the actions that it would take in redressing wrong worldwide.'[83] Similarly, *Falling Man* is a novel that is consumed by the event's importance to the present and unable to leave '9/11' in the past. The narrative begins just after Keith's escape from the North Tower and ends while he is still looking for a way out. Keith is stuck in a temporal loop that forces him to circle back to the event with no hope of a resolution or route into the future. Even the 'falling man' of the title is a fictional performance artist who suspends himself with a rope and harness in a recreation of Richard Drew's image of 'The Falling Man'.[84] The artist hangs provocatively from the buildings of the city, introducing his performance and its associations into the everyday lives of New Yorkers so that the event's symbolism becomes literally inescapable. Crucially, the 'falling man' is a disruptive presence in the everyday lives of DeLillo's characters but it is also a symbol of stasis because the performance does not recreate the act of jumping or falling but instead depicts a man hanging over the city in a suspended state.

DeLillo's characters are therefore stifled by the idea of the event's singularity and also by the unreliability of memory. Like the cacophonous noise echoing through the city, the impact of the event spreads at an alarming rate. From the opening line of the novel, the attacks open up the geography of the city so it becomes 'not a street anymore but a world, a time and space of falling ash and near night' (*FM* 1). Ideas of history and memory are nevertheless tied to the structure of the city and just as the famous skyline of New York is reconfigured by the attacks, memory is dissolved and personal identities erased. When Keith comes to rebuild his memories of the day, he is unable to fully access them and speaks only of constructs. 'It's hard to reconstruct', he says, 'I don't know how my mind was working' (*FM* 21). The trauma of '9/11' does not lie in forgetting in *Falling Man*, but rather in failing to remember anything beyond dissonance. Indeed, the speed with which observers have to process the event appears to inhibit the archivisation of memory. As Derrida suggests, the *mal d'archive* burns with a passion, never resting in its desire to uncover some kind of meaning from an event that will ultimately have no 'originary origin'.[85] The event therefore provides a grand narrative, a communal arc, reconstructing memories that the public may have forgotten but that appear pointedly necessary to the periodisation of the present. DeLillo wrote of this process in his essay, 'In the Ruins of the Future' (2001), when he suggested that the writer should attempt 'to give memory, tenderness and meaning to all that howling space.'[86] However, as *Falling Man* progresses, Keith is left with even fewer memories. He begins an affair in order 'to hear what he'd lost in the tracings of memory' (*FM* 91), yet this experience also fades. As memory is shown to be unreliable, there is nothing holding relationships together and no private sense of memory left for the characters to 'hear' in order to help them retrieve lost connections. The process of archivisation is therefore seen to fail and DeLillo traces its passing back to the noise of '9/11'.

What the essay 'In the Ruins of the Future' demonstrates most significantly is how noisy the 'totalising' qualities of '9/11' were to DeLillo as a writer of fiction. Despite the supposed impossibility of representing the event that he struggles with in *Falling Man*, DeLillo remains convinced of the event's enduring importance and that it is the 'job' of the novelist to record it. Describing how the physical destruction of Lower Manhattan seems to turn to threaten the fabric of reality, DeLillo writes that with reality compromised, the writer's thoughts should be consumed by assigning meaning to what has been left behind: 'In its desertion of every basis for comparison, the event asserts its singularity.'[87] DeLillo argues that it is the writer's job to form memories for the reader, to make meaning out of events that many struggle to comprehend, and to create art from the 'howling space' that remains. I would argue, however, that the contradiction at the heart of DeLillo's analogy is resonant of the noise of the event. The physical destruction of the World Trade Center left a hole in the New York skyline and a 'space' in the heart of Manhattan that was suddenly defined by its absence. As Manhattan resident Kenny Cummings complained, the void appeared to produce noise, even to howl, long after the site had been cleared and, similarly, DeLillo suggests that the mere existence of 'Ground Zero' speaks of what happened with such volume that the writer must create a work of equal noise in order to make sense of the din.

After the first flush of '9/11' fictions, the American novel remained concerned with the totalising noise of '9/11' and every novel set in New York City inevitably and nervously described the absent presence at 'Ground Zero'. In Jennifer Egan's Pulitzer-prize-winning *A Visit from the Goon Squad* (2010) characters glimpse the former World Trade Center site as they go about their day, noting the 'blazing freeways of light' where the Twin Towers once stood and suggesting that, after five years of having 'nothing there', the city remains stuck in the moment of the attacks.[88] In Gary Shtyengart's *Super Sad True Love Story* (2010), the author also imagines a future in which the Freedom Tower is complete and stands over the city as a symbol of imperialism: 'empty and stern in profile, like an angry man risen and ready to punch.'[89]

When publication of Amy Waldman's debut novel, *The Submission* (2011), coincided with the tenth anniversary of the attacks, it was hailed as the latest, greatest '9/11 novel'.[90] The novel opens as a committee meets to approve a permanent memorial on 'Ground Zero'. Two years after the attacks, artists, city planners and the bereaved struggle to choose between two final designs, 'The Void' and 'The Garden', concerned that the former will be seen as hopeless and that the latter will appear too soft. The events of 11 September 2001 are not included within the novel's action and although '9/11' is the novel's defining event, Waldman is more directly engaged with exploring the process of memorialisation: 'We have to think of history here, the long view, a symbolism that will speak to people a hundred years from now.'[91] Indeed, Waldman suggests that the processes of memorialisation will be remembered over the attacks themselves and each character in *The Submission* seems worried that any progress or movement away from the event and its initial 'trauma' risks forgetting the event's importance and the identities of those who died.

In my reading, *The Submission* also explores the ongoing tension between quiet and noisy responses to the event. History is a continual noise that runs loudly through everything, from personal names, 'the ring – theological, historical, hysterical – of Mohammed', to the legacy of the dead.[92] A mother whose son dies while rescuing people trapped in the towers goes so far as to suggest that the attacks have removed the quiet of grief:

> Sometimes I wish Patrick had died in a regular fire. No firefighter dies a private death, not if he dies on the job. But to have all these politics moved in – I don't like it, all ... the noise. Grief should be quiet. A memorial should have the silence of the convent.[93]

Set in 2003, though published in 2011, Waldman's novel remains consumed by the 'howling space' DeLillo described in October 2001.[94] Particularly in this passage, noise is explicitly linked to 'the politics' surrounding the event, making '9/11' almost impossible to ignore and cacophonous in its unrepresentability. Moreover, in suggesting that no firefighter dies a 'private death', Waldman's character links the noise of the tragedy to its public nature. For a brief moment, the residual sounds of '9/11' become unnatural, a disruption of recovery rather than the embodiment of a nation's ongoing experience. Perhaps most revealing of all, the design that is ultimately and controversially chosen to build over the horrors of 'Ground Zero' is 'The Garden', proposed by a secular Muslim American and selected to 'encourage contemplation', thus restoring an aesthetic of quiet to the memorialisation of an event that has been conceived primarily by its noise.[95]

## 'On a quiet day'

In September 2002, Indian novelist and activist Arundhati Roy concluded her lecture, 'Come September', with an entreaty to America:

> Welcome to the world [...] Perhaps things will become worse and then better. Perhaps there's a small god up in heaven readying herself for us. Another world is not only possible, she's on her way. Maybe many of us won't be here to greet her, but on a quiet day, if I listen very carefully, I can hear her breathing.[96]

Addressing the United States as a whole, Roy asked her audience to trust in the continuities of the wider world in an attempt to understand how history repeats itself. There is something transcendent, Roy suggests, that exists independent of the material world, that can be heard when the day is quiet but that will be ignored if individuals or, indeed, entire nations do not take the time to listen.

In this chapter, I have argued that the literary response to '9/11' represents a dismissal of reflection, calm and quiet and an attempt to meet the loud timbre of public tragedy with yet more noise. If each generation believes their present to be noisier than the last, I contend that the impulse to meet the noise of the present with increasingly louder forms of expression is symptomatic of a kind of exceptionalism that dismisses the present's continuity with the past and equates noise with a narrative of progress. That same noise is also symptomatic of an American exceptionalism that routinely ignored the nation's sonic footprint until it reverberated on US soil. As an event, '9/11' seemed to declare the tenor of a noisy new century but, as I have also argued, simultaneously limited the interpretative powers of contemporary writers to conceive of the diverse ways in which people experience the present. As David Simpson suggests, 'taking time' was the ultimate challenge to sustained reflection on the attacks because '[s]cholarly time looks its best when there are no critical events going on around it: then it can reflect and project and even hope to appear prescient.'[97] The speed with which '9/11' was connected with global politics, public crisis and worldwide military ambition denied the time for reflection that the novel and its criticism required for fullness of expression, diversity of opinion and sustained intellectual thought.

Similarly, I have argued that the teleological implications alluded to by Bhaba and Derrida are inherent in the association of the present with unprecedented levels of noise. Contrary to the idea of its singularity, the terrorist attacks on 11 September 2001 resonated with a broader, cultural noise that extended many pre-existing ideas about the experience of postmodernity and media culture. The events of 2001 seemed to loudly announce the twenty-first century but were contrarily articulated as a singular event that had captured the noise of the culture. It is this contradiction that, in turn, limited the fiction that represented the attacks. As I argue throughout *The quiet contemporary American novel*, the frozen temporality of the event can be countered by an aesthetic of quiet that problematises the need to shout and, in particular, to shout louder than the voices of previous generations. In contrast to the noise-filled novels of '9/11', the writers of quiet fictions display less concern about the novel's marginalised position and privilege fiction that is driven by moments of intensity within which nothing much happens. It is in this way that quiet novels evade residual expectations that fiction must represent topical event in order to speak of and to the present, thus innovating the expression of contemporaneity in the novel form through a reappraisal of older and, as I argue, quieter forms.

## Notes

1  Kenny Cummings, quoted in 'The Wailing of One World Trade Center', *Tribeca Citizen*, Community News (29 November 2013), http://tribecac itizen.com/2013/11/29/the-wailing-of-one-world-trade-center/. The first reports of the sound date back to Hurricane Sandy, the most destructive hurricane of the 2012 Atlantic hurricane season that hit New York City on 29 October.
2  For more on the construction of One World Trade Center, including debates about its name, see: Marita Sturken, 'Freedom Tower and the Mall', *Tourists of History: Memory, Kitsch, and Consumerism from Oklahoma City to Ground Zero* (Durham, NC: Duke University Press, 2006), pp. 244-286; Jon Anderson, *Understanding Cultural Geography: Places and Traces* (Abingdon: Routledge, 2010), pp. 181-182; Stephen E. Atkins (ed.), *The 9/11 Encyclopedia: Second Edition* (Santa Barbara, CA: ABC-CLIO, 2011), pp. 344-346.
3  Throughout this chapter and where necessary thereafter I refer to '9/11' in quotation marks and cite the date of the terrorist attacks in full as 11 September 2001. This decision is rooted in the widely held idea that terminology formulated by the Bush administration in the immediate aftermath of the attacks is ideologically problematic and perpetuates an idea of the events' exceptionalism by referring to the attacks as a symbol that removes the identifying year of the attacks and thereby implies the threat of its imminent repetition. The exceptionalism implicit in the lack of citation is explored throughout this chapter.
4  Aaron DeRosa, 'Analysing Literature after 9/11', *Modern Fiction Studies* 57:3 (fall 2011), p. 607.
5  Lauren Berlant, *Cruel Optimism* (Durham, NC: Duke University Press, 2012), 5. By referencing Berlant, I mean to purposefully avoid discussions of the United States as a trauma state. This discussion has, as

Alexander Dunst suggests, provided the 'first decade of the twenty-first century with one of its organizing metaphors' and trauma studies have become increasingly prevalent in modern scholarship as it speaks to the ideas of unrepresentability long held by post-structuralists. Dunst, 'After Trauma: Time and Affect in American Culture Beyond 9/11', *parallax* 18:2 (2012), p. 58. Over the past decade, trauma studies have extended the idea that '9/11' was collectively experienced and constitutive of a cultural trauma that left indelible marks on 'group' consciousness. Cathy Caruth is the most cited example in studies of '9/11' fiction because her work outlines the 'widespread and bewildering encounter with trauma' as a contemporary model of experience. Cathy Caruth, *Unclaimed Experience: Trauma, Narrative, and History* (Baltimore, MD: Johns Hopkins University Press, 1996), p. 11. Mark Seltzer has similarly written about the United States as a wound culture with a 'pathological public sphere' that has been born out of a public obsession with acts of violence. Seltzer, *Serial Killers: Death and Life in America's Wound Culture* (New York: Routledge, 1998), p. 6. For further reading on '9/11' and trauma studies see: Neil J. Smelser, 'Epilogue: September 11, 2001 as Cultural Trauma', in *Cultural Trauma and Collective Identity*, ed. Jeffrey C. Alexander (Berkeley: University of California Press, 2004); E. Ann Kaplan, *Trauma Culture: The Politics of Terror and Loss in Media and Literature* (Piscataway, NJ: Rutgers University Press, 2005); Yuval Neria R. Marshall and E. Susser (eds), *9/11: Mental Health in the Wake of Terrorist Attacks* (Cambridge: Cambridge University Press, 2007); Allen Meek, 'Virtual Trauma: After 9/11', in *Trauma and Media: Theories, Histories, and Images* (New York: Routledge, 2010), pp. 171–196; Victor Jeleniewski Seidler, *Remembering 9/11: Terror, Trauma and Social Theory* (New York: Palgrave Macmillan, 2013).

6  Jacques Derrida, *Archive Fever: A Freudian Impression*, trans. Eric Prenowitz (Chicago: University of Chicago Press, 1998), p. 68. In *Archive Fever*, Derrida considers the role of the archive in the process of periodisation, arguing that the archive is an economically invested logic that refines, complicates and adds emphasis to an event through a prolonged 'structural breakdown' (11). Most importantly for Derrida the process of archivisation cannot be divorced from the event itself as '[t]he archivisation produces as much as it records the event' (17). In the process of archivisation, the event is transformed into a 'token of the future' which is no more related to the present than the past might be, ibid., 18. Narratologist Mark Currie has since expanded the idea of archive fever to argue the present is always 'contaminated' by the 'commercial context' by which events are deemed worthy of our attention. Currie, *About Time: Narrative Fiction and the Philosophy of Time* (Edinburgh: Edinburgh University Press, 2007), pp. 10, 25. Like Derrida, Currie sees the attempt

to periodise contemporary experience by the passing of event as a commercially driven process that is not only exclusionary of wider experience but characteristic of a rush to dispose of the present into the past that denies the possibility of reflection in the present. I return to Currie's philosophy in Chapter 3.

7   Lauren Berlant, 'Intuitionists: History and the Affective Event', *American Literary History*, 20:4 (winter 2008), pp. 846, 845.
8   Ian McEwan, 'Beyond Belief', *The Guardian*, G2 (12 September 2001), p. 2.
9   'The Talk of the Town' is ordinarily comprised of brief, frequently humorous articles on New York life, but in this instance was entirely replaced with comment on the attacks by writers of fiction and political commentators. Extending the sobriety of the occasion, a specially commissioned cover image by Art Spiegelman depicted the black silhouette of the World Trade Center against an entirely black background. David Remnick (ed.), 'The Talk of the Town', *The New Yorker* (24 September 2001), http://www.newyorker.com/archive/2001/09/24/010924ta_talk_wtc.
10  Jonathan Franzen, 'The Talk of the Town', http://www.newyorker.com/archive/2001/09/24/010924ta_talk_wtc.
11  Susan Sontag, 'The Talk of the Town', http://www.newyorker.com/archive/2001 /09/24/010924ta_talk_wtc.
12  John Updike, 'The Talk of the Town', http://www.newyorker.com/archive/2001/09/24 /010924ta_talk_wtc.
13  For an extended discussion, see: Rachel Sykes, 'A Failure of Imagination? Problems in '"Post-9/11" Fiction' in *Recovering 9/11 in New York*, ed. Robert Fanuzzi and Michael Wolfe (Cambridge: Cambridge Scholars Press, 2014), pp. 248–263. Catherine Morley also provides a valuable survey in 'Plotting against America: 9/11 and the Spectacle of Terror in Contemporary American Fiction', *Gramma* 16 (2008), pp. 293–312.
14  Representations of 11 September 2001 quickly found a place in popular genres, including thrillers, science fiction and comic books. Lawrence Block's *Small Town: A Novel of New York* (New York: Orion Paperbacks, 2003) includes the destruction of the World Trade Center as part of the city's local texture. In the bestselling thriller, *Night Fall* (New York: Grand Central Publishing, 2004) by Nelson DeMille, the attacks coincide with the novel's climax and extend the basis of its network of FBI-based conspiracy theories. Marvel Comics were even quicker to respond. Three special issues, *Heroes: The World's Greatest Super Hero Creators Honor The World's Greatest Heroes* (New York: Marvel, 2001), *The Amazing Spiderman #36: The Black Issue* (New York: Marvel, 2001) and *A Moment of Silence* (New York: Marvel, 2002) raised over $1 million for disaster relief funds, further indicating how profitable representations

of the event could be. Perhaps predictably, all three volumes stress the need for action above the need for discussion, limiting the importance of words in response to the crisis. *A Moment of Silence*, for example, focuses on the prevalence of visual media in the recording of '9/11'. The volume features no super heroes and contains no words, telling four tales of 'real life' responses to the attacks solely through images. For more, see: Stefanie Diekmann, 'How Marvel Dealt with 9/11', *The Guardian* (24 April 2009), http://www.guardian.co.uk/culture/2004 / apr/24/guesteditors3; Andrew D. Arnold, 'The Most Serious Comix Pt. 2', *Time* (5 February 2002), http://www.time.com/time/arts/arti cle/0,8599,198966,00.html; Matthew J. Costello, 'Spandex Agonistes: Superhero Comics Confront the War on Terror', in *Portraying 9/11: Essays on Representations in Comics, Literature, Film and Theatre*, ed. Véronique Bragard, Warren Rosenberg and Christophe Dony (Jefferson, NC: McFarland and Company Inc., Publishers, 2011), pp. 30–43.
15  Philip Roth, *Everyman* (London: Random House, 2006), p. 135.
16  Jonathan Franzen, *Freedom* (London: Fourth Estate, 2010), p. 28.
17  Key studies of these early fictional responses include: Kristiaan Versluys, *Out of the Blue: September 11 and the Novel* (New York: Columbia University Press, 2009); Richard Gray, *After the Fall: American Literature Since 9/11* (Oxford: Wiley Blackwell, 2011); Arin Keeble, *The 9/11 Novel: Trauma, Politics and Identity* (Jefferson, NC: McFarland & Company Inc., 2014); Martin Randall, *9/11 and the Literature of Terror* (Edinburgh: Edinburgh University Press, 2014); Tim Gauthier, *9/11 Fiction, Empathy, and Otherness* (New York: Lexington Books, 2015); Christina Cavedon, *Cultural Melancholia: US Trauma Discourses Before and After 9/11* (Leiden: Brill Rodopi, 2015).
18  Fredric Jameson, 'Magical Narrative: Romance as Genre', *New Literary History* 7:1, Critical Challenges: The Bellagio Symposium (autumn 1975), p. 135.
19  Jeremy Green, *Late Postmodernism: American Fiction at the Millennium* (London: Palgrave Macmillan, 2005), p. 24; Peter Toohey, 'The Cultural Logic of Historical Periodization', in *Handbook of Historical Sociology*, ed. Gerard Delanty and Engin F. Isin (London: SAGE Publications, 2003), p. 206. Toohey describes the need to periodise as the desire for 'regularizing, packaging and calibrating the apparent disorder of historical record'.
20  Michiko Kakutani, 'Books of the Times; A Hero with 9/11 Peripheral Vision', *The New York Times* (18 March 2005), http://query.nytimes.com/gst/fullpage.html? res=9E01E0DD103 CF93BA25750C0A9639C8B63.
21  Ian McEwan, *Saturday* (London: Cape, 2005), p. 31.
22  Mohsin Hamid, *The Reluctant Fundamentalist* (London: Hamish Hamilton, 2007), p. 94.

23 Jonathan Safran Foer, *Extremely Loud and Incredibly Close* (London: Penguin, 2005), p. 257.
24 John Updike, *Terrorist* (London: Penguin, 2006), pp. 196, 28, 47.
25 In his piece for *The New Yorker*, Updike, who watched the attacks from a tenth-floor apartment in Brooklyn Heights, betrayed a larger anxiety about the visual nature of the attacks that marked many more responses. See: Richard Glejzer, 'Witnessing 9/11: Art Spiegelman and the Persistence of Trauma', in *Literature After 9/11*, ed. Ann Keniston and Jeanne Follansbee Quinn (London: Routledge, 2002), pp. 99–122; Randall, 'Introduction: Eyewitnesses, Conspiracies and Baudrillard', *9/11 and the Literature of Terror*, pp. 1–18; Sonia Baelo-Allué, 'The Depiction of 9/11 in Literature: The Role of Images and Intermedial References', *Radical History Review*, no. 111 (2011), pp. 184–193; Lewis Gleich, 'Ethics in the Wake of the Image: The Post-9/11 Fiction of DeLillo, Auster, and Foer', *Journal of Modern Literature* 37:3 (1 April 2014), pp. 161–176.
26 In the introduction to a special edition of *Modern Fiction Studies* published to mark the tenth anniversary of the attacks, editors John N. Duvall and Robert P. Marzec noted that from a total of seventy submissions, fourteen had focused on *Falling Man* with twelve more on *Extremely Loud and Incredibly Close*. John N. Duvall and Robert P. Marzec, 'Narrating 9/11', *Modern Fiction Studies*, 57:3 (fall 2011), pp. 394, 386.
27 Versluys, *Out of the Blue: September 11 and the Novel*, pp. 134, 1.
28 Kiran Desai and Susan Koshy, 'Postcolonial Studies after 9/11: A Response to Ali Behdad', *American Literary History*, 20, no. 1–2 (spring/summer 2008), 300–303; Michael Rothberg, 'A Failure of Imagination: Diagnosing the Post-9/11 Novel', *American Literary Studies*, 21:1 (spring 2009), pp. 152–158; Margaret Scanlen, 'Migrating from Terror: the Postcolonial Novel after September 11', *Journal of Postcolonial Writing*, 46:3–4 (2010), pp. 266–278; Peter Morey, '"The Rules of the Game Have Changed": Mohsin Hamid's *The Reluctant Fundamentalist* and Post-9/11 Fiction', *Journal of Postcolonial Writing*, 47:2, (May 2011), pp. 135–146; Susan Lurie, 'Spectacular Bodies and Political Knowledge: 9/11 Cultures and the Problem of Dissent', *American Literary History*, 25:1, Special Issue: The Second Book Project (spring 2013), pp. 176–189.
29 Elleke Boehmer and Stephen Morton, 'Introduction: Terror and the Postcolonial', *Terror and the Postcolonial: A Concise Companion*, ed. Elleke Boehmer and Stephen Morton (Oxford: Blackwell, 2010), p. 6; Rosalind Morris, quoted in Robert Eaglestone, '"The Age of Reason Was Over ... an Age of Fury was Dawning': Contemporary Fiction and Terror', *Terror and the Postcolonial*, p. 364.
30 Richard Gray, 'Open Doors, Closed Minds: American Prose Writing at a Time of Crisis', *American Literary History*, 21:1 (spring 2009), p. 129.

31　Ibid., pp. 129, 133, 135.
32　Gray, *After the Fall*, 55. In order to do this, Gray draws on significant work done in Global Southern studies.
33　Zadie Smith, 'Two Paths for the Novel', *New York Review of Books* (20 November 2008), http://www.nybooks.com/articles/archives/2008/nov/20/two-paths-for-the-novel/?pagination=false.
34　Lilian R. Furst, *Realism* (New York: Longman, 1992), p. 3.
35　Andrew O'Hagan, 'Don DeLillo, *Underworld*, and *Falling Man*', *The Good of the Novel*, ed. Liam McIlvanney and Ray Ryan (London: Faber & Faber, 2011), p. 37.
36　Brian McHale, *Pöstmödernist Fictiön* (London: Routledge, 1987), pp. 38–39.
37　Versluys, *Out of the Blue*, 3.
38　Pankaj Mishra, 'The End of Innocence', *The Guardian*, Guardian Review (19 May 2007), p. 4.
39　Franzen, 'Perchance to Dream: in the Age of Images, a Reason to Write Novels', *Harper's Magazine* (April 1996), p. 54.
40　Franzen, 'Why Bother?' in his *How to Be Alone* (London: Harper Collins, 2002), p. 80. 'Perchance to dream' was republished as 'Why Bother?' in 2002 with several key additions that extended the author's criticism of the growth of MFA programmes in the United States and attacked the growing prevalence of novels that represent interior life.
41　Kathy Knapp, *American Unexceptionalism: The Everyman and the Suburban Novel After 9/11* (Iowa City: University of Iowa Press, 2014), p. xiii.
42　Green, *Late Postmodernism*, p. 4; James Wood, 'Human, All Too Inhuman', *The New Republic* (24 July 2000), http://www.newrepublic.com/article/books-and-arts/human-all-too-inhuman. After the terrorist attacks, Wood would revisit the idea of 'hysterical realism', articulating the hope that it would be harder 'to bounce around in the false zaniness of hysterical realism or to trudge along in the easy fidelity of social realism.' Wood, 'Tell Me how Does it Feel?', *The Guardian* (6 October 2001), http://www.guardian.co.uk/books/2001/oct/06/fiction. In October 2001, Smith responded to Wood, arguing that some novelists might be able to write 'in a slightly quieter way' but that most needed to compete with the noisier aspects of the culture: 'it is difficult to discuss feelings when the TV speaks so loudly; cries so operatically; seems always, in everything, one step ahead.' Smith, 'This is How it Feels to Be Me', *The Guardian*, (13 October 2001), http://www.theguardian.com/books/2001/oct/13/fiction.afghanistan. Smith would later revise her opinion in 'Two Paths for the Novel'.
43　Berman, *All That is Solid*, p. 31.
44　Salman Rushdie, 'Outside the Whale', *Granta* 11: Greetings from Prague (spring 1984), p. 123.

45 Tom Wolfe, 'Stalking the Billion-footed Beast: A Literary Manifesto for the New Social Novel', *Harper's Magazine* (November 1989), p. 47.
46 Ibid., p. 50. In *The Bonfire of the Vanities* (1987), Wolfe had already written a story of comparable ambition, greed, racial and social politics. Take for example Sherman McCoy's view of Manhattan as he drives over the Triborough Bridge in New York: 'Just think of the millions, from all over the globe, who yearned to be on that island, in those towers, in those narrow streets! There is was, the Rome, the Paris, the London of the twentieth century, the city of ambition, the dense magnetic rock, the irresistible destination of all those who insist on being *where things are happening.*' Wolfe, *The Bonfire of the Vanities* (London: Vintage, 2010), p. 81.
47 Franzen, 'Perchance to Dream', p. 54; Don DeLillo, interviewed by Ann Arensberg, 'Seven Seconds', *Conversations with Don DeLillo*, ed. Thomas DePietro (Jackson: University of Mississippi Press, 2004), p. 45. Franzen criticises Wolfe for a shortness of vision but ultimately restates many of his central claims, blaming the critic for disconnecting novelistic practice from the social and seeking to both sanctify the role of novelist and to make his own claim for a New Social Novel.
48 Philip Roth, interviewed by David Remnick, 'Into the Clear: Philip Roth', *Reporting: Writings from* The New Yorker (London: Picador, 2007), p. 119.
49 DeLillo, quoted by Jonathan Franzen, 'Perchance to Dream', 54; Wood, 'Tell Me how Does it Feel?'.
50 DeLillo, *White Noise* (New York: Viking Press, 1985), p. 27.
51 Franzen, *The Corrections* (New York: Harper Perennial, 2007), pp. 3, 4.
52 Franzen, *The Corrections*, p. 4; DeLillo, *White Noise*, pp. 484, 153, 482.
53 Jacques Attali, *Noise: The Political Economy of Music*, trans. Brian Massumi (Minneapolis: University of Minnesota Press, 1977), p. 3.
54 Sven Birkerts, *American Energies: Essays on Fiction* (London: Faber & Faber, 1992), pp. 127–128. Two years later, Birkerts fatalistically and perhaps prematurely concluded that the representing experience was now impossible and that 'No one thinks any longer about writing the Great American Novel'. Birkerts, *The Gutenberg Elegies: The Fate of Reading in an Electronic Age* (London: Faber & Faber, 1994), p. 207.
55 Green, *Late Postmodernism*, p. 5.
56 Douglas Rushkoff, *Present Shock; When Everything Happens Now* (New York: Penguin, 2013), p. 75.
57 Green, *Late Postmodernism*, p. 4.
58 Elizabeth Renker, 'What Is American Literature?', *American Literary History*, 23:12 (2012), p. 248.
59 Ted Gioia, 'The Rise of the Fragmented Novel: an Essay in 26 Fragments', *Fractious Fiction* (17 July 2013), http://fractiousfiction.com/rise_of_the_ fragmented_novel. See also: Michael David Lukas, 'A Multiplicity of

Voices: On the Polyphonic Novel', *The Millions* (15 February 2013), http://www.themillions.com/2013/02/a-multiplicity-of-voices-on-the-polyphonic-novel.html.

60 Mark Greif, '"The Death of the Novel" and Its Afterlives: Toward a History of the "Big, Ambitious Novel"', *boundary 2*, 36:2 (2009), p. 27. James Wood first used the term 'Big, Ambitious Novel' in his review of Zadie Smith's *White Teeth* (2000). Wood, 'Hysterical Realism', *The Irresponsible Self: on Laughter and the Novel* (New York: Picador, 2005), p. 178. Greif extends Wood's claims, adding that these novels of ambition have a long history in the United States and emerge as a response to the 'death of the novel' as a concept.

61 Versluys, *Out of the Blue*, p. 3; O'Hagan, 'Don DeLillo, *Underworld*, and *Falling Man*', p. 37.

62 Safran Foer, *Extremely Loud and Incredibly Close*, p. 38.

63 Ibid., p. 235.

64 Jess Walter, *The Zero* (New York: Harper, 2006), p. 15.

65 'The Wailing of One World Trade Center', http://tribecacitizen.com/2013/11/29/the-wailing-of-one-world-trade-center/.

66 Amitav Ghosh, 'The Talk of the Town', http://www.newyorker.com/archive/2001/09/24/010924ta_talk_wtc.

67 Martin Amis, 'The Voice of the Lonely Crowd', *The Guardian* (1 June 2002), http://www.theguardian.com/books/2002/jun/01/philosophy.society.

68 Toni Morrison, 'The Dead of September', *Trauma at Home: After 9/11*, ed. Judith Greenberg (Lincoln: University of Nebraska Press, 2003), p. 1.

69 Ann Keniston, '"Not Needed, Except as Meaning": Belatedness in Post-9/11 American Poetry', *Contemporary Literature*, 52:4 (winter 2011), p. 658.

70 The author has rarely published poetry, releasing just one short collection, *Five Poems*, in 2002. Morrison's choice of form here reflects her uncertainty about the event's representation in fiction, echoing other American writers who voiced uncertainty about how to respond to major 'events' in fiction. See: Michael Thelwell, 'Modernist Fallacies and the Responsibility of the Black Writer', *Duties, Pleasures, and Conflicts: Essays in Struggle* (Amherst: University of Massachusetts Press, 1987), pp. 218–234; John Limon, *Writing After War: American War Fiction from Realism to Postmodernism* (Oxford: Oxford University Press, 1994); Sharon Monteith, 'Revisiting the 1960s in Contemporary Fiction: "Where Do We Go from Here?"' *Gender in the Civil Rights Movement*, ed. Sharon Monteith and Peter Ling (New York: Garland Publishing, 1999), pp. 215–238; Sally Bachner, *The Prestige of Violence* (Athens: University of Georgia Press, 2011).

71  John Cage, 'Lecture on Nothing', *Silence: Lectures and Writings* (Middletown, CT: Wesleyan University Press, 1973), p. 9.
72  Theodor W. Adorno, 'An Essay on Cultural Criticism and Society', trans. Samuel Weber and Sherry Weber, *Prisms* (New York: Columbia University Press, 1981), p. 34.
73  Lionel Trilling, *The Liberal Imagination* (New York: Doubleday, 1953), p. 256.
74  Adorno, 'Meditations on Metaphysics', *Negative Dialectics*, trans. E. B. Ashton (New York: Continuum International Publishing Group, 2005), p. 363. Adorno wrote about artistic guilt after trauma to qualify his often-paraphrased suggestion that writing poetry after Auschwitz was barbaric, the longer version of which reads: 'The critique of culture is confronted with the last stage in the dialectic of culture and barbarism: to write a poem after Auschwitz is barbaric, and that corrodes also the knowledge which expresses why it has become impossible to write poetry today.' Adorno, 'An Essay on Cultural Criticism and Society', p. 34. In *Negative Dialectics*, Adorno came to think of this as an overstatement, and offers this conditional, if potentially more damning, revision: 'it may have been wrong to say that after Auschwitz you could no longer write poems. But it is not wrong to raise the less cultural question whether after Auschwitz you can go on living.' Adorno, 'Meditations on Metaphysics', p. 363.
75  Ibid.
76  W. J. T. Mitchell, '911: Criticism and Crisis', *Critical Inquiry*, 28:2 (winter 2002), p. 568.
77  Homi K. Bhaba, *The Location of Culture* (London: Routledge, 1994), p. 140.
78  Ibid., p. 1. Only through consideration of time's 'everyday connotations' could homogeneity be dispelled and the potentiality of the present as a fully 'performative' and contentious space be restored as a mark of contemporaneity.
79  Jacques Derrida, 'A Certain Impossible Possibility of Saying the Event' (2001), trans. Gila Walker, *Critical Inquiry*, 33 (winter 2007), p. 445.
80  Ibid., p. 446.
81  Derrida, *Philosophy in a Time of Terror: Dialogues with Jürgen Habermas and Jacques Derrida*, trans. Giovanna Borradori (Chicago: The University of Chicago Press, 2003), pp. 85–86.
82  DeLillo, *Falling Man* (New York: Picador, 2007), p. 3. All further references will appear in the text as *FM*. DeLillo had written similarly about the sound of the attacks in his biographical essay, 'In the Ruins of the Future', published in *Harper's* in December 2001. He described the fall of the towers as a 'low drumming rumble' that echoed throughout the city. DeLillo, 'In the Ruins of the Future', *Harper's* (December 2001), p. 40.

83  Donald Pease, '9/11: When Was "American Studies after the New Americanists"?', *boundary 2*, 33:3 (2006), p. 101.
84  Richard Drew's series of images became known by this single shot, 'the falling man', which came to represent the 200 or so people who fell, or jumped, to their deaths that day. The image proved so shocking because images of falling people were heavily edited from broadcast television: their bodies were shown on the BBC five times, only once on NBC and CNN and never on the ABC network. In reality, the infamous 'falling man' was third from last in a series of images, yet three local newspapers published it on its own. One of the first editors defended his decision to publish by describing the photo as quiet: 'shocking, yet oddly peaceful'. He saw the image of a man, his tie slightly fluttering in the wind, resigned to his fate and taking control of his own destiny in the face of terrorism. See: Laura Frost, 'Still Life: 9/11's Falling Bodies', in *Literature after 9/11*, pp. 180–208; Tom Junod, 'The Falling Man', *Esquire* (September 2003), pp. 177–199; Laszlo Muntean, 'Naming the Unnamable: (De)constructing 9/11's "Falling Man"', in *Performing Memory in Art and Popular Culture*, ed. Liedeke Plate and Anneke Smelik (New York: Routledge, 2013), pp. 105–122.
85  Derrida, *Archive Fever*, p. 97.
86  DeLillo, 'In the Ruins of the Future', p. 40.
87  Ibid.
88  Jennifer Egan, *A Visit from the Goon Squad* (New York: Random House, 2010), pp. 12, 38.
89  Gary Shteyngart, *Super Sad True Love Story* (New York: Granta, 2010), p. 96. In *The Culture of Commemoration* (2006), David Simpson argues that the symbolic nature of the Twin Towers and the proposed structure of the Freedom Tower were destined to conflict, as the plans for the latter seemed 'rather more like a sword in the raised hand of a militant nation-state' than a monument of national grief and healing. Simpson, *The Culture of Commemoration* (Chicago: Chicago University Press, 2006), p. 58. Jean Baudrillard had described the Twin Towers similarly before their destruction, as 'blind communicating vessels' of cyberculture that were nothing more than 'the punch-card and the statistical graph'. Jean Baudrillard, *The Spirit of Terrorism and Requiem for the Twin Towers*, trans. Chris Turner (London: Verso, 2002), p. 41.
90  Waldman's background as a journalist has also been fetishised, her former profession used as evidence of *The Submission*'s truthfulness. See: Michael Prodger, 'The Submission', *The Financial Times* (25 August 2011), http://www.ft.com/cms/s/2/5cdbf726-ca57-11e0-a0dc00144feabdc0.ht ml#axzz2AKooUMVi; Marianne Corrigan, 'Could "Submission" Be America's Sept. 11 Novel?', *NPR* (6 September 2011), http://wap.npr.org/news/Books/139942267; and, particularly, an article by the first journalist to write about the impact of Richard Drew's photograph of the

'Falling Man', Tom Junod, 'The Submission', *Esquire* (2 December 2011), http://www.esquire.com/fiction/best-books-2011-1211-2.
91  Amy Waldman, *The Submission* (London: Random House, 2011), p. 9.
92  Ibid., p. 96.
93  Ibid., p. 89.
94  DeLillo, 'In the Ruins of the Future', p. 40.
95  Waldman, *The Submission*, p. 114.
96  Arundhati Roy, 'Come September', in her *War Talk* (Cambridge, MA: South End Press, 2003), p. 75.
97  Simpson, *The Culture of Commemoration*, p. 11.

# 3

# Quiet in time and narrative

In 2005, Marilynne Robinson's epistolary novel, *Gilead* (2004), won the Pulitzer Prize for fiction. Five years later, Robinson's former student Paul Harding received the same prize for his debut novel, *Tinkers* (2009). According to Harding, many publishers rejected *Tinkers* before Bellevue Literary Press finally distributed it in 2009. Perceived as 'just another graduate of the Iowa Writers' Workshop with a quiet little novel', publishers informed Harding that there was no readership for what they described as 'a slow, contemplative, meditative, quiet book.'[1] Marilynne Robinson presumed the same would be true while writing *Gilead* and, before the Pulitzer, spoke of the difficulties of publishing what she called 'meditative' fiction. 'It didn't seem as if there was any particular premium placed on inwardness or reflection at that point', she said, 'and that is the only kind of writing that has ever interested me.'[2] That these two strikingly similar novels should win the Pulitzer five years apart seems contradictory when their depictions of interior life were deemed to be unmarketable. Reviewers often describe Robinson as a 'quiet, modest' writer who evokes a surprisingly 'quiet power' through a distinctly 'quiet, ruminative style'.[3] Since winning the Pulitzer, Harding's tale of *Tinkers'* many rejections has also taken on the status of myth with journalists mocking publishers who lacked 'the nerve to imagine worldly success for so quiet and meditative a book'.[4]

This chapter examines the discrepancy between the prize-winning success of quiet fiction and repeated critical surprise at the trend's existence. Even Brett Easton Ellis, whose famously fast-paced and ultra-violent novels are characterised by an aesthetic noise, praised the 'meditative' prose of *Gilead* while admitting he couldn't finish reading it. *Gilead*, he told one interviewer, 'doesn't have that kind of propulsive energy going that I require. [It's] a very different experience from most contemporary novels. You have to get on its level.'[5] Contrary to Ellis' suggestion, *The quiet contemporary American novel* places Robinson's and Harding's quietly non-'propulsive' fictions within a larger contemporary trend that represents the lives of quiet characters, locations and states. I argue that the classification of either novelist as quiet reflects a cultural assumption that quiet fiction will be conservative, nostalgic and old-fashioned precisely because of the lack of an event-driven plot or contemporary social content. It frames quiet novels against the noise of the political now, demonstrated by the example of '9/11' in Chapter 2, and implies that their quiet stems from an historical, apolitical narrative that is disengaged from the cultural moment of its production.

Through analysis of texts by Robinson and Harding, this chapter then makes two propositions about what quiet fiction might be in its contemporary American form. First, I define quiet as a narrative aesthetic through analysis of Robinson's *Gilead* and its partner novels, *Home* (2008) and *Lila* (2014).[6] Building on the aesthetic conditions outlined in Chapter 1, I read each text for four quiet criteria and argue that a quiet text privileges the depiction of quiet characters, locations and interior life so that very little happens in the body of the text that might outwardly be described as action. The second strand of this chapter is then concerned with time and temporality in Robinson's and Harding's quiet texts. A quiet novel where very little happens and where narrative duration is based on the movement of thought and the invocation of memory is liberated, I argue, from the linear representation of time and otherwise committed to the portrayal of subjective experience. To illustrate, I read Robinson's *Gilead* and Harding's *Tinkers*, two similarly quiet novels, in light of the recent temporal turn in the philosophy of time and narrative, paying particular attention to what J. Hillis Miller classifies as the 'rhetorical interpretations of temporality in literature'. This I hope will situate both authors' understanding of time within another contemporary trend that also questions the relationship between topicality and contemporaneity, the event and noise, and perhaps most importantly, eventlessness and quiet.[7]

## Robinson's quiet aesthetic: *Gilead*, *Home* and *Lila*

Since the publication of her debut novel *Housekeeping* in 1980, Marilynne Robinson has garnered a reputation as a recluse and literary outsider. A 1992 profile in *The Iowa Review* describes the author as a mythical entity 'sprung into literature fully grown like Athena': a mess of tousled hair who arrives late to class because she is lost in her own thought.[8] The romantic conceit of Robinson's persona is important here because it informs the marketing and reception of her novels. Robinson largely encourages this depiction: she frequently notes her work's dissimilarity to much contemporary fiction, claims not to read modern literature, despite her position at the Iowa Writers' Workshop, and names Thoreau, John Calvin and Emily Dickinson as major influences.[9] Robinson's invocation of older writers has also allowed her to assert her place in a centuries-long tradition, referencing her own canon of literary outsiders and using her image as an eccentric to perform her place in its hierarchy.

This chapter focuses on the Gilead novels almost exclusively, but Robinson's debut may also be read as a quiet text. *Housekeeping* is a fragmentary and deeply meditative novel that charts the experiences of Ruthie and Lucille Stone after their mother's premature death and describes the progression of relatives who come to take care of them in the remote town of Fingerbone, Idaho. *Housekeeping*'s major characters are all quiet. The children's mother and her sisters are described as 'quiet daughters' who display introverted tendencies 'because the customs and the habits of their lives had almost relieved them of the need for speech.'[10] The 'lightless, airless' existence they live out in the 'quiet' fictional town of Fingerbone is set on the edge of a vast Thoreauvian lake that, following the conditions of my quiet aesthetic, adds to the quiet of their situation.[11] Interestingly, *Housekeeping* also dissects a traditional 'sense of home' to write more directly on the 'puzzling margins' of experience where the structure of the family 'house' embodies much of the transience that I argue is later attributed to time in *Gilead*.[12] This aspect of the novel is also quiet: according to Katy Ryan, Ruthie narrates her transition from settler to wanderer through the symbolic disorganisation of gendered domestic spaces and the 'quiet insistence on the transience of all things'.[13] The title of *Housekeeping* is, then, somewhat analogous to its content as Robinson suggests that the 'house' of the title must be broken down in order to live out a more peaceful existence. Indeed, somewhat paradoxically, Robinson suggests that the individual must compose their own definition of 'housekeeping' that draws from the lives of previous generations in order to escape the prescriptions of society's most antiquated traditions, privileging an inherited form of quiet over the oppressive and ultimately noisier constructs of mainstream society.

Although *Housekeeping* was awarded a PEN/Hemingway Award for best first novel, Robinson did not publish a second work of fiction for twenty-four years. In the interim, the author wrote and reviewed for *Harper's* and *The New York Times*, published *Mother Country: Britain, the Welfare State, and Nuclear Pollution* (1989), a controversial examination of the public health dangers of the Sellafield nuclear plant, and *The Death of Adam* (1998), a collection of essays that she described as 'contrarian in method and spirit' and for which she received the National Book Award.[14] Between 1980 and 2004, however, Robinson published just two short stories, 'Orphans' (1981) and 'Connie Bronson' (1986), which she had written in the 1970s and subsequently dismissed as 'juvenilia'.[15] When *Gilead* was finally published in 2004, Robinson's 'quiet' career became a unique selling point. *Time* magazine reported that '[t]he anticipation of Robinson's follow-up has been urgent, loud and public', a statement that both suggests the public demand for meditative fiction had grown and that Robinson's quiet fiction was in some way creating noise.[16]

The Gilead novels complicate and expand *Housekeeping*'s examination of quiet states through a cast of characters who live in or return to the fictional town of Gilead, Iowa.[17] For Jeffrey Gonzalez, Robinson's later fiction retains the 'meditative flavor' of *Housekeeping* through 'a more developed system of ethics' that allows the narrator, Reverend Ames, to skip between a vast array of theology, philosophy and literature.[18] Read together, *Gilead*, *Home* and *Lila* focus on two Christian families, the Ameses and the Boughtons, and narrative episodes overlap around 1956. *Gilead* was the first to be published in 2004; it is an epistolary novel written from the perspective of Congregationalist minister John Ames in the months after he is diagnosed with heart failure. The text of *Gilead* lasts from the 'fine spring' of 1956 to the beginning of winter and, published just four years later, *Home* begins in the same spring and ends within a few days of *Gilead* when a 'light frost' descends on the town.[19] *Home* retells the events of *Gilead* from the household of Ames' oldest friend and confidante, the Presbyterian minister Robert Boughton, whose daughter Glory is forced to return 'home' at the age of thirty-eight to live 'a quiet life in a quiet place' (*H* 16) and care for her elderly father. *Home*'s third-person narrative is often focalised through Glory's perspective but her younger brother, John 'Jack' Ames Boughton, is the black sheep and would-be 'prodigal son' (*G* 84) whose search for redemption structures both *Gilead* and *Home*. A third novel, *Lila*, published in 2014, provides the history of Ames' second wife and covers the longest period, beginning thirty years before *Gilead* and skipping between the poverty of Lila's childhood in the 1920s, her early adulthood in a St. Louis whorehouse, her marriage to Ames in the 1940s and the present moment in 1956. Through a closely focalised third-person perspective, Robinson revisits themes of drifting, transience and gender identity last explored in *Housekeeping*, but while the end of Robinson's debut sees the Stones finally put 'an end to housekeeping', *Lila* depicts the opposite transition as the second Mrs Ames struggles to escape her vagrant past and make Gilead her physical and spiritual home.[20]

Read together, the Gilead novels are quiet in aesthetically similar ways. *Gilead*, *Home* and *Lila* focus on the same cast of quiet characters in the same rural location, retelling the history of Gilead from different but unanimously quiet perspectives. Read individually, however, each novel's quiet is subtly different. *Gilead* is the first and quietest of the trilogy. This is due to many aspects of Ames' situation, from the integration of all narrative incidents within one central fading consciousness to the love of quiet fostered by the religiosity and studiousness of Ames' nature. *Gilead*'s religious content has been a major preoccupation for critics who have framed Robinson's portrayal of Christianity as a largely benevolent force that is 'short on doctrine and long on wonder, mystery, and wisdom'.[21] Ames' beliefs are also important to a quiet reading of the novel because they commit him to a lifetime of contemplation and daily attempts to understand 'omniscience, omnipotence, judgment, and grace' (*G* 147). Ames is quiet, then, by profession and by nature; he is not simply withdrawing as he nears the end of life but has always been comfortable viewing the world from a distance. He has a deep appreciation of reflective states, often sitting quietly with Lila to appreciate the 'celestial consequences' (*G* 10) of life's minutiae. Indeed, he considers the 'quiet presence' (*G* 236) of Lila and Robby to be a reward for decades of loneliness following the death of his first wife and child in 1905. For forty years, the parsonage was marked by what Glory calls a 'stricken quiet' (*H* 82) that drove Ames to his study to 'read out of loneliness' (*G* 38). In the present, however, Ames seeks solitude because he loves the quality of attention that quiet brings, the 'hoard of quiet' (*G* 151) that can be found in peaceful environments and 'the silent and invisible life' (19) that reflection reveals to him. Ames' quiet is based in joy and *Gilead* is the quietest of Robinson's novels because, as a narrator, Ames is largely unconcerned with the noise of the world and happy with the smallness of his life.

*Gilead*'s epistolary form further structures the quiet of its prose. Janet Altman suggests that the aesthetic features of epistolary fictions rely largely 'on the relationship of internal writer to internal reader' and *Gilead* is technically quiet because the interiority of its narrative style provides little dialogue.[22] When the novel begins, Ames' letter has two primary functions: first, to record 'the way I think' (*G* 35) and second, to write a history of his father and grandfather whose political disagreements during the Civil War and Reconstruction overshadow Ames' intellectual life in the present. Ames believes that the letter will pass on aspects of his interior life to his son including childhood memories, inherited stories and a lifetime of knowledge accumulated by reading. He alludes freely to scripture, philosophy and fiction and assumes a fluency in theological works that he is uncertain Lila, his 'unschooled' (*G* 78) wife, will teach Robby. Ames' letter can be read as a kind of inheritance that consolidates the religious, studious and familial quiet, love of reflection and pleasure in meditation that he has learnt from his family but will not live to teach his son. For Lila, too, quiet is a favoured trait that is lost if it is not cultivated. In her third Gilead novel, Robinson reveals how much Lila understands the project of Ames' 'begats':

> And she would tell [Robby] he was a minister's son, so he might blame her because she couldn't give him what his father would have given him, the quiet gentleness in his manners, the way of expecting the people would look up to him. She couldn't teach him that.[23]

Both Lila and Ames believe the 'quiet gentleness' of the Ames family will die with the Reverend but only Lila acknowledges the privileged position of men who choose to be quiet and expect others to listen. Aesthetically, *Gilead*'s quiet is a product of Ames' character, age, religiosity and studiousness as well as its epistolary form, eventless prose and the integration of narrative incident within one central consciousness. However, *Gilead* is quieter than either *Home* or *Lila* because of the privilege and security that Ames inherits from the generations of quiet men who lived, studied and worshipped in the parsonage before him.

*Home* retells a story already partially told in *Gilead*, recounting the difficulties of Jack, Glory and their father, Reverend Boughton, as they attempt to live together after twenty years apart. *Home* also meets my conditions for a quiet aesthetic: Robinson focusses first on quiet characters, second on a quiet location, third, although to a lesser extent, on interior life so that, fourth, nothing really happens in the novel. All three Boughtons enjoy quiet activities: Boughton reads dense tomes of German theology, Glory studies her Bible every day and Jack spends his evenings reading Karl Marx and, most significantly, W. E. B. Du Bois. Like Ames, Boughton is old, infirm and habitually contemplative, often 'praying before the commencement of prayer' (*H* 71) and sleeping most of the day. However, *Home* lacks the interiority of Robinson's previous work and abandons the restricted perspective of Ames for a third-person narrative that is supplemented with long passages of description and dialogue. The novel is aesthetically noisier than *Gilead*, first because the majority of the narrative takes place outside of consciousness and second because the quiet of *Home* is troubled by negative affect, anxiety and anger. Unlike Ames, Boughton is furious about the indignities of old age and feels trapped in his 'empty and quiet' (*H* 7) house after the death of his wife. Jack is similarly heartbroken, returning to Gilead after a forced separation from his African American fiancée, Della, and their young son, Robert. Even Glory, the only character through whom the narrative is focalised, feels pressured into a caretaking role as the only single woman in a conservative Presbyterian family. Despite her Masters' degree in English and years spent away from Gilead as a teacher, Glory bites her tongue 'twenty times a day' (70), avoids intellectual debate and is so quiet that sometimes her father forgets she is present. Glory's quiet borders on silence, a state abided rather than enjoyed and one radically different from the communicative quiet Ames appreciates in *Gilead*.

*Home* therefore contains the briefest suggestion that quiet is gendered, even racialised. The struggle for civil rights is a driving force of Robinson's second Gilead novel, which picks up the discussion of segregation introduced in *Gilead*'s final pages. Throughout *Gilead*, the political backdrop of the 1950s is curiously absent and Ames' only political declaration, 'If I live, I'll vote for Eisenhower' (*G* 107), suspiciously empty. It is only at the end of *Gilead*, when Jack confesses to Ames that he wants to return to Iowa because of the state's lack of anti-miscegenation laws, that Ames is thrown into a spiritual crisis and forced to address the political apathy that ensures his life is untroubled by noise.

By comparison, *Home* amplifies the political events excluded from Ames' letter: Jack follows news on the 1956 civil rights demonstrations over segregation in Montgomery and argues with his father about the 'provocation' (*H* 214) of non-violent protest. Jack's quiet is characterised by an 'incandescence of unease' (*H* 215) and although Robinson describes him as 'quiet' (*H* 31, 37, 120, 133, 164, 196, 217, 256) more than any other character, this quiet is undermined by what he cannot admit: his relationship with Della and the existence of their mixed-race son. Indeed, *Home* is full of quiet people who endure rather than thrive in Gilead's quiet spaces. Glory cannot confess to the failed engagement that brought her home and, as Boughton grows weaker, he becomes confused, believing that his wife is still alive and their house should be full with the noise of eight children: he asks Glory why his children have become 'so quiet!' (*H* 304) and mistakes the peace around him for a sign that something is wrong. Although they are quiet, then, the Boughtons are never peaceful and in *Home*, it is clearest that quiet is only valuable as an expressive state when it is chosen and not when it is compelled. As Kevin Everod Quashie suggests, quiet has the potential to provide a refuge for the 'suppressed textualities' of the disenfranchised because the ideal of public selfhood is not available to everyone.[24] However, Quashie underestimates the importance of audience: that is, in order for a quiet person to be heard they must encounter an active listener. At the end of the novel, the Boughtons' 'unreadable quiet' (*H* 13) remains uncommunicative while Robinson's references to the political landscape of the 1950s hint, and only hint, at an African American community, just outside Gilead, who are denied the privilege of quiet altogether and must shout in order to be heard.

*Lila*, finally, offers a third interpretation of quiet. In many ways, it is the most ambitious of the Gilead novels, covering the longest timespan and the greatest geographical distance. Unlike the Ames and Boughtons in *Gilead* and *Home*, Lila has no family to tie her to one place and she spends her early life drifting with vagrants and criminals who cannot keep her safe or provide her with the education she craves. The novel's first line evokes the poverty that Lila is born into: 'The child was just there on the stoop in the dark, hugging herself against the cold, all cried out and nearly sleeping' (L 3). Lila is quiet in this instance because she is exhausted from shouting and Robinson notes that her family also 'fought themselves quiet' inside the house. In fact, everything about Lila's poverty is loud; her early years are composed of shouts, screams and a 'pounding at the screen door' that only subsides through exhaustion. On the novel's second page, Lila is rescued by the enigmatic Doll who commits them to a life of wandering to escape the child's neglectful family and Doll's criminal past. However, Lila's life as a vagrant exposes her to many more locations in which quiet is inconsistent and unreliable. When Lila sleeps rough, every noise startles her: the crickets 'so damn loud' (L 56), the rain 'too loud' (L 60) and the people she travels with constantly noisy (L 59). The aesthetic qualities of noise and quiet are unpredictable to Lila and from the enforced 'quiet' (L 189) of a St Louis whorehouse to the quiet people she meets in Gilead, Lila believes that quiet masks much louder realities.

In my reading, the third Gilead novel is also reflexive about the principles of a quiet aesthetic and *Lila* might ultimately be 'about' the difficulties of quiet as a mode of engagement in the present. If *Gilead* is the quietest of the trilogy and *Home* is the loudest, *Lila* narrates the transition from loud to quiet in which the future Mrs Ames learns that the 'quiet of the world' doesn't always sound 'like mockery' (L 112). Of all Robinson's characters, Lila changes the most. She works as an itinerant labourer, cleaner, and unsuccessful prostitute; moves from a life of homeless poverty to the parsonage of Gilead; and, in the reader's eyes, evolves from the marginal and 'gentle' soul glimpsed in *Gilead* (228) into the obstinate, difficult, and 'hard woman' (L 51) of *Lila*. Slowly, she also begins to embrace the quiet of her character and finds pleasure in Gilead's 'quiet evening streets' (L 122). Lila's arrival in Gilead does not 'cure' her insecurities and she continues to occasionally dwell on the 'roar and wrench' (L 112) of existence. However, as Sarah Churchwell suggests, if *Lila* is the 'least political' of Robinson's novels, it is 'lit at moments by a visionary wonder' that make it the 'most emotional'.[25] The quiet of Gilead and a relationship with Ames provide Lila with a feeling of security she has never experienced, leaving her open to and capable of a more peaceful relationship with herself and others. '[H]ere she was', Robinson writes, 'in the Reverend's quiet house, as calm and safe as the good man could make her' (L 218). Robinson describes the relationship between Lila and Ames as a form of sustenance 'like rest and quiet, something you live without but you needed anyway' (L 79–80) and towards the end of *Lila* the calm of *Gilead*, which *Home* undermines, is reinvoked in the aesthetic quiet of the text.

## *Gilead, Tinkers* and narrative atemporality

Since *Gilead*'s publication, many critics have enigmatically referred to the quiet of Robinson's prose. Novelist Ali Smith describes *Gilead* as 'careful' and 'crepuscular'; literary critic David James calls *Gilead*'s partner novel *Home* a 'crystalline' novel; Robert E. Kohn suggests that 'radiance' best captures the quiet tenor of Robinson's prose; and James Wood argues that Robinson's fiction is 'sanguine' and 'deeply unfashionable' when compared to the work of her peers.[26] The publication of Harding's *Tinkers* in 2009 received comparatively little fanfare and very limited critique. Harding was a first-time author and a recent graduate of the Iowa Writers' Workshop with no publications to his name. Distributed by a small, independent press, *Tinkers* sold 7,000 copies and was not picked up for review by *The New York Times* until after it received the Pulitzer, a prize Harding only found out he had won by checking the prize's website.[27]

The popular success of quiet novels can be a slow burn. As I discussed in Chapter 1, the 2006 reissue of John Williams' *Stoner* (1965) surprised many critics when it became an international bestseller. Like *Tinkers*, *Stoner* was not widely reviewed when it was first published, only briefly noted by *The New Yorker* and sold 2,000 copies before vanishing into obscurity. The commercial success of both novels in the first decade of the twenty-first century was therefore conceived as a victory for small presses and what Harding describes as 'quiet, metaphysical novels'.[28] Contrarily, however, because *Tinkers* and *Stoner* were perceived as quiet outliers of a publishing industry that is largely attracted to noise, the aesthetic qualities of quiet again went unidentified.

The same can be said of the obvious links between Robinson and Harding. Critics have not yet read *Gilead* and *Tinkers* side by side, although their pairing seems to be inevitable.[29] The authors met when she was his teacher in a summer writing class at Skidmore College in 1996 and then at the Iowa Writers' Workshop, a programme for which she recommended him. *Gilead* and *Tinkers* are also strikingly similar as quiet novels. Both protagonists, Ames in *Gilead* and George Washington Crosby in *Tinkers*, are housebound and dying. In *Gilead*, Ames is a quiet man who pursues prayer and meditation as a pastime and for a living; *Tinkers* is narrated omnisciently but often focalised through the consciousness of amateur horologist George Washington Crosby in the final days of his life. Robinson's novel is set in the small town of Gilead, Iowa; Harding's is set in the equally rural and fictional village of Enon, Massachusetts.[30] In many respects, and despite its third person narration, *Tinkers* is even quieter than *Gilead*. Bed-ridden for the entirety of *Tinkers*, George often falls into periods of unconsciousness during which he is physically unable to communicate. As Larry D. Bouchard points out, the 'action' of Harding's 'slow' novel 'simply involves a mind and spirit dissolving over time and transcendental nature'.[31] Both novels are technically quiet therefore because the interiority of their narrative style provides little dialogue and most each novel's 'action' takes place within the protagonist's consciousness as he faces his imminent end.

The plotless narrative of both *Gilead* and *Tinkers* is the most complex feature of any quiet fiction and an aspect of both narratives that critics frequently reference but never directly address. Peter Boxall lists *Gilead* amongst a group of twenty-first-century fictions centring on elderly protagonists and argues their narrators are symptomatic of a 'late' postmodernism that explores 'discordance between newly passing time and the expired narratives with which we have made time readable.'[32] David James distinguishes Robinson and Harding as 'crystalline' novelists, a term that he applies to writing that seems both old and new and reanimates the idea of 'the sublime' as an aesthetic of contemporary experience.[33] Both Boxall and James discuss a kind of narrative stillness that characterises the passing of time in *Gilead* and *Tinkers* but both stop short of suggesting that either novel is quiet. Jeffrey Hart comes closest to addressing the quiet that I argue structures *Gilead* and *Tinkers* when he notes: 'not a great deal happens [in *Gilead*], except that everything happens.'[34] Indeed, Hart conceives Heidegger's concept of Being as the 'balm' of Robinson's prose and argues that Robinson's fictive exploration of consciousness facilitates a plot that 'does not drive the reader urgently ahead', representing a third possibility between 'bellicosity' and 'pacifism' that restores the individual's capacity for reflection in the present.[35]

The third possibility Hart alludes to but does not name is where I also argue quiet resides. As this study suggests, the representation of quiet people and states has the potential to act as a 'balm' for contemporary readers when it maintains the usefulness of reflection against the rush of society, retrieves moments of existence from the belligerent drive of a future-oriented present and holds these moments in a suspended state for further engagement. As Kathryn Hume suggests, readers may respond favourably to Robinson's prose because it provides relief from a barrage of plot-driven contemporary novels that not only 'scream in your ear' but 'do the mental equivalent of pissing on your shoes, holding a knife to your throat, or spouting nuclear physics at you as well.'[36] Rather than making the narrative unfashionable or 'out of time', as James Wood suggests of *Gilead*, I argue that a quiet aesthetic actually roots *Gilead* and *Tinkers* more firmly in the narrative present.[37] In Hart's winning contradiction 'not a great deal happens, except that everything happens' and the quiet narrative is thus distant from the portrayal of national or topical event that characterises, dates and arguably limits the historical present of many noisier fictions.

For example, much of the eventlessness of Robinson and Harding's prose is linked to its vague temporal setting. All three Gilead novels are undated. 1880, the year of Ames' birth, is one of very few dates referenced in *Gilead* and, at the beginning of the novel, Ames states that he has lived seventy-six years in Gilead from which the reader can deduce he is writing in 1956. *Home* makes more explicit reference to the 1950s in which the novels take place. As previously noted, the narrative voice alludes to contemporary adverts and films and Jack takes every opportunity to discuss 'the [racial] troubles in the south' (*H* 162) with his father.[38] *Lila* occupies a more ambiguous present than either *Gilead* or *Home* in which the American Dust Bowl of the 1930s is simply referred to as 'the times they began to get caught in the dust' (*L* 16). All three Gilead novels are therefore temporally abstracted from both the 1950s in which they are set and the twenty-first century in which we read them.

*Tinkers*, by comparison, opens in the near present, although it is similarly undated and, like Ames' remembrances, George's deathbed hallucinations lead the reader back into the past through three generations of Crosby men.[39] The effect of this temporal abstraction is to place both *Tinkers* and *Gilead* in an ambiguous present in which the political and cultural 'now' is vague scenery to the emotional landscape of the characters. Michael Schmidt calls this aspect of *Gilead* 'anachronistic'; Tessa Hadley describes *Gilead* as 'old fashioned'; Susan Petit argues that the characters of *Gilead* and *Home* suffer from a kind of 'historical amnesia' that papers over the injustices of the past and neglects the noise of the present.[40] I contend that the atemporality of both Robinson's and Harding's fiction is the product of a quiet aesthetic that removes contemporary noise from the character's experience of the present. By focusing on the interior lives of quiet characters who live in a quiet location, *Gilead* and *Tinkers* are untethered from the representation of noise, event and the progression of narrative action that typically constitutes a novel's plot. These 'historical' narratives are therefore pointedly non-topical: Schmidt, Hadley and Petit all acknowledge that the Gilead novels are set in the past but are not immediately identifiable with a particular historic 'moment'.

The notion of narrative atemporality returns us to a larger point about the critical reception of quiet and noisy novelists. As I argued in Chapter 2, writers like Don DeLillo, Jonathan Franzen, Thomas Pynchon and Philip Roth are often seen as the century's key chroniclers because within a culture declared to be loud, quiet is seen as reticence, at best, and conservatism, at worst. Robinson has acknowledged this association of creativity with noise and volume with authority in her non-fictional writing. In 'Writers and the Nostalgic Fallacy' (1985), Robinson defended the 'meditative' fiction she prefers to read and write from the 'literature of expostulation, of Catastrophe'.[41] Interestingly, Robinson frames her discussion in terms of quiet and loud, arguing that it should not be necessary for the novelist to engage in a shouting match in order to be heard. 'Among people carried along in a canoe toward a waterfall', she writes, 'the one who stands up and screams is not the one with the keenest sense of the situation.' Her fiction is political, she claims, in its very avoidance of contemporary detail, and by doing so she suggests that our engagement with the present might benefit from the reinstatement of quiet and reflection, especially at times of social upheaval. It is this aspect of both Robinson's and Harding's prose that reviewers often describe as 'quiet'. As this chapter suggests, quiet fiction represents life between events, shifting focus from louder instances or actions and reprioritising the subjective as a locus for experience. It is, in other words, a reflective engine of narrative that renders stories of forward movement less persuasive by valuing reflection as an active state of presence.

## The temporal turn

Attention paid to the subjective portrayal of temporality is crucial to understanding the quiet aesthetic outlined in *Gilead* and *Tinkers*. In their focus on old-age, interiority and the selective recall of memory both novels evoke the recent temporal turn in philosophy located in the so-called 'space-time crises' of the late twentieth century.[42] The temporal turn shares several features with my quiet aesthetic, most notably the argument that time, like quiet, is a fundamental if neglected concern of Western thought. In *The Deconstruction of Time* (1989), philosopher David Wood hints that spatial and linguistic turns in scholarship have finally been exhausted and rejects the idea of an objective gauge of temporality to argue the end of the century is already 'whispering loudly that the temporal turn is upon us'.[43] Like Robinson, Wood frames his discussion of time and presence in terms of volume and argues that if temporality is a mere whisper of contemporary thought its study will soon be loudly felt.[44] Similar to Jeffrey Hart's appraisal of the Heideggerian 'balm' of Robinson's fiction, Wood advocates for a return to Heidegger's conception of time's horizonality in *Being and Time* (1926), suggesting that philosophy should move as Heidegger did 'to a thinking that would no longer be *about* something so much as speaking out of a certain engagement' with its subject matter.[45] In this way, and as this chapter argues, Wood's study bears similarities to the doctrines of political and philosophical quietism outlined in Chapter 1. He argues that time has always been a major concern of Western philosophy but that over the course of the twentieth century the study of time and temporalities was side-lined by attention paid to the metaphysical values of unity and certainty. Rather than considering the larger mechanised structure of temporality, Wood therefore argues that the temporal turn should reside in an 'ordinary conception of time' which might eschew the will to conclude that characterises event-driven narratives and focus instead on the quietly lived experience of the individual.[46]

Literary critics including Mark Currie and Jesse Matz have since extended Wood's idea that 'the art of time' should be reconsidered phenomenologically as the study of conscious experience from the first-person perspective.[47] To these critics, temporality is what Matz calls 'an open question' that can be applied to a diverse range of texts. While science and philosophy work to achieve an accepted definition of time, literary critics have argued that works of literature often achieve the opposite and are, as J. Hillis Miller observes, 'sui generis, different from all the others'.[48] Notably, the study of time in narrative is philosophically therapeutic to these critics; it carries no common objective or narrative drive beyond the exploration of texts as 'phenomenological instruments through which to transform temporal realities, pragmatic opportunities that makes time more truly an open question'.[49] Indeed, the study of time might also be described as an objectiveless exercise that is, like a quiet aesthetic, a means of interpreting the present beyond the narrative drive of progress, providing ways of thinking about duration that prioritises subjective experience through a focus on reflective modes of engagement with the present. The way in which a narrative is 'about' time is just as often indirect. Just as Wood paraphrases Heidegger's idea of time's horizonality to suggest a 'certain engagement' with its subject, so time does not always seem to be what is 'at stake' in the narrative to be one of the text's central concerns. It follows that the quiet narratives of *Gilead* and *Tinkers* are not 'about' the twenty-first-century moment in which they were written yet what the temporal turn reveals about the centrality of time to narrative, and vice versa, is that the relationship between two concepts does not need to be explicit to be important. Perhaps, that is an analysis of time's rhetorical interpretations can engage with the discursive nature of quiet prose without reducing the discussion of time in narrative to the identification of a narrative arc that depends on the passing of event in the build-up to a conclusion.

The quiet temporalities of both *Gilead* and *Tinkers* express initial similarities. The limitation of time, for instance, indicated by the protagonist's imminent death makes time's passing both precious and more vital. The novels each capture the pleasures of the narrator's final days as he 'notice[s] them all, minute by minute' (*G* 106–107). Both also describe the narrator's attempts to compose a family history. Ames' recollections range from the 'present' moment in 1956 back as far as 1850 through anecdotes of his father and grandfather yet it remains possible to read *Gilead*'s timeline as linear because it, like *Home*, technically only spans several months. Consider, for example, this statement about Ames' birth:

> I, John Ames, was born in the Year of Our Lord 1880 in the state of Kansas, the son of John Ames and Martha Turner Ames, grandson of John Ames and Margaret Todd Ames. At this writing I have lived

seventy-six years, seventy-four of them here in Gilead, Iowa, excepting study at the college and at seminary.

And what else should I tell you? (*G* 10–11)

The gauging of time is idiosyncratic in this passage. The repetition of the 'Ames' surname, taken from the French for friend (*amie*) or the Hebrew for burden, reasserts itself as though to repeat 'I am.' With Ames' waning participation in the present, names are concrete and painful indicators that he is losing his active participation in the world (Ames' wife, Lila, is named only once in the novel; his son is not named at all). For the Reverend, names have a necessary association with the past and are only explicitly stated for characters who are elderly or retrieved through his oldest memories. Not only is time established in relation to Ames' existence but in this early passage there are already gaps in the narrative that Ames is reconstructing, revealed by the phrase: 'excepting study at the college and at seminary' (*G* 11). This omission of detail about his only time away from Gilead indicates that although the reader perceives Ames' narrative as a stream of consciousness, he is actually engaged in the art of self-composition and, as I explore in Chapter 5 of this book, mimicking the conventions of memoir.

While Ames is viscerally aware of his approaching death, and keen to document what time he has left, as *Tinkers* begins George Crosby is already entering his final hours. The novel opens by initiating a countdown, 'George Washington Crosby began to hallucinate eight days before he died' (*T* 6), and time is subsequently gauged by how much remains. The wealth of topics explored in *Tinkers*' otherwise restricted narrative is made possible by Harding's representation of George's encroaching death and by George's increasingly unconscious state. Through flashbacks and a third-person narration that skips between the experiences of George, his father, Howard, and his unnamed grandfather, Harding moves freely through over a century of a family's life, representing the present moment without a sense of contingency and despite the fact that the ailing narrator is presented with 'a different self every time he tried to make an assessment' (*T* 18) of himself. Indeed, narrative time is made to seem limitless as Harding explains the science of horology, looks back at the present moment from the perspective of a future archaeologist and slips between the minds of people long dead to inhabit the thoughts of three generations. Moreover, all of this is made possible, rather than limited, by George's ailing body, which gradually excludes the noise of the world around him as it shuts down.

The temporal sweep of Harding's novel incorporates past, present, and future in a continuous living present that shows less anxiety about life's impermanence than *Gilead*. As death looms beyond the present moment of the protagonist's consciousness, and eternity cannot be imagined, Harding describes the human presence on earth as fading against the permanence of the natural world. Individuals then appear only as 'brief disturbances of shadows or light, or as a slight pressure, as if the space one occupied suddenly had had something more packed into it' (*T* 134) and human existence is reduced to an intensification of pre-existing elements, holding no fixed definition of self and meaning so that the depiction of consciousness must be considered as the accumulation of unconnected elements rather than a stable whole. Skipping back to a time when he was not bedridden, Harding also describes George's attempt to document his final thoughts. George chooses a tape recorder and, like Ames, he begins with hesitancy, expressing displeasure with the 'cheap microphone', 'cryptic' labels and 'heavy' levers (*T* 21–22) that distract him. Soon, the recording of his life takes on a similar form to Ames' letter and George begins to compose his legacy:

> He began formally: My name is George Washington Crosby. I was born in West Cove, Maine, in the year 1915. I moved to Enon, Massachusetts, in 1936. And so on. After these statistics, he found that he could think only of doggerel and slightly obscene anecdotes to tell. (*T* 22)

Despite initial hesitation, there is a moment during the process of recording when George loses himself, recording 'almost without being conscious of doing so' (*T* 23). Yet the tape ultimately provides a mechanised rendering of time that preserves nothing of what George intends. Harding stresses the fictionality that George perceives in the act of recording: how 'he imagined that his memoirs might sound like those of an admirable stranger' and how they come across as 'mockery' (*T* 23–24). His voice is left 'thin and remote' (*T* 22) and the tape fails to record his disparate memories of 'blue snow and barrels of apples and splitting frozen wood' (*T* 23). Dissatisfied, he abandons the project and throws the tape into the burning stove, questioning the validity of his attempt at self-representation.

It is notable here that this quiet protagonist should choose a method of recording his legacy that creates noise. Tellingly, it is the thinness of his voice that distresses George the most and the act of recording demonstrates the problem of the archive as characterised by Derrida when he suggests that the act of recording becomes a 'token of the future' and is no more related to the present than the past might be, speaking rather to an eagerness to imagine how the present will be perceived from a future time.[50] George similarly resents the act of recording, which, once composed, appears to him to be a conceited attempt to project his importance into the future. While Ames' letter to his son is an attempt to control how he is remembered by passing on an almost familial sense of quiet, George's tape only confirms to him that his presence on earth is fading and, further, that this is how it was meant to be.

Ames and George differ, then, in their experience of the present and particularly over the prospect of extending their relevance into the future. Each novel also differs in its direct handling of time. Ames, for example, often considers the nature of time idiomatically. He stresses its passing in reference to quiet pastimes, the 'time to read' (*G* 45), or his religious beliefs, stating that 'the Sabbath is set apart so that the holiness of time can be experienced' (*G* 102). Reading, writing and praying are therapeutic for Ames; each act of reflection helps to restore the feeling of joy in the present and the experience of wonder to the passing of time. As he nears the end, Ames considers his lifelong commitment to work and public life, concluding that activities conducive to quiet states are the only satisfactory modes of existence. Still, the prospect of his imminent departure from the world hovers over the text and as a result Ames alludes to time in a distracted and repetitive way. Early in *Gilead*, as Ames introduces his thoughts on death and dying, he starts repeating the idioms that will recur throughout the novel: 'a long time ago', 'the wrong time', 'at the time', 'from time to time' (*G* 7). Ames repeatedly refers to time in the quotidian sense, illustrating the extent to which he feels robbed of a future with his son and expressing a fundamentally Heideggerian sense of time's every day importance.[51]

Although Robinson's use of the first-person perspective instils the narrator with a practical understanding of his own experience of time, Ames is kept from fully considering time in its abstraction. By comparison, Harding writes more directly, and sometimes more abruptly, about George's personal experience, discussing temporality in its mathematic and abstracted senses, its public and private forms. While George lies dying, he imagines what his visitors may be saying to him, when he finds he is no longer able to listen. This episode of quiet is a construction of George's mind: his guests are not intentionally quiet but the noise that they produce is incompatible with George's conscious experience. Demonstrating both the indefiniteness of speech and the interpretive potential of quiet, George replaces uttered conversation with a description of time's experiential qualities. 'I was just thinking', his guest is imagined to say, 'that I am not very many years old, but that I am a century wide. I think that I have my literal age but am surrounded in a radius of years. I think that these years of days, this near century of years, is a gift from you' (*T* 159). The entire scenario of George's hallucination is confusing to the reader and even more difficult to explain because the imagery muddies the terms in which the reader might understand temporality in the novel. Years become days and periods of time take on spatial dimensions as George's vision and his imagining of conversation overwrites the noises externally produced within the quiet of the protagonist's mind. Despite its complexity, however, the passage reveals Harding's interest in breaking apart distinctions between linear and non-linear time and also between temporality and spatiality, reaching beyond the confines of George's brain through 'a radius of years' and back across many centuries.

Prioritising what Miller calls the 'rhetorical interpretations of temporality in literature' is not, then, to ignore the thematic implications of Paul Ricœur's 'phenomenology of time experience', which removes time from its purely linear connotations and informs any study of how novelistic temporality is gauged.[52] According to Ricœur, temporality can be divided into cosmological time, the linear progression of time from birth to death, and phenomenological time, the qualification of time as past, present and future. The conceit that Ricœur first describes in his essay 'Narrative Time' (1980) and returns to in the three-volume study, *Time and Narrative* (1983–5), is the root of his philosophy: that is, 'the ordinary representation of time as a linear series of "nows" hides the true constitution of time.'[53] The individual's self-awareness means that personal experience of time is framed by the moment's position in a continuum; this makes the present part of the past and also part of the future. Time and narrative are then perceived to be interweaving and, importantly to Ricœur, narrative time in the novel cannot be static. Using *Tinkers* as an example, as

George lies dying in his family home the house around him begins to fragment as his consciousness' differentiation between the past and the living present breaks down. 'Nearly a ghost', George's perception of time no longer distinguishes between tenses, as every part of his life is overhauled into the current moment: 'George imagined what he would see, as if the collapse had, in fact, already happened: the living room ceiling, now two stories high, a ragged funnel of splintered floorboards ... and pointing towards him in the center of all of that sudden ruin' (*T* 8–9). The passage recalls Ruthie and Sylvie's destruction of the family home in Robinson's *Housekeeping*: both novels suggest that in order to live outside of society's loudest and most repressive structures the individual must be at peace with their private interpretation of time. What Ricœur's theorising also helps to explain is just how quiet novels use moments from the past, present and future to create the moment in which the action of the novel takes place, unmarked by the anxiety that Derrida associates with the event and the archive. This is not to suggest a collaborative theory of temporality between all novels of interiority, or even between all quiet fictions.[54] Yet it is to claim that in the narrative unity between past, present and future, as Ricœur suggests, we might 'move beyond historicality itself to the point at which temporality springs forth in the plural unity of future, past, and present.'[55] In this way, I argue that *Gilead* and *Tinkers* both hint at the difficulties of representing or even conceiving of the present while paradoxically speaking both to and about a sense of the contemporary that locates the main body of the narrative in the past.

## Horological time

Narrative temporality and composition of the present is most obviously a consideration for Harding because *Tinkers*' central character has an obsession with clocks. As an amateur horologist, George finds great comfort in the mathematical construction of time: the clock 'cast[s] familiar shadows' for George and offers reassurance for him through contemplation of its 'deeper mysteries' (*T* 180). Indeed, George considers the nature of existence to be more easily contemplated in mechanical measurements. The hands of the clock may be repetitious and unrelenting but they are also familiar, comforting and a reminder of his previous life and existence in the present.

The figure of the clock in *Tinkers* recalls a similar obsession in many modernist fictions and hints at the legacy of literary modernism in the quiet novel's explication of time. By the early twentieth century, the introduction of World Standard Time made the clock an obvious and immediate symbol for the standardisation of temporality, as well as for the wider context of industrialisation. As historian Stephen Kern explains:

> The affirmation of private time radically interiorized the locus of experience. It eroded conventional views about the stability and objectivity of the material world and of the mind's ability to comprehend it. Man cannot know the world 'as it really is', if he cannot know what time it really is. If there are as many private times as there are individuals, then every person is responsible for creating his own world from one moment to the next, and creating it alone.[56]

Kern equates the standardisation of public time with the impulse to consider interiority because, he writes, temporal strictures of objectivity contrarily reveal their falsity. Arguably, the quiet novel echoes the affirmation of subjectivity that Kern reads in modernism's engagement with the private experience of time by locating the narrative drive of its fiction so internally. His suggestion that every person might contain his own world, for example, is reiterated in *Gilead* as the Reverend Ames suggests that '[e]very single one of us is a little civilisation' (*G* 224). In this phrase, Robinson appropriates an aesthetic concern of modernity, mapping the emotionally expansive landscape of interiority against the breadth of 'civilisation' and diagnosing the interior environment as a nation to explore. By extension, it might also be claimed that a focus on private temporalities undermines the importance of narrative event as a structuring device in fiction. If, that is, 'every person is responsible for creating his own world from one moment to the next' then external gauges of time are made incidental to the real 'civilisation' contained within the individual.

The continuing relevance of 'stream of consciousness' technique to the quiet contemporary American novel will be explored in more detail in Chapter 4. However, the obsession with clocks particular to *Tinkers* recalls a number of earlier texts. Placing himself within a hierarchy of 'quiet' writers, Harding has said of Proust that his fiction 'explodes time' through the process of apprehending 'the mind in a moment' as if to suspend time in a moment of reflection but then violently expand it.⁵⁷ In his prose, Proust intended to undercut clock time, slowing down and then magnifying experience so that his prose could quietly follow memory rather than the passing of external event.⁵⁸ To other modernist practitioners, the clock was also a figure of fear and dread. In Charles Baudelaire's 'L'Horloge' (1857), the clock removes all pleasure from existence, personified as an enemy that cannot be beaten: 'dieu sinister, effrayant, impassible, / Dont le doigt nous menace et nous dit: *Souviens-toi!*'⁵⁹ Sixty years later, Virginia Woolf's *Orlando* (1928) depicts the clock as constant antagonist to her eponymous hero. The chiming of the clock continually upsets Orlando's thoughts and even threatens to assault her physical body: 'the clock ticked louder and louder until there was a terrific explosion right in her ear.'⁶⁰ In his 1920 novel, *Women in Love*, D. H. Lawrence also reflects the mechanics of the timepiece in maddening detail. For Lawrence's characters, the clock is personified as it was for Baudelaire and, as in Woolf, it is merged with the body:

> Oh God, the wheels within wheels of people, it makes one's head tick like a clock, with a very madness of dead mechanical monotony and meaninglessness [...] Gerald could not save her from it. He, his body, his motion, his life – it was the same ticking, the same twitching across the dial, a horrible mechanical twitching forward over the face of the hours [...] across the eternal, mechanical, monotonous clock-face of time.⁶¹

Here, Lawrence's personification of the clock compromises its threatening overtones and the 'twitching' hands of the dial add uncertainty to its menace. The clock is therefore shown to be broadly threatening to these modernist writers, often personified, sometimes deified but always unrelenting as an antagonist for their characters.

As a recurring device in the text, *Tinkers* introduces and overstates the concept of mechanical time represented by clocks and clock making, although Harding does so with greater ambiguity than many of his modernist predecessors.⁶² The memories of George's life that *Tinkers* presents mixed with the memories of his father and grandfather and focalised through a third-person voice, are interspersed with extracts from a fictional handbook, *The Reasonable Horologist*. Harding suggests that 'The clock resembles the universe' (*T* 179) for George who demonstrates a sustained desire for chronology by filling his house with timepieces and draws power and, as previously stated, comfort from fixing clocks. Repairing the time pieces of a local bank, a place where he finds respite in the structure of fixed 'rates and principals' (*T* 165), George is able to feel as if he has some control over time and its passing; that time is in some way tameable. However, what is a comfort for George becomes hell for his grandchildren who are driven to 'near madness' by the 'tyranny of time' (*T* 160) in his home. Sitting with their grandfather, they feel trapped by his collection of time pieces and in the quiet of George's bedroom they can only 'listen to the way that the tickings of the different clocks, which not only lined the walls but were also crowded onto several folding card tables, an old cot, and the shelves of a built-in bookcase, fell into and out of beat with one another' (*T* 168). George's clocks play out a mechanical symphony that is ever so slightly out of sync and feels like a 'tyranny' to characters who do not share his interest in horology. So, while George can take comfort in his personal interaction with its mechanisms, his clocks are further confirmation of the idiosyncratic value that Harding attributes to the experience of temporality and the sonic qualities of its passing.

Beyond the device of clock making, the representation of time as it is experienced must also recall some philosophical concerns of literary modernism, particularly the philosopher Henri Bergson whose work influenced writers including Joyce, Woolf and Katherine Mansfield.[63] Specifically relevant to a discussion of a quiet aesthetic, Bergson's theory of duration (*la durée*) suggests that time, like quiet, is difficult if not impossible to gauge and that individual consciousness is not quantifiable and must be considered as a process. In *Creative Evolution* (1907), Bergson writes that if we are to discuss the human experience of time we must acknowledge that time is, itself, an evolution: 'The more we study the nature of Time, the more we shall comprehend that duration means invention, the creations of forms, the continual elaboration of the absolutely new.'[64] According to Bergson, duration is the substance of reality itself and must be considered as a continually shifting process of renewal that gauges the passing of time with elasticity. In this way, the present is divorced from linearity, left ungoverned and, most importantly, uninterrupted by event in the organic shifts of time's duration.

For Bergson, selfhood also gathers continuously, dependent on memory and supplemented by the past. In its application to fiction, time might, therefore, be most successfully represented as a composite of past, present and future moments that are continually in development. In the next chapter, I suggest that discoveries in turn-of-the-century neuroscience conceive of consciousness as a similarly dynamic structure that constantly assimilates and evolves over time. However, in this chapter, I have argued that time is formulated in quiet fiction by the 'continual elaboration' that Bergson suggests. It is important to remember that the idea of accumulation is quite different from commonly held ideas of invention and originality. As I contend throughout *The quiet contemporary American novel*, the impulse to meet the noise of the present with ever louder forms of expression is symptomatic of a kind of exceptionalism that dismisses the present's continuity with the past and equates noise with narratives of progress. However, if noise is not conflated with a common idea of innovation, then quiet can be more clearly defined as a mode of discussion that draws together elements of the past, present and future in a composite depiction of the contemporary age. In this formulation, the past need not be triumphed over or conceived as outdated but might continue to quietly coexist in the present. Any parallels between *Gilead* and *Tinkers* and traditions of literary modernism are therefore illustrative of the continuity between past and present that a quiet aesthetic also represents. Here, I believe it becomes clearer how Robinson's literary persona, her aversion to contemporary literature, and her stated interest in Calvin, Thoreau and Dickinson as literary antecedents are important to an appraisal of her quiet fictions. Like Bergson's conception of selfhood, quiet fiction develops continuously and, thus enabled by its liberation from the linear depiction of temporality, is distinguished by a refusal to noisily declare its originality as a viable contemporary form.

## Quiet locations; quieter histories

The final strand of this chapter links the quiet portrayal of time to the idea of contemporaneity in the quiet novel. In doing so, it should become clearer how the tendency to think of Robinson and Harding as old-fashioned novelists is consistent with a culturally ingrained tendency to read the present moment as inevitably noisier than the past. While neither *Gilead* nor *Tinkers* directly reveal the date in which they are set, by setting the majority of each novel in the past both Robinson and Harding avoid the representation of digital technologies and allow forms of new media to feature only in the background.

The displacement of technology is further compounded by the age of the narrators who feel alienated by the advances of their time. Just as George is unable to understand his tape recorder, and is unaware of anything more advanced than the cassette, Ames mentions technology only in passing as he wonders if he can protect his son from its effects. For Ames, television seems to be a backward step and 'quite two-dimensional beside radio' (*G* 143). Neither protagonist therefore celebrates the innovations of their present moment and consequently a large extent of the noise associated with contemporary culture is excluded from both narratives.

The quiet location of these novels is also purposefully distant from contemporary society. Reverend Ames describes the Iowan prairies as the only environment in which he can participate in being uninterrupted: 'Here on the prairie there is nothing to distract from the evening and the morning, nothing on the horizon to abbreviate or to delay' (*G* 281). Indeed, the location of Gilead is the most unifying characteristic of Robinson's quiet novels; it is what Joan Acocella describes as a 'dusty, no-account little town', a place where dogs take naps in the middle of Main Street and Ames can walk past every house in an hour (*G* 71).[65] Characters respond to the quiet of this setting in different ways. To the Boughtons, Gilead's quiet is a 'curse of sameness' (*H* 293) but to Lila this tiny 'no-name place' (*L* 213) offers an escape from her past. Again, it is the ability to choose a life in Gilead that makes its quiet a privilege. Ames is the town's most loyal resident: he decides to stay long after his grandfather, father and brother have all left and shows no interest in exploring the world beyond Iowa. Yet even Ames comes to describe Gilead as a town of 'no-account' and, after his confrontation with Jack, speculates that there could be 'a hundred little towns like it' (*G* 264). As a location, Gilead is therefore a device that further distances Robinson, her characters, and her prose from the political noise of the 1950s. As Ames gradually realises, Gilead could be any small town in mid-century America and, to varying degrees, the quiet location of Robinson's fiction evokes an ambiguous past that is distant from both the politics of the 1950s and the 2000s in which Robinson is writing.

Yet the quiet of Gilead is more complex and, indeed, more 'political' than a cursory reading indicates. In an essay on the forgotten history of abolitionism in the American Midwest, Robinson states that the 'imaginary' town of Gilead is modelled on Tabor, a small

# Quiet in time and narrative

settlement in south-west Iowa that was founded by the abolitionist preacher John Todd in the 1850s:

> [Tabor] was intended to serve, and did serve, as a fallback for John Brown and others during the conflict [between anti-slavery and pro-slavery factions] in Kansas ... A more typical feature of the settlement was a little college, no longer in existence, which educated women as well as men. Some of these women travelled to distant countries, Korea, for example, to establish women's education there. History has ebbed away from Tabor since then, but it would be difficult to underestimate the impact of this one little settlement on American culture and world culture.[66]

Gilead is not, then, just one of a 'hundred little towns' but a singular and historically important settlement that was established during a time of great abolitionist urgency in the pre-Civil War United States. Robinson stresses the forgotten intellectual history of the region and claims she is interested in Iowa as a site of intellectual and physical activity whose national and international importance has since been forgotten. The history of Tabor, and therefore Gilead, is full of noise, action and event but Robinson notes that the passage of time has subdued the political tenor of the region until its history has become a whisper.

*Gilead* and *Home*, in particular, hint at the wider, historical noise that features heavily in Robinson's non-fiction and that is located just outside each character's experience of the present. Ames is the quietest of Gilead's residents, the most removed from his contemporary moment; his letter is a history of disengagement from contemporary events. He admits to burning a sermon about the influenza pandemic of 1918 in which he described the mass fatalities as an act of God rescuing young men from 'committing murder' (G 48) in the war. Similarly, Ames recalls how his grandfather took him to see Bud Fowler, the first African American player in professional baseball, at Keokuk in 1885. Claiming to remember very little about Fowler himself, Ames gives the briefest mention to the introduction of 'the Negro Leagues' (G 54), set up the same year to combat the exclusion of black players from major and minor league baseball and claims to have lost interest in Fowler once segregation was in place. Ames skims over the major political events of the late nineteenth and early twentieth centuries through avoidance and elision and gradually reveals himself to be a political quietist in its most negative and accusatory sense, a man who burns his only incendiary sermon and rarely expresses discomfort at the social, economic and racial inequality he witnesses. Robinson therefore hints at the limits of quiet as a form of engagement while simultaneously demonstrating one of the strengths of her aesthetic. At the end of *Gilead*, Ames angrily mourns Iowa's forgotten radicalism, an 'old urgency that is forgotten now' (*G* 267), suggesting that the quiet of his existence has turned to passivity when it should have turned to action. Robinson's use of quiet presents multiple interpretations of the relationship between thought and activity, the past and the present, passivity and action. Most importantly, however, the Gilead novels examine and explore the varied states of quiet as a diverse and valid object of study with severe moral and ethical limitations.

*Tinkers'* setting is comparatively nomadic. George's father Howard is a tinker who often travels through the woods of Massachusetts and trades with a mysterious character known as Gilbert the Hermit, reminiscent of the 'simple and natural man' who calls at Thoreau's cabin in *Walden* (1854).[67] Like Thoreau, Gilbert's relationship to nature is governed by water and when he meets Howard each year to buy supplies it is always on 'the first day that the ice went out of the ponds' (*T* 23). The relationship between the two men is quiet: first, because they rarely speak and, second, because Gilbert adheres to a natural calendar that works outside the strictures of mechanical time. Eventually, the men devise a routine so efficient that they no longer speak at all, trading and smoking together in complete silence. The peaceful and inherent quiet that Thoreau projects onto his 'quiet' visitor in *Walden* is therefore mirrored in Howard's relationship with Gilbert who is quiet because he reaches an equilibrium with the natural world. Eventually, when Gilbert fails to show up for their regular meeting, Howard returns to their spot where he is silent for a final time, alone. Recalling the state of reflection that the two created together, Howard feels as though the woods communicate to him, even informing him that Gilbert's absence is the result of his death:

> As he smoked, he listened to the voices in the rapids. They murmured about a place somewhere deep in the woods where a set of bones lay on a bed of moss, above which a troop of mournful flies had kept vigil the previous autumn until the frosts came and they, too, had succumbed. (*T* 27)

Harding makes it unclear whether Howard imagines Gilbert's fate or if he is, indeed, in communion with nature. It is notable, however, that both men find a reflective quiet through acceptance of a calendar that works outside both the human experience of time and the mechanical noise of society. For both characters, the 'murmur' of the woods is only accessible by inhabiting a location that allows the listener the time and space in which to comprehend and then reflect on the smaller sounds that noisier environments subsume.

As stated in my Introduction, the type of rural quiet explored in this chapter appears elsewhere in contemporary fiction. Denis Johnson's 2012 novella, *Train Dreams*, is driven by the kind of non-reflective quiet that shares the isolated, transcendent rurality with *Gilead* and *Tinkers* but lacks their attention to interiority.[68] Similarly divorced from the noise of contemporary society, Elizabeth Strout's *Olive Kitteridge* (2008) depicts a small town in rural Maine where characters enjoy 'the sweetness of time that contained no thoughts of a beginning and no thoughts of an end'.[69] The portrayal of rural locations links the quiet of *Gilead*, *Home* and *Lila*, *Tinkers* and *Enon*, *Train Dreams* and *Olive Kitteridge*; all of these novels share a fascination with the temporal structure of the natural world, which I examine more closely in Chapter 4's discussion of Richard Powers' *The Echo Maker* (2006). Significantly, the quiet novel's engagement with rural environments and small towns disorders and demotes the noise of contemporary urban experience. A quiet novel avoids the claims to contemporaneity that trail many noisier narratives through a commitment to subjectivity that reaffirms an affinity with non-urban locations and finds a schema for experience that progresses independent from external structures like, for instance, the event.

It is in this way, too, that quiet novels are often rich in the acceptance of uncertainty. As J. Hillis Miller contends, temporal definitions of narrative analysis often rest on the idea of human temporality as a vast and 'unknowable thing'.[70] *Tinkers* conceives of all experience as 'unimaginable and unknowable' (*T* 120) while *Gilead* contrasts consciousness with the 'known and nameable' (*G* 203) outside world, concluding that what is easily nameable is inadequate to fully represent experience. As I have argued throughout this chapter, the quiet novel is ultimately 'about' the unknowable and subjective representation of time, just as it is 'about' the overhauling of the past in the present moment, the depiction of present experience as a composite of tenses and the quiet mundanity of every day experience. In

*Gilead*, this allows Robinson to critique the construction and elision of regional political histories, using the character of Ames to demonstrate the unreliability of historical record. *Tinkers*, by comparison, is more concerned with how time can be abstracted from everyday mechanisms and how we live within memory. The third-person perspective allows a broader range of narrative subjects than *Gilead* and eschews the temporal and spatial limitations imposed by *Gilead*'s quiet 'retreat' into consciousness. Read together, both novels work against noisier trends in contemporary culture that stress the social relevance of setting a novel in the present and structure narrative by the passing of event. That is, both Robinson and Harding depict the historical present in terms of its continuities rather than its ruptures, its reflective processes rather than its major events, reclaiming the time for contemplation as the present moment unfolds and privileging, while also interrogating, quiet as an aesthetic of their texts.

## Notes

1. *Tinkers* was eventually published by an offshoot of the Bellevue Literary Review, becoming the first novel in thirty years to win the prize through a small press. Paul Harding quoted in Motoko Rich, 'Mr. Cinderella: from rejection notes to the Pulitzer', *The New York Times* (18 April 2010), http://www.nytimes.com/2010/04/19/books/19harding.html?pagewanted=all.
2. Marilynne Robinson, quoted in Meghan O'Rourke, 'A Moralist of the Midwest', *The New York Times* (24 October 2004), http://www.nytimes.com/2004/10/24/magazine/24ROBINSON.html.
3. 'An Iowan Troy', *The Economist* (13 January 2005) http://www.economist.com/node/3555878; Peter Hitchens, 'Some Reflections on the Novels of Marilynne Robinson', *The Daily Mail* (8 January 2015), http://hitchensblog.mailonsunday.co.uk/2015/01/some-reflections-on-the-novels-of-marilynne-robinson.html; Sameer Rahim, 'Lila by Marilynne Robinson', *The Telegraph* (12 October 2014), http://www.telegraph.co.uk/culture/books/bookreviews/11151458/lila-by-marilynne-robinson.html.
4. Paul Harding, 'The Q&A: Paul Harding', Alexander Benaim, *Intelligent Life*, http://moreintelligentlife.com/blog/alexander-benaim/qa-paul-harding-author-pulitzer-prize-winner.
5. Brett Easton Ellis, interviewed by Robert Birnbaum, 'Brett Easton Ellis', *The Morning News* (19 January 2006), http://www.themorningnews.org/article/bret-easton-ellis.

6 At the time of writing, Robinson has published three Gilead novels but suggests that '[p]eople should be prepared to say quartet and not trilogy'. Robinson, quoted in Ron Charles, 'Robinson Confident of a Fourth Gilead Novel', *The Washington Post* (31 March 2015), http://www.washingtonpost.com/blogs/style-blog/wp/2015/03/31/marilynne-robinson-confident-about-a-fourth-gilead-novel/.
7 J. Hillis Miller, 'Time and Literature', *Daedalus*, 132:2, On Time (spring 2003), p. 90. In 1989, David Wood suggested that a century-long turn to linguistics would soon be followed by a 'spiralling return' to time and narrative and this temporal (re)turn is apparent in many recent publications that attempt to account for time in its subjective dimensions. See: Wood, *The Deconstruction of Time* (Evanston, IL: Northwestern University Press, 2001), p. xxxv; Mark Currie, *About Time: Narrative, Fiction and the Philosophy of Time* (Edinburgh: Edinburgh University Press, 2007); Jan Meister and Wilhelm Schernus (eds), *Time: From Concept to Narrative Construct* (Berlin: De Gruyter, 2011); Claudia Hammond, *Time Warped: Unlocking the Mysteries of Time Perception* (London: Harper Perennial, 2012); Christine Ross, *The Past is the Present; It's the Future Too: The Temporal Turn in Contemporary Art* (New York: Continuum, 2012). Hikaru Fujii, *Outside, America: The Temporal Turn in Contemporary American Fiction* (New York: Bloomsbury, 2013).
8 Anne E. Voss, 'Portrait of Marilynne Robinson', *The Iowa Review*, 22:1 (winter 1992), pp. 22, 25.
9 O'Rourke, 'A Moralist of the Midwest'.
10 Robinson, *Housekeeping* (London: Faber & Faber, 2005), p. 15.
11 Ibid., p. 9.
12 Ibid., pp. 39, 4.
13 Katy Ryan, 'Horizons of Grace: Marilynne Robinson and Simone Weil', *Philosophy and Literature* 29.2 (October 2005), p. 349.
14 Marilynne Robinson, 'Introduction', in *The Death of Adam: Essays on Modern Thought* (New York: Houghton Mifflin Harcourt, 1999), p. 1.
15 Marilynne Robinson, 'The Art of Fiction #198', http://www.theparisreview.org/interviews/5863/the-art-of-fiction-no-198-marilynne-robinson.
16 Michele Orecklin, 'On Her Time', *Time Magazine* (22 November 2004), http://www.time.com/time /magazine/article/0,9171,995700,00.html.
17 There is a real town of Gilead in Iowa but it is located north-east of the fictional town in which *Gilead* is set. Gilead is also the name of the totalitarian Christian nation in Margaret Atwood's 1985 novel, *The Handmaid's Tale*. Both Robinson and Atwood write in opposition to a rising tide of Christian fundamentalism but given Robinson's stated aversion to contemporary literature it cannot be claimed Atwood's novel bore any influence on the latter. Enon is an entirely fictional town and is also the setting for *Tinkers*' partner novel, *Enon* (2013), just as Gilead is

the setting for *Gilead*'s partner novels *Home* and *Lila*. Made more significant by their singular location, the names of these towns also reflect the biblical and Calvinist traditions that both novels are informed by. Gilead refers to the hymn, 'There Is a Balm in Gilead', that originated before the Civil War as an African American spiritual and draws on its Hebrew translation that means hill or mound of testimony. Enon is represented in John 3:23 as Aenon, a town close to where John practices baptism. It is also the Greek word for 'springs' and means a mass of darkness, a fountain, or an eye. I would add that the naming of both Gilead and Enon implies a sense of heightened perception, of improved sight gained from the perspective of higher ground. Susan Petit, 'Names in Marilynne Robinson's *Gilead* and *Home*', *Names*, 58:3 (September 2010), p. 139.

18  Jeffrey Gonzalez, 'Ontologies of Interdependence, the Sacred, and Health Care: Marilynne Robinson's Gilead and Home', *Critique: Studies in Contemporary Fiction*, 55:4 (2014), p. 373.
19  Marilynne Robinson, *Gilead* (London: Virago, 2004), p. 6; Robinson, *Home* (London: Virago, 2008), p. 332. All further references referred to in text as *G* and *H*, respectively.
20  Robinson, *Housekeeping*, p. 204.
21  Christopher Douglas, 'Christian Multiculturalism and Unlearned History in Marilynne Robinson's *Gilead*', *Novel: A Forum on Fiction*, 44:3 (fall 2011), p. 339.
22  Janet Altman, *Epistolarity: Approaches to Form* (Columbus: Ohio State University, 1982), p. 144.
23  Marilynne Robinson, *Lila* (London: Virago, 2014), p. 255. All further references appear in text as *L*.
24  Kevin Everod Quashie, *The Sovereignty of Quiet: Beyond Resistance in Black Culture* (New Brunswick, NJ: Rutgers University Press, 2012), p. 15.
25  Sarah Churchwell, 'Marilynne Robinson's Lila – A Great Achievement in US Fiction', *The Guardian* (7 November 2014), http://www.theguardian.com/books/2014/nov/07/marilynne-robinson-lila-great-achievement-contemporary-us-fiction-gilead.
26  Ali Smith, 'The Damaged Heart of America', *The Guardian* (16 April 2005), p. 26; David James, 'A Renaissance for the Crystalline Novel?' *Contemporary Literature*, 53:4 (winter 2012), p. 845; Robert E. Kohn, 'Secrecy and Radiance in Marilynne Robinson's *Gilead* and *Home*', *The Explicator*, 72:1 (2014), p. 8; James Wood, '*Gilead*: Acts of Devotion', *The New York Times* (28 November 2004), http://www.nytimes.com/2004/11/28/books/review/28COVERWOOD.html.
27  Lynn Neary, 'For a Tiny Press, the Pulitzer Arrives Out of Nowhere', *NPR*, Books (16 April 2010), http://www.npr.org/templates/story/story.php?storyId=126054322.
28  Paul Harding, 'Second Coming', *Boston Globe* (25 August 2013), http://

www.bostonglobe.com/magazine/2013/08/24/author-paul-harding-his-follow-tinkers/WCY3CQ7ucDjM7IPEpRPvYN/story.html.
29 David James' reading of *Tinkers* briefly references Robinson's third novel, *Home*, but does not expand on the association between Robinson and Harding and does not mention *Gilead* at all. James, 'A Renaissance for the Crystalline Novel?', p. 845. Larry D. Bouchard makes the comparison between the two authors in a footnote, referring largely to the centrality of death to *Gilead* and *Tinkers*. Bouchard, 'Belief, Revelation, and Trust: Faith and the Mind's Margins in Ian McEwan's *Saturday* and Paul Harding's *Tinkers*', *Christianity and Literature*, 63:4 (summer 2014), p. 463.
30 Following Robinson's Gilead novels, Harding published *Enon* as a partner novel to *Tinkers* in 2013. *Enon* centres on the death of Kate Crosby, the daughter of Charlie, George's grandson who appears briefly in *Tinkers* when he reads to George at his bedside. *Enon* begins loudly, with a car crash that sets off a chain of events from Kate's death through the breakdown of Charlie's marriage, his eventual dependence on prescription medication and the stark and difficult process of his rehabilitation with which the novel ends. Harding therefore underscores what would otherwise constitute a quiet, first-person narrative with the cacophonic experience of grief and addiction. Although Charlie spends the majority of *Enon* seeking out quiet spaces, composing an internal history of the area and meditating on the lives of his ancestors, he suffers continually and the prose is harried and, arguably, noisy as a result.
31 Bouchard, 'Belief, Revelation, and Trust', p. 456.
32 Peter Boxall, 'Late: Fictional Time in the Twenty-First Century', *Contemporary Literature*, 53:4, Fiction Since 2000: Post Millennial Commitments (winter 2012), p. 701.
33 Like Boxall, James links the trend for crystalline fictions to a period of late postmodernism that, in response to deconstruction, seeks to intensify 'attention to the aesthetic dimensions of ordinary experience'. James, 'A Renaissance for the Crystalline Novel?', p. 857.
34 Jeffrey Hart, *The Living Moment: Modernism in a Broken World* (Evanston, IL: Northwestern University Press, 2012), p. 100.
35 Ibid., pp. 99, 107. Heidegger's concept on Being is most relevant to *Gilead* because Ames' letter is an attempt to make sense of his life and to leave behind some kind of moral compass for his son. Indeed, Ames refers to 'Being' twice in the novel, the most significant of which reads as follows: 'We participate in Being without remainder. No breath, no thought, no wart or whisker, is not as sunk in Being as it could be. And yet no one can say what Being is' (*G* 203). To Ames, the act of Being is absolute proof that God exists, although it is unlikely that Ames is a disciple of Heidegger's.

36 Kathryn Hume, *Aggressive Fictions: Reading the Contemporary American Novel* (Ithaca, NY: Cornell University Press, 2011), p. ix.
37 Wood, 'Acts of Devotion', http://www.nytimes.com/2004/11/28/books/review/28COVERWOOD.html.
38 *Home* also provides evidence of Ames' political beliefs beyond the allusions found in *Gilead* and amplifies our understanding of the Reverend's quieter thoughts. Glory describes arguments between Ames and Boughton as 'incomprehensible ... shouting matches' (*H* 222) while Boughton's account of their fights complicates the quiet persona that Ames writes for himself in *Gilead*. '[Ames] pretends to be mulling it over', Boughton claims, 'but I know he will vote Republican again. Because his grandfather was a Republican! ... Whose grandfather was not a Republican?' (*H* 43). Boughton presents himself as a moderate outsider and suggests that his family, who arrived in Iowa in 1870, could not understand the 'fanaticism' (*H* 213) of abolitionists like Ames' grandfather. Whether or not Boughton is right about the vehemence of Ames' convictions, and his surprisingly thoughtless support of the Republican party, *Home* periodises *Gilead* and connects both novels with the political noise of the 1950s that Robinson's quiet aesthetic would otherwise exclude.
39 Both novels recount similar histories of patrilineal relationships, expressed through centuries of religious and family ritual. More than three generations in *Gilead* become ministers and George's grandfather is remembered similarly as an 'inept' and 'mumbling' (*T* 131) preacher.
40 Michael Schmidt, *The Novel: A Biography* (Cambridge, MA: Harvard University Press, 2014), p. 559; Tessa Hadley, 'An Attic Full of Sermons', *London Review of Books*, 27:8 (21 April 2005), p. 19; Petit, 'Field of Deferred Dreams: Baseball and Historical Amnesia in Marilynne Robinson's Gilead and Home', *MELUS*, 37:4 (2012), p. 119.
41 Marilynne Robinson, 'Writers and the Nostalgic Fallacy', *The New York Times*, Book Review (13 October 1985), p. 34.
42 By the beginning of the twenty-first century, the idea that temporality had been a neglected area of study had been expressed in a variety of disciplinary fields. The temporal turn in sociology also widely argued that 'unless we consciously make the time to consciously reflect, we run the grave risk of becoming further in thrall to technological time, both to clock time and increasingly to the times of a globalised digital network that is oriented toward speed and efficiency'. Robert Hassan, 'Globalization and the "Temporal Turn": Recent Trends and Issue in Time Studies', *The Korean Journal of Policy Studies*, 25:2 (2010), p. 99. For more, see: Jon May and Nigel Thrift (eds), *Timespace: Geographies of Temporality* (London: Routledge, 2001); Alan Bluedorn, *The Human*

*Organization of Time: Temporal Realities and Experience* (Stanford, CA: Stanford University Press, 2002); Barbara Adam, *Time* (Cambridge: Polity, 2004); Robert Hassan, *Empires of Speed* (Leiden: Brill, 2009).

43 Wood, *The Deconstruction of Time*, p. xiv.
44 Wood by no means marked the end of the linguistic or spatial turns but rather heralded temporality's future importance. The political geographer Edward Soja published *Postmodern Geographies* (1989) the same year, applying Henri Lefebvre's conception of space as a social product of capitalist gain, to deconstruct 'the temporal prisonhouse of language'. Edward Soja, *Postmodern Geographies: The Reassertion of Space in Critical Social Theory* (London: Verso, 1989), p. 2.
45 Wood, p. xv.
46 Ibid., p. 19.
47 Ibid., p. 4; Jesse Matz, 'The Art of Time, Theory to Practice', *Narrative*, 19:3 (October 2011), p. 275.
48 Miller, 'Time in Literature', p. 87.
49 Matz, 'The Art of Time, Theory to Practice', p. 275.
50 Jacques Derrida, *Archive Fever: A Freudian Impression*, trans. Eric Prenowitz (Chicago: University of Chicago Press, 1995), p. 18.
51 In *Being and Time*, Heidegger argues that it is the task of philosophy to destroy ontological concepts and compose 'ordinary' meanings of time, history, being, etc. that can be more universally understood: 'Tradition takes what has come down to us and delivers it over to self-evidence; it blocks our access to those primordial "sources" from which the categories and concepts handed down to us have been in part quite genuinely drawn. Indeed, it makes us forget that they have had such an origin, and makes us suppose that the necessity of going back to these sources is something which we need not even understand.' Martin Heidegger, *Being and Time*, trans. Max Verlag (Albany: State University of New York Press, 2001), p. 21. For more, see: Steven Heine, *Existential and Ontological Dimensions of Time in Heidegger and Dogen* (Albany: State University of New York Press, 1985); Ted Sadler, *Heidegger and Aristotle: The Question of Being* (London: Athlone Press, 1995); Andrew Feenberg, *Heidegger and Marcuse: The Catastrophe and Redemption of History* (Abingdon: Psychology Press, 2005).
52 Miller, 'Time and Literature', p. 90; Paul Ricœur, 'Narrative Time', *Critical Inquiry*, 7:1, On Narrative (autumn 1980), p. 172.
53 Ricœur, 'Narrative Time', p. 170.
54 Nor am I suggesting that temporality is unified between the novels of either author. Time in *Housekeeping*, for example, is highly gendered; standardised and linearly progressive when male-led, temporality falls into cyclical, seasonal patterns once the male head of the family is removed: 'They had no reason to look forward, nothing to regret. Their

lives spun off the tilting world like thread off a spindle, breakfast time, suppertime, lilac time, apple time.' Robinson, *Housekeeping*, p. 13.
55 Ricœur, 'Narrative Time', p. 171.
56 Stephen Kern, *The Culture of Time and Space: 1880–1918* (Cambridge, MA: Harvard University Press, 1983), p. 314.
57 Harding, 'The Q&A: Paul Harding', http://moreintelligentlife.com/blog/alexander-benaim/qa-paul-harding-author-pulitzer-prize-winner. Harding also names Thomas Mann as a major influence, although several reviewers also compared *Tinkers* to William Faulkner's *As I Lay Dying* (1930), if not in style then in the organising principal of a central character's death and brief reference in the text to the 'old Budden place' that might recall the Bundrens of Faulkner's text. See: Jay Parini, 'Tinkers', *The Guardian*, Guardian Review (25 September 2010), p. 10; Kimberley Jones, 'As He Lay Dying', *The Austin Chronicle* (24 September 2010), http://www.austinchronicle.com/books/2010-09-24/as-he-lay-dying/.
58 Of the seemingly infinite sources on Proust, time and clocks, see: Margaret Mein, *Proust's Challenge to Time* (Manchester: Manchester University Press, 1962); Julia Kristeva, *Proust and the Sense of Time* (New York: Columbia University Press, 1993); Clark Lunberry, 'A Body Bending: Removing the Boots of Beckett and Proust', in his *Sites of Performance: of Time and Memory* (London: Anthem Press, 2014), pp. 3–14.
59 'Terrifying, impassive, sinister God, / Whose threatening fingers say to us: *Remember!*' Charles Baudelaire, 'L'Horloge', *The Flowers of Evil* (Oxford: Oxford World Classics, 1993), p. 160.
60 Virginia Woolf, *Orlando* (Oxford: Oxford World Classics, 1998), p. 284.
61 D. H. Lawrence, *Women in Love* (London: Penguin Classics, 2007), p. 523.
62 Emphasising the importance of horology to *Tinkers* and its partner novel, in *Enon* Charlie recounts an extended memory of fixing a clock with George, his grandfather; a 'tall clock' that the latter is hypnotised by. Harding, *Enon*, pp. 64–67.
63 For more on Bergson's relationship with modernism, see: Paul Douglass, *Bergson, Eliot, and American Literature* (Lexington: University Press of Kentucky, 1986); Mary Ann Gillies, *Henri Bergson and British Modernism* (Montreal: McGill Queen's University Press, 1996); Paul Ardoin, S. E. Gontarski and Laci Mattison (eds), *Understanding Bergson, Understanding Modernism* (London: Bloomsbury, 2013).
64 Henri Bergson, 'Creative Evolution', in *Henry Bergson: Key Writings*, ed. Keith Ansell-Pearson and John Mullarkey (London: Continuum, 2002), p. 176.

65 Joan Acocella, 'Lonesome Road', *The New Yorker* (6 October 2014) http://www.newyorker.com/magazine/2014/10/06/lonesome-road.
66 Marilynne Robinson, 'Who Was Oberlin?' in her *When I Was A Child I Read Books* (London: Virago, 2013), p. 180.
67 Henry David Thoreau, *Walden* (Princeton, NJ: Princeton University Press, 2004), p. 146.
68 More comparable, perhaps, to the quiet of Williams' *Stoner*, but more deeply indebted to transcendentalist notions of temporality, *Train Dreams* is a novel of quiet surfaces that lacks equal attention to the quieter depths of interiority. The protagonist, Robert Granier, lacks both family history and context. Sent as an infant to become an itinerant labourer in the American Midwest, Robert knows little of his origins and the third-person narration affords the reader no more detail than Robert possesses: 'As far as he could ever fix it, he'd been born sometime in 1886, either in Utah or in Canada'. Johnson, *Train Dreams* (London: Granta, 2012), p. 26. As the book moves chronologically through Robert's life, he barely finds further context; he loses his young family and when he dies, no-one misses him. Robert's life is therefore lived quietly and exists purely in the present 'rhythm' of the seasons, to such an extent that the narrative ends with his final breath (p. 57).
69 Elizabeth Strout, *Olive Kitteridge: A Novel in Stories* (New York: Random House, 2008), p. 11.
70 Miller, 'On Time in Literature', p. 90.

# 4

# The quiet novel of cognition

In 2002, the literary journal *Poetics Today* published a special issue to mark what the editors called a 'new phase' in literary theory.[1] In their introduction to the volume, the editors argued that cognitive science had emerged as a major influence on contemporary criticism, 'demystifying traditional humanist and religious concepts of supposedly timeless categories, such as self, identity, and morality.'[2] Indeed, at the turn of the twenty-first century science experienced what was phrased as a 'turn' to subjectivity with many researchers newly dedicated to studying the structure of the brain and the experience of interiority. In the same year that *Poetics Today* described cognitivism as a phase of literary theory, cognitive philosopher John Searle declared consciousness to be 'the most important problem in the biological sciences' and literary critic Joseph Tabbi called the depiction of cognitive operations 'our time's literary defamiliarization par excellence'.[3] Although novelist David Lodge also resurrected C. P. Snow's 'two cultures' debate to prove that the 'new' cognitive obsession of the 'natural sciences' was a traditional object of philosophy and literature, for at least the first decade of the twenty-first century the field of cognitivism seemed to offer a way forward,[4] granting new legitimacy to a focus on interiority in both literature and science and conceiving of consciousness as the next and inwardly conquerable frontier.

This chapter discusses novels of cognition, a term intended to connect the discussion of a quiet aesthetic with early twenty-first century debates about the place of cognitive approaches within literary studies. On a cursory level, novels of cognition narrate the discoveries of cognitive science: as Stephen J. Burn argues, writers of such novels interpret 'the nonliterary realities' of a contemporary culture that is permeated by scientific explanation.[5] The influence of cognitivism is apparent in a number of American novels published in the first decade of the twenty-first century, dating back to the publication of Jonathan Lethem's *Motherless Brooklyn* in 1999 and continuing through Richard Powers' *The Echo Maker* (2006), Lynne Tillman's *American Genius; a comedy* (2006), Rivka Galchen's *Atmospheric Disturbances* (2008) and John Wray's *Lowboy* (2009). The writers listed above all texture their novels with contemporary theories of mind; notably, the scientific and philosophical works of Daniel Dennett, Israel Rosenfield, V. S. Ramachandran and Antonio Damasio.[6] Many cognitive fictions are also 'accounts of brain damage' as Powers notes in *The Echo Maker*, reflecting cognitive science's belief that we learn more about the human brain when it is recovering from a traumatic incident.[7] As Daniel Dennett writes in his most popular work, *Consciousness Explained* (1991), '[p]eople are extraordinarily good at overcoming brain damage, and it is *never* a matter of "healing" or the repair of damaged circuits. Rather, they discover new ways of doing old tricks.'[8] By elaborating the workings of a 'damaged' consciousness, these cognitive scientists, philosophers and novelists depict the brain as a site that constantly repairs and rewires itself, positioning conscious experience as something both extraordinary and mundane while suggesting that every brain is at constant risk of 'damage' because of the contingency that undermines its day-to-day activities.

Of greater interest to this volume and the aesthetic of quiet it proposes, the novel of cognition also recalls the modernist 'stream' or 'novel of consciousness' whose rich and ambiguous history overlaps with the quiet novels discussed throughout this study. Although broadly applied to fiction that is in some way set within the protagonist's mind, scholarship increasingly limits the 'novel of consciousness' to literary modernism. Violeta Sotirova dates the form back to Jane Austen's use of free indirect style but argues that the modernist novel 'emerges as a novel of consciousness' through the 'unmediated presentation' of inner life.[9] Similarly, in *Consciousness and the Novel* (2002), David Lodge discusses the legacy left by the 'modernist experimental novel of consciousness and the unconscious', suggesting that modernist fiction's lack of plot is a direct result of the period's fascination with the repressed desires outlined by the then burgeoning field of psychoanalysis.[10] Of course, I am interested in the novel of consciousness as a quiet form, structured by thoughts and subdued modes of conversation that would otherwise remain hidden. This chapter argues that the novel of cognition briefly reanimated the novel of consciousness at the turn of the twenty-first century. Proceeding by a similarly internal engine of narrative, these cognitive fictions largely replace the movement of plot or external event with a succession of cognitive processes and, set roughly a century after the advent of literary modernism, transform the modernist fascination with psychoanalysis into a literary preoccupation with contemporary neuroscience.[11]

This chapter therefore applies the terms of my quiet aesthetic to one of the 2000s' pre-eminent trends to examine what happens when fictions of interiority depict pointedly *un*quiet states of mind.[12] Taking *The Echo Maker* and *American Genius; a comedy* as representative of the trend's diversity, I read the novel of cognition as a quiet contemporary American form; one that privileges the experience of a quiet protagonist, in a quiet location, to whom very little happens. What Powers attempts, and what I argue Tillman more successfully achieves, is an intellectually expansive mode of interiority that is more structurally unstable than the quiet narratives discussed so far. *The Echo Maker* and *American Genius* push at the boundaries of contemporary understanding, questioning the borders between fact and fiction, asking what it is like to have consciousness and, ultimately, what it means to be 'quiet'. However, to borrow a phrase from Powers, both authors create an 'inside out' form of interiority that incorporates vast quantities of knowledge within the body of what I argue are otherwise quiet texts.[13] The novel of cognition is quiet, then, despite the playfulness with which Powers and Tillman depict the boundaries of the mind and despite the noise included within the shifting borders of consciousness. Indeed, the novel of cognition is quiet in this instance because both Powers and Tillman accept consciousness as a continually changing structure, defined by its elaborately but fundamentally quiet processes and its deeper connections to our ongoing political and evolutionary histories.

## The cognitive turn

The novel of cognition is a quiet novel set in a cultural moment when scientists believed an analysis of brain chemistry might finally 'explain' consciousness. Yet the language of science and cognition is rarely characterised as quiet. To many critics, scientific discovery is part of the deafening noise of progress and its inclusion in American fiction is an indication of the novel's volume, linked to what Don DeLillo once called 'the big social novel' or what James Wood refers to as 'the Great American Social Novel'.[14] As delineated in Chapter 2, these cavernous texts promise to halt the death of the novel by noisily proclaiming the breadth and necessity of the form and are often accompanied by what Wood calls the 'obligatory acknowledgements page' where the author credits the scientific, political and sociological tomes that underpin the text.[15] Stephen J. Burn suggests that what he calls the 'neurocentric' trend complicates and expands existing models of postmodernism, grounding the novel in 'a fluid, rapidly changing reality' that is defined by the 'solitary, "nervous" nature' of America's global position in a multi- and mass-media culture.[16] Similarly, Joseph Tabbi argues that cognitive fictions organise a wider 'cultural noise' within the quiet of an interior narrative thus fragmenting the subject's interiority and, it could be argued, filling consciousness with a deafening noise.[17]

Alongside cultural readings of science as a noisy form of knowledge, many cognitivists also stress the fundamental volume of the brain's activity. While neuroscientists Edmund T. Rolls and Gustavo Deco argue that 'the brain is inherently noisy', psychiatrist Norman Doidge describes the 'noisy brain' as one that is unable to distinguish neuronal signals from the 'background noise' of consciousness.[18] For Doidge, the mind is noisy when it is 'distressed and firing irregular, noisy signals' and this description chimes with the 'accounts of brain damage' found in many contemporary novels of cognition.[19] Still, scientific language is not anomalous to a quiet aesthetic and many quiet novelists dispute the division between the humanities and the sciences in their non-fictional works by challenging distinctions between types of knowledge and even types of authorship. Marilynne Robinson's essay collections act as public defences of the relationship between religion and science; Paul Harding has studied and written about physics; Ben Lerner, whose novels I discuss at length in Chapter 5, frequently appropriates scientific discourse in both his fiction and poetry.[20] That is to say, once freed from the strictures of plot and narrative action, the quiet novel can hypothetically include anything: the texts in this study alone entertain a wide range of social, political and scientific theories as a meditation on the depth of internal life and draw no distinction between noisy and quiet forms of knowledge.

As this chapter posits, cognitivism can also be read as a quiet science. In the ambitiously titled *Consciousness Explained*, Daniel Dennett dismisses the noisy desires of psychoanalysis as 'warm-up exercises' for cognitivism's fresh understanding of consciousness at a biological level.[21] Dennett is one of many to suggest, first, that newly discovered neural processes happen below the threshold of consciousness where the individual has no awareness and, second, that consciousness occupies the brain in its entirety. Historian and philosopher Israel Rosenfield similarly rejects the notion, made popular by psychoanalysis, that most of the brain's activities are unconscious. In *The Strange, Familiar and Forgotten: An Anatomy of Consciousness* (1993), Rosenfield, like Dennett, argues that the structure of the brain is tantamount to the structure of consciousness: it is 'ever evolving and ever changing, intrinsically dynamic and subjective.'[22] For a diverse range of philosophers and scientists, it then follows that a discussion of objectivity can no longer preoccupy the philosophy of mind because consciousness is an entirely subjective structure, according to their discoveries. Cognitivists therefore dispute the traditional opposition of conscious and unconscious thought, subjective and objective perspective, in the attempt to reach a new and fundamentally biological understanding of consciousness as a state that occupies the whole brain.

Of particular relevance to the argument expressed in this chapter, cognitive science shares several key elements of a quiet aesthetic. First, in their research methods and interests, cognitivists are scholars and often introverted people who, second, seek out and value quiet environments. Since the turn of the twenty-first century, science has also broadly experienced its own interest in quiet with researchers increasingly concerned with the role of solitude and contemplation in the sciences.[23] Dennett identifies the same need for 'peace and quiet' as a primal instinct of the individual, which must be prioritised over and above the prescriptions of a noisy society.[24] Specifically, he understands quiet to be a cognitive structure, an evolutionary instinct without which the individual cannot survive: 'built from millions of associations' and 'thousands of memes'. Third, then, and as I argue of all quiet narratives, cognitivists emphasise narratives of continuity over rupture and work particularly to uncover the evolutionary processes that inform contemporary experience. Literary critic Brian Boyd describes the relationship between evolution, cognitivism and culture as symbiotic, claiming that culture tracks 'changes in the environment more rapidly than genes do.'[25] Cognitivists also conceive the 'Quiet Mystery' of consciousness as a powerful storytelling engine made more potent by what neurologist Antonio Damasio describes as the 'quiet remodelling' or 'quiet renetworking' of the brain that restructures neural pathways from minute to minute but works virtually unnoticed.[26] In sum, cognitive systems are quiet, discreet and unobtrusive but most importantly these processes are not rarified or singular but common to all conscious experience. As a discussion of the novel of cognition demonstrates, cognitivists seek a language by which to understand and normalise the contingencies that ground universal experience and see consciousness, in the words of philosopher Barry Dainton, as a 'weakly unified' system made up of processes that continually and quietly reformulate the mind.[27]

If cognitive processes are quiet, however, their cultural impact has been noisy. By the beginning of the twenty-first century, references to neurological processes had permeated popular and intellectual discourse and 'neurocentric' terms had passed into everyday speech. Minor references to cognitive processes also began to appear in a variety of Anglo-American fictions. In *The Corrections* (2001), Jonathan Franzen describes emotion as a number of stimulated 'neurofactors' and identifies in his characters the 'genetic bases' that cause clinical depression.[28] Similarly, the paired characters and narratives of Jennifer Egan's *Look at Me* (2001) connect via the neural operations of the 'bicameral mind' and the motivation of Egan's characters is often located biologically, like the 'cerebral lobe'.[29] The rise of cognitivism is also evident in a number of amnesia and bipolar disorders portrayed in genre fictions, thrillers and mystery novels in the early 2000s, including Mark Haddon's Whitbread Award-winning *The Curious Incident of the Dog in the Night-time* (2003). Christopher, the novel's narrator, is a fifteen-year-old boy who exhibits symptoms common to a diagnosis of Asperger's syndrome. Describing the mind as 'a complicated machine', Christopher believes that cognitive analogies explain the world to him better than emotion and he relies on these analogies to express himself throughout the novel.[30]

The novel of cognition goes further than the noisy fictions of Franzen, Egan and Haddon who allude to but never expand on the advances of cognitive science. Rivka Galchen's debut novel, *Atmospheric Disturbances*, is narrated by psychiatrist Leo Liebenstein who freely debates the usefulness of psychoanalysis as a contemporary 'science' and acknowledges how 'eager' the brain is 'to perceive order' in the world.³¹ Leo's flaw as a narrator is that he is loyal to the objective presentation of science, believing that he can work 'outside' his own habits and overcome his 'lonely point of view'.³² Galchen's narrator therefore overlooks the subjectivity of consciousness that cognitivists prioritise and is critically unable to diagnose his own mental condition as it deteriorates into psychosis. At the other end of the patient–doctor spectrum, John Wray's *Lowboy* is focalised through the 'claustrophobic brain' of William, a sixteen-year-old boy who escapes from a mental institution.³³ *Lowboy* is composed in sections that last less than a page, moving rapidly through the unstable and distorted viewpoint of a schizophrenic young man who knows that the disturbance he is suffering is the result of 'an electrical difference in the brain'.³⁴ William associates quiet with the suppressive weight of his medication and after his escape, he remains particularly sensitive to the 'shimmering tent of noise' that surrounds him in the city.³⁵ Similarly, Jonathan Lethem's *Motherless Brooklyn* reimagines the classic detective novel through a first-person protagonist who suffers from Tourette's syndrome. The narrator, Lionel Essrog, values quiet as a rare commodity and though the 'frenzy' of his mind makes it neurologically unlikely, he frequently yearns to '[b]e quiet'.³⁶ Tellingly, in the novel's opening paragraph, Lionel does not describe the symptoms of his illness as loud shouts but as 'suppressed' noises: 'words escaping silently, mere ghosts of themselves.'³⁷ Lionel's narration therefore expresses the unheard quiet of a disorder that psychologists define by its volume and Lethem suggests that attention to quiet might offer Lionel salvation from social, personal and even biological forms of noise.

### *The Echo Maker*: the quiet of Capgras

Broadly speaking, and as this brief survey indicates, the cognitive turn in literature and science reanimated philosophical categories of selfhood and identity, providing a biological language for affective and reflective processes that had not previously existed. In many ways, a surge of interest in cognitive science can also be read as a reanimation of older categories that is expressively similar to a quiet aesthetic: cognitivism is at once old and new, traditional and innovative, and it was quickly, if only briefly, integrated within the landscape of contemporary fiction.

Richard Powers' ninth novel, *The Echo Maker*, is fiction's fullest account of cognitivism's crowning moment and a representative example of how the cognitive trend can be read for its quieter qualities. In *The Echo Maker*, Powers alternates between brief fragments of temporally non-linear internal life and a primarily third-person narration focalised through the perspectives of Mark Schluter, his sister, Karin, and a 'famous' neurologist, Dr Gerald Weber. The novel begins in the winter of 2002, in the year that *Poetics Today* declared a 'Cognitive Revolution' had taken place in both the sciences and humanities. Powers recounts much of his wider reading in the sciences through the character of Weber who is working at a moment when 'neuroscience basked in its growing instrumental power' (*EM* 240).[38] Alongside this grander narrative, Powers tells a much smaller or, arguably, a quieter story of personal trauma. After he crashes his truck late at night outside his hometown of Kearney, Nebraska, Mark is diagnosed with Capgras syndrome, a rare condition in which the patient believes those closest to him have been replaced by imposters or clones.[39] Suffering under Capgras' signature 'misidentification delusions' (*EM* 75), Mark doubts the authenticity of his sister, his dog and his home. Capgras does not make Mark forget, per se, but it does alter his emotional association to significant people or objects in his life leaves him unable to connect his family and his most familiar possessions with an emotional memory-response.

In my reading, *The Echo Maker* is a quiet novel in which a sudden event disrupts the processes of the mind and turns the narrative inward. Yet the novel might equally be described as noisy because it is broad, ambitious and complex. To contextualise Mark's condition, Powers filters the interior lives of Mark, Karin and Weber through the vast metafictional frames of contemporary neuroscience and environmental degradation, demonstrating the 'treacherous' (*EM* 130) and cacophonous pressures daily facing the mind and other quiet environments. Charles B. Harris praises the novel as 'a feat of metaphorical dexterity' in which Powers fuses 'the synaptic networks that constitute the self with the biosphere's densely textured, interacting ecosystems.'[40] Indeed, Powers typically structures his novels around a series of oppositions that reflect his proclivity for scientific research, spanning topics like molecular genetics, artificial intelligence, virtual reality and game theory.[41] His 1995 novel *Galatea 2.2* is the semi-autobiographical account of Powers' tenure as the 'token humanist' in the Center for the Study of Advanced Sciences at the University of Illinois at Urbana-Champaign.[42] Powers' fictional protagonist, named after the author, arrives at the university in the early 1990s when academic attention is converging through 'several intersecting rays' on 'the culminating prize of consciousness' long adventure: an owner's manual for the brain.'[43] In the body of the text, Powers recounts feelings of awe as cognitivists begin to understand the mind as 'a model-maker, continuously rewritten by the thing it tried to model.'[44] A discussion of narrativity therefore grounds the novel's scientific investigations: that is, the groundbreaking discoveries of cognitivism depict the mind as a quiet generator of fiction, just as 'Powers' is nicknamed 'Marcel' by his co-workers after Proust, a figure who many cognitivists see as a major contributor to contemporary science.[45] Despite constant cross-pollination between the arts and sciences, however, in the body of the novel he is writing Powers resolves never to write fiction again, briefly suggesting that the novel lacks the capacity to represent the 'efficiently lonely' age of the Internet and recommitting himself to science.[46]

*The Echo Maker* marks a significant stylistic break for Powers and, in many ways, addresses the author's fears for the novel's future. In an interview given to Stephen J. Burn between the publication of *The Time of Our Singing* in 2003 and *The Echo Maker* in 2006, Powers claimed he had developed a style he described as 'double-voiced interiority', a narrative mode that would represent the interior life of a character 'as if it were externally narrated'.[47] Powers believed his use of interiority would be innovative in the field of contemporary fiction and a pioneering inversion of 'field and ground, coming at the old themes of narrative, self-construction, and interdependent intelligence from the inside out'. Despite the author's claims, the interiority of *The Echo Maker* is never truly innovative; although Powers does not draw the comparison, his conception of an interiority that is 'double-voiced' directly recalls Mikhail Bakhtin's concept of heteroglossia, a term that has since been expanded on by scholars wishing to explore the postmodern identities of oppressed and minority cultures.[48] However, by turning the narrative inward, Powers' ninth novel is certainly his quietest. The 'double-voiced interiority' that is evident in *The Echo Maker* allows the narrator to be both omniscient and interior, depicting the conscious experience of the novel's characters in a hybrid form that retains many features of high realism practised by Powers and his noisier contemporaries.[49] This form of interiority is louder than the narratives considered in previous chapters. While *Gilead* and *Tinkers* focus on the interior lives of subdued and elderly protagonists, Powers narrates consciousness from multiple, younger and significantly 'brain-damaged' (*EM* 555) perspectives who are often anxious and sometimes highly disturbed.

Like all novels of cognition, however, *The Echo Maker* meets my criteria for a quiet aesthetic. Powers' protagonists are introverted and quiet but by a circuitous route: it is the noise of Mark's car crash, the 'squeal of brakes, the crunch of metal on asphalt, one broken scream' (*EM* 4), that focuses the narrative on quiet. Prior to his accident, Mark leads a relatively outgoing if unambitious life. At the age of twenty-seven, he is a 'lively personality' (*EM* 153), living locally in Kearney where a taste for 'thrills, sports, war, and their many combinations' (*EM* 111) provide noisy distractions from the boredom of his day-to-day life. Mark's accident subdues him thereafter and literally represents the threat that the outside world poses to the quiet of all conscious experience. Placed briefly in a coma, Mark is even physically unable to speak because his brain is temporarily divorced from his body and his screams are completely 'soundless' (*EM* 12). Yet, while he is unconscious, Mark's interior monologue overcomes the spatial and temporal limitations imposed by this temporary paralysis. Existing outside of time and space, his conscious experience seems to be a dimension that '[l]asts forever' with 'no change to measure' (*EM* 12) and the present of his traumatised mind becomes a composite of past and present experiences. Pointedly, time seems temporarily broken to Mark and throughout the novel, he will wonder if this is the moment in which he died. However, as he slowly comes back to consciousness, Mark imagines receiving instructions to *'[b]e patient, be a patient'* (*EM* 23) from an unknown recess and, critically, the accident forces Mark and those around him to take stock of their lives. It slows them down, in other words, and teaches them to *'[b]e patient'*, reminding the novel's characters that the constant drive onwards, to the next event, relationship or professional milestone, loudly suppresses and diminishes the value of reflection in their lived experience of the present.

Powers' attention to the dynamic range of experience is also an important feature of *The Echo Maker*, an idea that Colson Whitehead acknowledges when he describes the novel as 'a quiet exploration of how we survive, day to day.'[50] Mark's crash is a noisy 'event', for example, but the diagnosis of Capgras that it brings about is powerful because it is rare, inaudible and difficult to diagnose. When Mark is unable to comprehend how Capgras has changed him, he becomes angry and violent, prone to guttural exclamations and animalistic noises that resemble 'the squeal of a dog' (*EM* 80) being run over. The processes that change the mind may happen quietly but *The Echo Maker* notes how their traumatic effects are often cacophonous and wide reaching.

In the aftermath of the crash, Mark's condition also becomes the focal point for other crises of identity. Karin Schluter and Gerald Weber are quiet characters who enjoy reading, writing and studying until, that is, Mark's diagnosis causes them both to doubt the legitimacy of their formerly 'quiet, stable' (*EM* 69) existences. Over the course of the novel, Weber loses faith in his ability as a scholar and Karin believes she actually is the 'Kopy Karin' (*EM* 152) that Mark, under the delusions of Capgras, accuses her of being. As Luc Herman and Bart Vervaeck suggest, Powers' alternation between perspectives is here emblematic of a 'form of contamination' in which each character's point of view is no longer counted as a separate mental world.[51] Although Capgras is first introduced as a rare and mysterious side effect of Mark's traumatic brain injury, Powers gradually extends its specificity, first to the people around Mark and ultimately to the entire human race so that the reader can no longer tell who amongst the characters is mentally well or if, indeed, any of them are ill. Weber, for instance, acknowledges that '[t]he self bled out' (*EM* 485), paraphrasing Daniel Dennett's suggestion that advances in contemporary neuroscience make the belief in a boundary between consciousness and 'the outside world' both 'naïve' and old-fashioned.[52] Through a cognitive lens, we might therefore claim that every 'external' event in *The Echo Maker* also occurs within the consciousness of Powers' central characters, who all believe that the boundary between consciousness and the outside world is non-existent. Finally, and with consciousness portrayed 'from the inside out', *The Echo Maker* reaches its noisiest point as Powers frames Capgras as a metaphor for the fragmented, anxious and dissonant experience of all contemporary life.

### *The Echo Maker*: the quiet of Kearney

At this juncture, it seems wise to return to and, again, interrogate the noise commonly attributed to narratives infused with scientific knowledge. The novel of cognition has been criticised for ceding ground to the sciences, with some critics accusing the trend of denigrating fiction by filling it with 'fact.' Journalist Marco Roth argues that the 'special perceptions and heightened language' of the trend refits the quiet of a modernist aesthetic for the depiction of 'special cases' thus losing the ability to capture the rhythms of the everyday in eventless prose.[53] Reading Capgras as a metaphor for the disorientation of society also risks romanticising the portrayal of cognitive illness by overlooking the everyday realities that its sufferers face. As Susan Sontag argues in her influential study *Illness as Metaphor* (1978), all metaphorical descriptions of illness can act as a form of silencing. Of particular note to the discussions of traumatic brain injury and mental illness foregrounded in this chapter, Sontag suggests that the elegance of allegory suppresses the noisier, uncomfortable realities of pain and illness and when used as 'stereotypes of national character' metaphors of illness also become devices of exceptionalism that cultivate anxiety and ignorance.[54]

It could, therefore, be argued that ethical issues plague the novel of cognition and taint the quiet aesthetic it presents with a narrative of personal trauma that has more similarities with '9/11' or any 'state of the nation' novel than the quiet of *Gilead* or *Tinkers*. Colson Whitehead's review of *The Echo Maker* suggests as much, describing the text as a 'wise and elegant post-9/11 novel' that is 'quiet' because of its attention to the everyday feelings of loneliness and alienation common to American citizens after 2001.[55] This argument is extended by literary critic Ann Keniston who compares *The Echo Maker* to Jess Walter's *The Zero* (2006), published in the same year and also featuring what Keniston defines as a 'Traumatic Brain Injury (TBI)', common to many post-9/11 texts. Noting that these novels are 'otherwise quite different', Keniston argues that the recurrence of TBI in 'post-9/11' fiction hints that the 'attacks' cultural afterlife – at least as of the mid-2000s – is evident through a series of disruptions to and distortions of memory'.[56] Keniston then examines both novels for their reinforcement of 'positivist, (neuro)scientific discourse' and a 'sense of radical uncertainty', suggesting that the recurrence of TBI, if not the entire genre of cognitive fiction, is 'at least implicitly political'.

The portrayal of mental unrest is not unique to the novel of cognition, or to the trend's 'post-9/11' context. While Marco Roth criticises cognitive fiction for fixating on 'special cases', cognitive scientists and contemporary novelists share a long-held fascination with the fragmented mind which manifested itself strongly, once again, in literary modernism. Indeed, the cognitive turn in literary scholarship pays particular attention to novels written in the early twentieth century. Alongside cognitive science's noted preoccupation with Proust, critics like Patricia Waugh describe the portrayal of mental disturbance as one of the 'quieter achievements' of the modernist canon, reading cognitivism as a tool to retrospectively liberate authors like Woolf and Joyce from 'the disabling myth' of modernism's '"inward turn"' as an expression 'of a purely private self'.[57]

Many modernist novels can also be said to depict instances of mental disturbance as the inability to process unwanted sounds. Woolf's 1931 novel, *The Waves*, is a classic stream of consciousness novel in which characters search for 'quiet, gravity, control' and pointedly delve inwards to create meaning because they are acutely sensitive to the noise of others.[58] On hearing the voice of a concert soprano, for instance, Rhoda, one of the novel's central characters, does not directly respond and instead asks existential questions about the nature of that noise: 'She has provided us with a cry. But only a cry. And what is a cry?'[59] Many of Woolf's characters seek conditions in which to stabilise their mental environments: as I noted of Mrs Dalloway in Chapter 1, they seek out moments of solitude and spaces for independent reflection. Woolf also reflects on the difficulties of quiet when illness affects the mind. In *The Waves*, Rhoda is particularly alert to interactions with others. She enters the novel with the words 'I hear a sound' and from this point until her eventual suicide the character is uniquely sensitive to noise.[60] During the day, Rhoda feels ill at ease because the noise of other people disrupts her stream of thought. 'Listen', Woolf writes from Rhoda's perspective, 'a whistle sounds, wheels rush, the door creaks on its hinges. I regain the sense of the complexity and the reality and the struggle'.[61] However, when the day is over Rhoda finds herself alone and better able to consider the present and the quotidian:

> How much better is silence; the coffee-cup, the table. How much better to sit by myself like the solitary sea-bird that opens its wings on the stake. Let me sit here for ever with bare things, this coffee cup, this knife, this fork, things in themselves, myself being myself.[62]

By referring to the 'stake' on which bird feeders are raised, Rhoda suggests that the 'silence' of the empty room is not only free of noise but also nourishing to her. Left alone with 'things' that are nothing more than 'themselves', Rhoda can comprehend the fullness of the moment; even the book she is reading lies discarded on the floor as she attempts to empty out her present from the sources of overstimulation that regularly threaten her internal peace. In reflection, that is, Rhoda is unable to conceive of herself in relation to others. She not only rejects her friends but finds herself unable to read, a pastime that traditionally offers a quiet source of refuge. In this gesture, *The Waves* offers little hope for the production of a sustainable quiet and in Rhoda, Woolf portrays an introvert who is unable to escape, either externally or internally, from the noise of society.

Much like a quiet aesthetic, I argue that the cognitive turn in its literary and scientific manifestations is not a turn away from the outside world but an examination of its complexity from within the mind of the individual. Whether or not we label Powers a noisy novelist, *The Echo Maker* demonstrates a mode of writing that focuses on the lives of quiet individuals, processes and, as I discuss in this section, locations. Like Woolf and, indeed, Marilynne Robinson, Powers writes quietly and from within consciousness without losing his social focus. The quietest element of *The Echo Maker* is therefore the novel's attention to consciousness but, like all quiet fictions, this attention liberates the narrative from the inclusion of national or topical event that characterises the historical present of many noisier fictions. For example, although the novel is set between the US invasion of Afghanistan in 2002 and Operation Iraqi Freedom in 2004, Powers treats the events of 11 September 2001 and the subsequent 'War on Terror' lightly. On the night that Mark has his accident, a television in the corner of the waiting room contextualises the novel's historical moment as Karin watches pictures of 'mountain wasteland scattered with guerrillas. Afghanistan, winter, 2002' (*EM* 9). Contemplation of the outside world temporarily disassociates Karin from her own body; distracted by the television, she does not notice how hard she is digging her fingernails into her hand until she bleeds from the wound. With the wider event happening '[o]ff in the corner', Powers incorporates minimal political content, acknowledging its peripheral or subliminal influence on the primary subject of consciousness but never directly engaging with the 'event' itself. Both Tim Lustig and Charles Harris argue that the events of 11 September 2001 'indirectly' cause Mark's accident when, towards the end of the novel, Powers reveals that Mark swerved his car to avoid a TV reporter who is traumatised by the events in New York and heads suicidal into his path.⁶³ Lustig's reference to *The Echo Maker*'s 'indirect' relationship with '9/11' is important here, as is Ann Keniston's observation that Powers only 'indirectly' refers to the World Trade Center site.⁶⁴ In this deliberate indirectness, Powers keeps the contemplation of this national 'event' at a distance from the narrative present of his characters, providing only 'the shadow' (*EM* 344) of a shared trauma and no direct relevance or representation. As Lustig admits, Powers seems to 'shrink' from making even the most general accusations of failure against American foreign policy and the television remains 'muted' (*EM* 9) as a result of the news' decentralisation.⁶⁵

Importantly, the characters of *The Echo Maker* also live in a quiet location where they can avoid national event. A city in decline, Kearney is quiet despite being urban: even its residents describe the city as a 'vacant, floating terrain in the dead center of nowhere' (*EM* 144). Despite or perhaps because of its vacuity, Karin and Weber find themselves drawn to the city and both characters see Kearney as a place in which they can 'rewrite' (*EM* 552) the lives they have made elsewhere. Powers claims to have chosen Kearney as the location for *The Echo Maker* because it is a 'terra incognita in many readers' mental landscapes'; a location that is neither identifiably American nor modern despite its position at the geographical heart of the nation.⁶⁶ More pressing to the aesthetic of quiet noted here, it is a location in which industrial decline has divorced the city from the noise of industrial progress. At the edges of Kearney, Nebraska's famous Platte River further accentuates the quiet of the city's deterioration. The Platte is a 'calming' (*EM* 7) environment for many residents as well as a unique habitat that draws half a million sandhill cranes to Kearney every year.⁶⁷ The migratory pattern of the birds is a major part of the region's mythology: '[t]his year's flight', Powers writes, 'has always been. Something in the birds retraces a route laid down centuries before their parents showed it to them' (*EM* 4). Dramatising their migration as a social act, Powers both personifies the cranes and describes their behaviour as 'prehistoric' (*EM* 125, 534); guided by an instinct that was built into consciousness when the birds were 'feathered dinosaurs' (*EM* 351). The Platte River temporarily hosts 'dense bird cities' (*EM* 123) as they await their flight further south. However, when the birds eventually 'scatter' (*EM* 123) it is as part of an instinctive and primeval ritual programmed deep into their neural pathways. Like Karin and Weber, the birds will always return to Kearney because something old and quiet rules their migration, a set of neurologically programmed desires hidden deep within their brains that they, like their human neighbours, know very little about.

In my formulation, Powers' distrust of progress, specifically urban development, makes *The Echo Maker* a pointedly quiet novel. As the advancement of a process to its conclusion, progress is a noisy idea, structured by a reliance on event and a drive to conclude. Indeed, as I have argued, Kearney is a perilously quiet city, slowly emptying of industry as production moves out but also surrounded by an increasingly endangered natural resource. Powers' disapproval of the capitalist cycles of boom and bust is made clear as he describes the 'gamut' of franchises that plague the city. 'Progress', he writes, 'would at last render every place terminally familiar' (*EM* 210) by slowly eradicating Kearney's regional identity. Ironically, the presence of the cranes also threatens to destroy the Platte River they migrate to as Powers depicts a team of local conservationists battling contractors' plans to develop the land into 'a sprawling tourist village for crane peepers' (*EM* 437). Powers is also explicit about his distrust of ecotourism as the prospective saviour of the environment: he describes his characters prophetically 'gazing across the wetlands, past the progress that will destroy them' (*EM* 539) and exhibits a kind of archive fever as his prose foretells the Platte's demise.

The opposition between quiet and noise plays out most revealingly in Powers' representation of a public debate over the fate of the river. The developers, who are all traditionally 'extrovert' personality types, buoyed by 'humor, style, unlimited budgets, sophistication, subliminal seduction' (*EM* 438), can project their argument above their bookish opponents. When the public debate fails to reach a decision, the developers also seem to exploit the quiet manners of the conservationists and by planning to 'sit on the proposal for a few months, then slip out a ruling when no one is looking' (*EM* 440), the developers subtly, and quietly, get what they want. The triumph of progress, in this case, seems to be inevitable: as Karin listens to the debate, she even believes that she is taking 'the combat inside herself' (*EM* 439), both internalising and perhaps also attempting to quieten the competing shouts around her. It is in this instance, too, that Karin makes the connection between the chaotic nature of consciousness and the environmental conflict happening around her. As if in an epiphany, she suggests, 'the whole race suffered from Capgras' and speculates that their instinct to fight, to shout over one another, is an 'instinctive ritual' that, like the migratory instinct of the sandhill cranes, is built so deep into consciousness that no one knows it is there. Just as Mark becomes violent and noisy under the delusions of Capgras, a neurological disturbance that is unique to him, the conclusion of *The Echo Maker* suggests that his symptoms are present in all of those who are too quick to sacrifice discussion and contemplation for the noisier promise of conflict.

### *American Genius; a comedy*: the quiet of contingency

*The Echo Maker* concludes with the pessimistic suggestion that our enduring quieter instincts and environments are continually overwritten by the noise of progress. However, Lynne Tillman's fifth novel, *American Genius; a comedy*, is an elaboration and embodiment of the cognitive processes that Powers describes. Lacking *The Echo Maker*'s external focalisation, the prose of *American Genius* is much quieter and its 'intense drama of interiority' unfolds in the extended internal monologue of a single protagonist who is eventually, but only occasionally, named as 'Helen'.[68] Fast paced and discursive, the narrative flies through what Patrick O'Donnell describes as a 'digressive assemblage of associations and contingencies' as uneven segments of varying length both invite and reject the idea that a stable conscious experience is possible.[69]

Important to an aesthetic of quiet, the plot of *American Genius* is not event driven. The novel's segments each follow chronologically from the last, forming a fragmented account of the final few weeks of Helen's voluntary residency within an unspecified community. While *The Echo Maker* charts one year in the life of the Schluters, the duration of Helen's rehabilitation is undefined, relying as much upon the reader's assumptions as on the detail Tillman provides. When she decides to leave the community, Helen offers no other reason than 'It's time, I think', proposing a further ambiguity where the reader seeks resolution.[70] The narrator implies that she has run out of possibilities for self-development during her stay and claims the community has become too familiar to find out 'what I think I am' *(AGAC* 156) or 'what I might also become' *(AGAC* 288). Such vague allusions to unity do not entirely ring true but rather reinforce Helen's unwillingness to settle on fixed definitions. By the end of the novel, Helen has left the confines of the facility to continue in her old routines, which are largely comprised of worrying about her mother and going for facials. The final clause of the novel, 'and she goes on' (*AGAC* 292), implies perpetuation rather than change, embodying the narrative's obsession with repetition and the possibility of continuity but offering no conclusive account of Helen's recovery.

In this way, too, *American Genius* continues Tillman's career-long experimentation with the rhythms of thought. As Eric Rasmussen suggests, the 'cognitive aesthetic' of *American Genius* engages with 'the space and time of turbulent thinking' and challenges the limits of the psychological realism that Tillman has broached throughout her career.[71] Tillman's fictional art critic, 'Madame Realism', first appears as a character in a 1984 short story of the same name, presented as an absolute third-person observer who, like Powers' narrator in *The Echo Maker*, is almost completely invisible. Madame Realism reveals very little of herself but frequently comments on the mechanisms of fiction and, later, in *The Madame Realism Complex* (1992), Tillman explicitly connects the function of narrative with the process of thought: '[S]tories do not occur outside thought. Stories, in fact, are contained within thought. It's only a story really should read, it's a way to think.'[72] Tillman wrote this description at a time when advances in cognitive science were just beginning to describe the mind as an engine of narrative. In *Consciousness Explained*, which Dennett published in 1991, the author goes to great lengths to explain how the brain turns experience into a 'coherent "narrative"', composed in fragmentary or multiple drafts that play 'short-lived roles in the modulation of current activity'.[73] Ten years later, V. S. Ramachandran also argued that the desire to narrativise distinguishes human consciousness because it seeks 'to construct an autobiography, imparting a sense of narrative and meaning to its life.'[74] For Tillman, as for Dennett and Ramachandran, stories do not exist without the brain, or vice versa. Most significantly, narrative cannot be understood or communicated without both experience of the mind and a simultaneous analysis of its processes.

Tillman's fiction similarly suggests that stories might be our best chance to comprehend the relationship between personal and public histories or, as I argue, between what it quietly and loudly apprehended. Tillman's fourth novel, *No Lease on Life* (1998), for example, reflects the author's interest in quiet people and noisy environments through the narration of a notably quiet woman named Elizabeth.

An underpaid proof-reader and lifelong underachiever, Elizabeth is forced to live in a New York tenement where the noise of her surroundings transforms her into a 'vigilante, citizen executioner'.[75] The novel charts twenty-four increasingly frustrating hours during which Elizabeth fights the external disturbance of rising street noises and illegal rent hikes. Rather than moving between the many voices of the tenement, Tillman focuses on the internal life of her single protagonist as she fends off the intrusions of the outside world and, importantly, Elizabeth does not seek out a quieter environment than the tenement she lives in. Instead, Tillman's narrator retreats to her room, where she can be 'separated from the world' and invoke quiet strategies for self-preservation that include reading and tidying.[76] As the noise of the city continues to invade her personal space, Elizabeth increasingly retreats into hallucination and fantasy to escape the increased volume of her location. In *No Lease on Life*, and as I discuss at length in Chapter 5, the distance between internal and external environments is seen to shrink as city sounds threaten the quiet of those individuals who prefer reflective activities and environments.

In *American Genius*, however, as in many novels of cognition, Tillman integrates the noisier elements of society within a quiet aesthetic. Helen is a quiet character, a former historian, who frequently studies and enjoys time alone. Helen's narrative is composed of what she describes as 'reclusive, evanescent moment[s]' (*AGAC* 232), periods of time in which nothing particular happens but that provide her with clarity and shelter, thus forcing 'the world's horror [to] leave temporarily.' As Kasia Boddy points out, Helen is '[u]ndoubtedly self-obsessed' but the particular nature of her self-obsession is 'partly a way of dissolving the barrier between social and psychological discourse'.[77] Critically, then, *American Genius* references a vast array of topics, quoting from American history and transcendentalism, the science of dermatology, design, psychology and, of course, neuroscience.[78] The narrator knows, for example, that bee stings are poisonous because of 'formic acid and a neurotoxin' (*AGAC* 209) and that the 'neural routes of the brain' (*AGAC* 132) dictate her everyday habits. However, Tillman does not prioritise the discoveries of cognitivism over other forms of knowledge. Helen's familiarity with neural processes is therefore passing and never threatens to overwhelm the validity of Tillman's fiction with more detail than it is natural for Helen to remember. Rather, the narrative represents ideas as they occur to Helen. With striking similarity to Marilynne Robinson's depiction of the Reverend Ames in *Gilead*, who narrates ideas that occur to him as he wanders 'to the limits of [his] understanding', Helen often resolves to 'let my mind wander as far as it could, since I mean always to untether it from its ordinary course' (*AGAC* 132).[79] The subjects she touches on are diverse and discursive, like Ames' patterns of thought, but Tillman presents them within a stream of consciousness that shows each thought flowing into another, sometimes illogically and without discrimination.

Most evocative of the mind's continued reprocessing of information, as well as its habit of misfiring and misremembering, Helen's narration is prone to misdirection and deviation. She continually returns to the same motifs and phrases but never settles on a single resolution to the dilemmas she poses for herself. Peter Nicholls calls this aspect of Tillman's style a 'syntax of equivocation' and a stylistic embodiment of fallacious reasoning.[80] An encounter with a fellow resident in the library best exemplifies the complications of Helen's internal syntax. The event passes uneventfully but once Helen has returned to the quiet of her room, she interprets the minutiae of their encounter in a typically discursive fashion:

> The brand of jeans that the odd inquisitive woman wears could have meaning, since everything means something, even if it is not anything much, negligible, or hardly worth mentioning, and, even though interpretations change and often meanings are temporary, especially those about a brand, her jeans still affect my relationship to her, since much harbors in trivialities, though not as much as in profound words and acts, whose significance can also be debated and more likely is. (*AGAC* 154)

Every aspect of the scene is 'debated' by Helen and her distracted, multi-clausal sentences defy any 'profound' or lasting meaning. The incredible sensitivity of Helen as a narrator is also obvious in this passage. Helen notices the brand of jeans that the woman is wearing in the sentence's first clause but this seemingly trivial fact is undercut by four clauses that successively cast doubt on any meaning that the act of noticing may hold; until, that is, a conjunction shifts the emphasis of the sentence onto a wider consideration of 'meanings'. Lost amidst the complexity of the sentence is also a vague reference to the 'profound' but as it is left to the sentence's penultimate clause, its resonance is undercut by the weight of Helen's previous qualifications. Profundity becomes 'debatable' and, as Nicholls points out, ambiguity, or equivocation, 'becomes habitual, a reflex of thinking itself.'[81] If occasionally anxious about the repercussions of all uncertainties, Helen ultimately embraces the equivocation of her conscious experience while Tillman's attention to cognitive processes seems to suggest that she has no choice but to do so.

*American Genius* is therefore a disquisition on the habit of thinking and the process of reflection in which contemplation is an end in itself. Much like *The Echo Maker*, a focus on consciousness is also the quietest element of the novel. *American Genius* is entirely intradiegetic and the narrative voice slips between discursive and dramatic modes as Helen presents many versions of herself: 'I was good, bad, indifferent, young, cruel, sensitive, a helper, a hindrance, a victim, a victimizer, hero, bystander' (*AGAC* 283). Tillman's emphasis on equivocation, then, points to the narrative construction of character but ultimately denies the reader a point of fixity. This idea is illustrated, time and again, through Helen, who is unnamed for the majority of the novel and thus denied a differentiated personal identity. In comparison to the quiet of the interior narratives discussed in Chapter 3, Paul Harding's *Tinkers* opens with the name of the protagonist, George Washington Crosby, and, in *Gilead*, the Reverend Ames situates himself both historically and geographically, announcing early in the novel: 'I, John Ames, was born in the Year of Our Lord 1880 in the state of Kansas.'[82] For Ames, this declaration and naming legitimises the project of writing down his story within the larger history of the region and his genealogy. Yet Tillman denies her narrator such definition and waits 200 pages to reveal the protagonist's name in the fleeting allusion to a letterbox: 'the wooden slot, with "Helen" marked on it' *(AGAC* 200). Considering the wealth of information deployed in the novel, this omission of specificity and authority is suggestive, emphasising Helen's structural unfixity and her ambivalence towards narratives of history and progress. Although she often comments on the state of the world, Helen seems uninterested or unable to tie elements together. 'I like history', she admits, 'but it is slow. I am fast and quickly lose interest in things, and some people, and this dismays me, but I start and stop many reasonable pursuits' *(AGAC* 86). History is a process of narrativisation that feels slower to Helen than the pace at which she exists. Even as she identifies as a historian, Helen's lack of attention commits her to a life of contingency, a fundamentally unstable lifestyle that rises and falls with the waves of consciousness and writes an idiosyncratic history of the present.

If *American Genius* has a 'story', then, it lies in Helen's elaboration of her conscious processes. A quiet character who has, perhaps, lost her way in an attempt 'not to appear mad' (*AGAC* 94), Helen's withdrawal into an unnamed community teaches her the processes of reflection she has learnt to suppress. The reader learns little about the environment in which she lives: it is rural, 'not far from' (*AGAC* 141) Lowell, Massachusetts, but pointedly not attached to the town. Indeed, it is understood that the residents of Lowell are fearful of Helen's community because the retreat or hospital in which she lives is filled with 'unstable' characters who are rarely referred to by anything other than their eccentricities. Helen's closest friend is a man known only as 'The Count', who compulsively and poignantly collects timepieces, while other peripheral characters are known only by Helen's perception of them: 'the Turkish poet', 'the Magician' or 'the disconsolate woman'. Within this community, the residents spend their time on therapeutic activities including reading, writing and meditation that seem to at least temporarily calm them. Yet because of the proximity of other, primarily anxious people, Tillman's narrative is often fragmentary, sometimes paranoid and threatened by the noise of other residents. 'I'm the one who makes noise', Helen says, 'who flushes the toilet most often, going to the bathroom in the middle of the night, because I can't sleep, I'm afraid to dream, to surrender' (*AGAC* 9). In this instance, quiet seems like a 'surrender' to Helen and mental stillness is equated with the failure to fully live or to heal. However, by the end of the novel, Helen's mind has calmed substantially. Over the course of her stay, the text of *American Genius* presents the continual elaborations, negations and deviations of Helen's mind, but it is only at the novel's finale that the reader is shown how therapeutic the exercise has been. Before leaving the facility, Helen remarks: 'I needed dinner, which marked the end of a day during which I had or hadn't accomplished anything' (*AGAC* 289). Although the schedule of the institution continues to mark her sense of time, an acknowledgement of Helen's lack of accomplishment and of the aimless ways in which she passes her days demonstrates a calmer mind with greater toleration of ambiguity.

## *American Genius*: the quiet of cognition

Helen's sense of resolution and peace at the end of *American Genius* is somewhat at odds with the ominous conclusion of *The Echo Maker*. Powers' aversion to homogenised notions of progress, made obvious by his fatalistic denouncements of both urbanisation and ecotourism, might oppose his passion for scientific discovery if cognitivism had not shown consciousness to be better understood as a system prone to constant modulation. Processes of slow, incremental change are, I argue, infinitely quieter than teleological notions of progress; where progress invokes rupture, change evokes constant elaboration rather than invention and ongoingness rather than the sense of an ending. Most importantly, the desire for change is not dependent on the will to conclude and it is a process that cognitive scientists claim to both uncover and accept. V. S. Ramachandran describes the 'plasticity of the cortex' as its defining feature, thus making change an inevitable part of existence.[83] As Ramachandran notes, a series of daily 'rapid changes' write and rewrite consciousness to such an extent that the acceptance of almost constant change must also be part of any novel of cognition.[84] While narratives of progress loudly deny the time for reflection in the present, change can happen incrementally and, I argue, quietly, normalising the experience of contingency and transformation so that it is no longer traumatic to the mind of the individual.

Of course, some novels are better at this than others. Powers' characters are ultimately unnerved by 'how intoxicatingly pointless existence could be' (*EM* 48) but in *American Genius* Helen resolves to 'accept temporariness' (*AGAC* 124) and to further reappraise concepts that are traditionally thought to be stable. Cognitive scientists have shown, for instance, that memory may not be a cognitively secure unit, stored safely within consciousness like a library. As neurologist Israel Rosenfield writes, '[w]hen I form an image of some event in my childhood, I don't go into an archive and find a pre-existing image, I have to consciously form an image.'[85] In *American Genius*, Helen also seems aware that memory does not have a singular 'pre-existing image' and that it is always reconstructed in the present. She is particularly distrustful of the trappings of memory: 'Memory revamps itself. The temporary is contemporary, flowing in the veins, though humans behave as if permanence beat steadily in every transaction and feeling' (*AGAC* 158). The free rhyme, 'temporary is contemporary', seems trivial but it also invokes a Steinian relationship with rhyme and repetition that runs throughout Tillman's prose.[86] Specifically, it invokes Gertrude Stein's sense of joy at the idea of a diverse and contingent 'continuous present' that might liberate the individual from the strictures of memory and allow them to 'fully' exist in the present.[87] Through the long, digressive, repetitive and shifting sentences of *American Genius*, Tillman makes sense of impermanence, acknowledges the difficulties of living, truly, in the present, and, by acknowledging the 'revamps' of memory, suggests that the acceptance of contingency is the only way to live quietly.

Ultimately, *American Genius* may also owe more to the modernist 'novel of consciousness' than *The Echo Maker*. Through the character of Weber, Powers describes consciousness as a deceptive process that self-presents as an unbroken stream, constituted by a serial phenomenon in which neural processes overwrite its underlying fragmentation. However, Tillman embeds the portrayal of cognitive fragmentation within a single stream of consciousness narrative that evades resolution on a sentence-by-sentence level and enacts the processes that Powers goes to great lengths to describe. Similar to the mountaintop sanatorium described by Thomas Mann in *The Magic Mountain* (1924), in *American Genius* the lives of the 'perfectly healthy and ordinary' are indistinguishable from the mentally unwell and Tillman embraces the advances of cognitivism that explain how this is possible.[88] It is in this way, too, that the title of *American Genius; a comedy* reveals its author's larger intent. In an interview, Tillman claims that her novel provides ways to 'think about being an American now', rejecting critics who would read *American Genius*' immersion in consciousness as a withdrawal from the world.[89] In the novel's title, we might also think of Stein's conception of genius, which Tillman admits has particularly influenced her writing. '[T]he essence of genius', Stein suggested, is 'of being most intensely alive'.[90] The quiet protagonist of *American Genius* may therefore be Tillman's way of writing about national identity without shackling her narrative to the portrayal of event or a particularised notion of the 'contemporary'. Set in an unknown location, at an unknown time, and never mentioning the date at which the novel is set, the only indication of the period in which the novel takes place is the technology Helen alludes to, particularly the computers and cell phones that other people own but that she claims to have no time for. Like the Reverend Ames in *Gilead*, Helen does not venture into political debate because she finds it repetitive and pointless. While her friends 'parrot TV and radio commentators' *(AGAC* 50), Helen instead believes that received ideas of 'history' and 'politics' are too hastily drawn, unreflective and unoriginal. The prose of *American Genius* is therefore packed with knowledge and trivia that Helen accumulates through continuous study, yet she divines that the texts she reads generally neglect 'tenacious unwritten histories' (*AGAC* 7) and that an alternative history exists only in the individual's perception of the present. In this way, Helen can declare herself to be 'exceptionally present' *(AGAC* 82) without demonstrating any knowledge of America's 'contemporary' situation.

It also follows that temporality is a lesser concern for Tillman than it was in the novels of Robinson, Harding or even Powers. In *Gilead* and *Tinkers*, the quiet, dying protagonist is subject to the 'tyranny of time' that looms ominously over the novel.[91] In *The Echo Maker*, the rapid spread of Capgras threatens to deny the characters time. Weber, for instance, often refers to 'what time he had left' (*EM* 129) and strictly rations his 'time and interest' (*EM* 169) to calculate the work he can achieve before death. In *American Genius*, however, Helen has an air of ambivalence towards the passing of time. '[I]t may be that there's no time', she says 'only the peculiar, winsome present, in which I seem to be alive' *(AGAC* 89). This, again, appears to be based in Tillman's preference for equivocation: Helen admits that there may be no time, but she also suggests that time 'is unimportant here, and seemingly grows more insignificant every day' *(AGAC* 52). Notably, Helen's contemplation reflects the freedom afforded her from within her quiet and isolated community. Time does not matter to her because time is allowed not to matter and with the noise of civilisation, or the noise of industrial and economic development that Powers so disdains, kept at a distance, she is able to be 'exceptionally present' in ways that the protagonists of many noisier fictions cannot.

Perhaps, too, the 'syntax of equivocation' that Peter Nicholls notes in Tillman's prose provides an apt description for all quiet fictions.[92] Ames' thoughts in *Gilead* are particularly slow and leisurely. A typical narrative episode begins with an account of the Reverend's sleep, followed by a mental exercise or debate. On one occasion, Ames imagines what it would be like to ask himself for advice, running over an 'equivalency of considerations that is interesting in theory but resolves nothing'.[93] Importantly, Ames' thought experiments do not have goals: he sets out to achieve 'nothing' beyond the exploration of his conscious mind and records the process for his son and the reader to experience. *Lila*, too, often depicts long contemplations that are circuitous or discursive, where Robinson's prose is animated by what Amy M. King describes as the will to 'be at peace and pay attention' rather than the reader's desire to reach the end of the story.[94] After leaving St Louis, and freeing herself from the oppressive 'quiet' of the whorehouse, Lila is wary of the peace she finds in Iowa and continually waits 'for something to happen' to her.[95] It is completely by chance that Lila then passes through Gilead where she meets and eventually marries Ames. The 'event' of Ames' marriage is therefore seen as the result of Lila's whim to leave St Louis, travel to Iowa and pass through the town. Importantly, these discursive thoughts and actions convey a kind of quiet in their lack of purpose. Just as Ames' acts of contemplation need not necessarily turn to action to be productive, so Robinson's quiet fiction is driven by attention to the everyday acts that may or may not result in an outward form of action.

If, finally, the novel has long been described as a 'chamber of consciousness', to borrow a phrase from Henry James, in a novel of cognition the walls of the chamber are shifting and also permeable.[96] In *The Echo Maker* and *American Genius; a comedy*, the boundary between internal and external environments is pushed and tested, expanding my definition of a quiet novel by uncovering the complex and often discordant recesses of conscious experience and challenging the traditional division between what is internally and externally felt. In *The Echo Maker*, characters acknowledge consciousness as a dynamic structure and Powers integrates contemporary detail into what he describes as an 'inside out' form of interiority that shares many aesthetic qualities with other quiet fictions. However, Powers' distaste for urban development twinned with his passion for the ecosystems that Kearney's developers threaten to spoil leaves the prose of his quiet fiction anxious, disjointed and pessimistic. *American Genius*, on the other hand, follows the digressive thoughts of a woman whose greatest subject is herself, tracing her disquisitions on religion, the Manson family, chairs and American history, without ever considering the events of the present. Helen is highly educated, yet devotes herself to 'pondering and reflection' (*AGAC* 237) with no aim or end in mind. Together, Powers' and Tillman's novels of cognition detail the machinations of consciousness in order to drive the narrative forward without the passing of action or event, illustrating how reading for quiet requires a philosophical interest in process rather than progress, incremental change rather than dramatic breaks and continuities rather than ruptures. In this study's final chapter, I consider how novels by Teju Cole and Ben Lerner extend the aimless intellectualism of Ames and 'Helen' against the noisy environment of the city, wandering further than either quiet protagonist but, in the process, reaching the limits of quiet as an ethical and philosophical position.

## Notes

1 Alan Richardson and Francis F. Steen, 'Literature and the Cognitive Revolution: An Introduction', *Poetics Today*, 23:1 (spring 2002), p. 3. Literature was late to catch on to the advances of cognitivism. In 1998, Richardson argued that theorists of the late twentieth century would be remembered as an amusing footnote to science's larger discoveries: 'That [cognitive science] remains news to many working in literature departments has already become something of an embarrassment; it will steadily prove more so.' Richardson, 'Brains, Minds, and Texts: A Review of Mark Turner's *The Literary Mind*', *Review*, 20 (1998), p. 39.
2 Richardson and Steen, 'Literature and the Cognitive Revolution', p. 4.
3 John Searle, 'Consciousness', in his *Consciousness and Language* (Cambridge: Cambridge University Press, 2002), p. 58; Joseph Tabbi, *Cognitive Fictions* (London: University of Minnesota, 2002), p. xv.
4 David Lodge, *Consciousness and the Novel: Connected Essays* (Cambridge, MA: Harvard University Press, 2002), p. 16. As it is used here, the term 'two cultures' originates from Snow's 1959 Rede Lecture, in which he argued that a gulf had arisen between scientific and literary intellectuals, with science proving the more fundamental to society.
5 Stephen J. Burn, *Jonathan Franzen at the End of Postmodernism* (London: Continuum, 2008), p. 26. Burn is a champion of Powers and of cognitive studies: he was guest editor for a special issue of *Modern Fiction Studies* devoted to 'Neuroscience and Modern Fiction' and is finishing a monograph about the American novel in the age of neuroscience. Burn also edited *Intersections: Essays on Richard Powers* (New York: Dalkey Archive Press, 2008), the first essay collection to be published on Powers' work.
6 Daniel Dennett, *Consciousness Explained* (London: Penguin, 1991); Israel Rosenfield, *The Strange, Familiar and Forgotten: An Anatomy of Consciousness* (New York: Knopf Doubleday Publishing, 1992); V. S. Ramachandran and Sandra Blakeslee, *Phantoms of the Brain: Probing the Mysteries of the Human Mind* (New York: Harper, 1998); Antonio

Damasio, *The Feeling of What Happens: Body, Emotion and the Making of Consciousness* (New York: Random House, 2000).
7   Richard Powers, *The Echo Maker* (London: Vintage, 2007), p. 67. All further references will appear in text as *EM*.
8   Dennett, *Consciousness Explained*, p. 192.
9   Violeta Sotirova, *Consciousness in Modernist Fiction: A Stylistic Study* (London: Palgrave Macmillan, 2013), pp. 26–27.
10  Lodge, *Consciousness and the Novel*, p. 209. By contrast, Monika Fludernik disparages the 'so-called *novel of consciousness*' and argues that narratology greatly exaggerates the form's potential as 'the purest example of internal focalization'. Fludernik, *An Introduction to Narratology* (Oxford: Routledge, 2009), p. 79. Despite her objection to the term, Fludernik also dates the form to the end of the nineteenth century.
11  William James originally conceived his 'stream' of consciousness technique as a theory of mind that would express how a linear 'stream' of experience disguises the fact that consciousness is 'chopped into bits'. William James, 'The Stream of Consciousness', in his *Writings: 1878–1899* (New York: Library of Congress, 1992), p. 159. Any 'stream' of consciousness is therefore only as 'quiet' as the thoughts it represents. As Kevin Everod Quashie also posits, the various patterns of consciousness represented in quiet aesthetic embody 'a dramatic and poetic presentation of the speaker's most intimate thoughts' that rise and fall with the currents of contemplation. Kevin Everod Quashie, *The Sovereignty of Quiet: Beyond Resistance in Black Culture* (New Brunswick, NJ: Rutgers University Press, 2012), p. 31.
12  Psychologists often use unquiet, loud and noisy to describe instances of mental disturbance: for instance, Eustace Chesser's *Unquiet Minds: Leaves from a Psychologist's Casebook* (New York: Roy Publishers, 1952) and William Sargant's *The Unquiet Mind: The Autobiography of a Physician in Psychological Medicine* (Boston: Little Brown, 1967). This dynamic reading of consciousness is also reflected in a number of contemporary memoirs: see Kay Redfield Jamison, *An Unquiet Mind: a Memoir of Moods and Madness* (London: Vintage, 1996); Andy Behrman, *Electroboy: A Memoir of Mania* (New York: Random House, 2011); Daniel Smith, *Monkey Mind: A Memoir of Anxiety* (London: Simon & Schuster, 2012).
13  Powers, interviewed by Stephen J. Burn, 'An Interview with Richard Powers', *Contemporary Literature*, 49:2 (summer 2008), p. 175.
14  Don DeLillo, quoted in Jonathan Franzen, 'Perchance to Dream: In the Age of Images, A Reason to Write Novels', *Harper's Magazine* (April 1996), p. 54; James Wood, 'Tell Me how Does it Feel?' *The Guardian* (6 October 2001), http://www.guardian.co.uk/books/2001/oct/06/fiction.
15  Wood, '*Lowboy*', *The New Yorker* (30 March 2009), http://www.newyorker.com/arts/critics/books/2009/03/30/090330crbo_books_wood.

16  Burn, 'Reading the Multiple Drafts Novel', *MFS Modern Fiction Studies*, 58:3 (fall 2012), p. 448.
17  Tabbi, *Cognitive Fictions*, pp. xxv, xv.
18  Edmund T. Rolls and Gustavo Deco, *The Noisy Brain: Stochastic Dynamics as a Principle of Brain Function* (Oxford: Oxford University Press, 2010), p. 78; Norman Doidge, *The Brain's Way of Healing: Remarkable Discoveries and Recoveries from the Frontiers of Neuroplasticity* (London: Penguin, 2015), p. 103.
19  Doidge, *The Brain's Way of Healing*, p. 105; Powers, *The Echo Maker*, p. 67.
20  In the essay collections, *The Death of Adam: Essays on Modern Thought* (New York: Picador, 1999), *Absence of Mind* (New Haven, CT: Yale University Press, 2010), *When I Was a Child I Read Books* (London: Virago, 2013) and *The Givenness of Things* (London: Virago, 2015), Robinson synthesises ancient and religious concepts as an expression of contemporary experience with particular reference to contemporary sciences. Robinson believes that an understanding of science enlarges the individual's conception of God's grandeur in the present and argues that '[i]f the old, untenable dualism is put aside [between religion and science], we are instructed in the endless brilliance of creation. Surely to do this is a privilege of modern life for which we should all be grateful.' Robinson, 'Freedom of Thought', in *When I Was a Child I Read Books* (2013), p. 11. Lerner's poetry collections, *The Lichtenberg Figures* (Port Townsend, WA: Copper Canyon Press, 2004), *Angle of Yaw* (Port Townsend, WA: Copper Canyon Press, 2006) and *Mean Free Path* (Port Townsend, WA: Copper Canyon Press, 2010), are informed by and named after his reading in physics and the history of science. However, Lerner freely admits to referencing scientific ideas *because* he has no understanding of them and claims that he is, instead, thematically interested 'in the way we arrived at this position in which there is such a division between the cultures of sciences and what are called the humanities or the arts.' Lerner, by Luke Degnan, 'Phoned-In #4', *BOMB Magazine* (19 March 2010), http://bombsite.com/issues/1000/articles/4500.
21  Dennett, *Consciousness Explained*, pp. 10, 17.
22  Rosenfield, *The Strange, The Familiar and The Forgotten*, p. 8.
23  The Silences of Science is an AHRC-funded research network based at Imperial College London that examines the paradox between collaboration and independent scholarship in scientific discovery. Physicist Felicity Mellor argues that contemporary science overemphasises the value of interdisciplinarity and cooperation, ignoring quiet as a mode of communication: 'Loud proclamations can obfuscate as well as inform', she argues, and 'noise can itself become a form of silence.' Mellor, 'Shhhh? Scientists Need to Talk about not Talking', *The Guardian* (15

January 2014), http://www.theguardian.com/science/political-science/2014/jan/15/shhhh-scientists-need-to-talk-about-not-talking.
24 Dennett, *Consciousness Explained*, p. 384.
25 Brian Boyd, *On the Origin of Stories: Evolution, Cognition, and Fiction* (Cambridge, MA: The Belknap Press of Harvard University Press, 2009), p. 25.
26 Damasio, *The Feeling of What Happens*, pp. 251, 228.
27 Barry Dainton, *Stream of Consciousness: Unity and Continuity in Conscious Experience* (Abingdon: Routledge, 2000), p. 102.
28 Jonathan Franzen, *The Corrections* (New York: Harper Perennial, 2007), pp. 183, 207.
29 Jennifer Egan, *Look at Me* (New York: Random House, 2001), pp. 391, 34.
30 Mark Haddon, *The Curious Incident of the Dog in the Night-time* (London: Vintage, 2004), p. 146.
31 Rivka Galchen, *Atmospheric Disturbances* (London: Harper Collins, 2008), pp. 138, 85.
32 Ibid., pp. 71, 50.
33 John Wray, *Lowboy* (New York: Canongate, 2009), p. 5.
34 Ibid., p. 90.
35 Ibid., p. 162.
36 Jonathan Lethem, *Motherless Brooklyn* (New York: Faber & Faber, 2004), pp. 78, 24.
37 Ibid., p. 1.
38 Richardson and Steen, 'Literature and the Cognitive Revolution: An Introduction', p. 3.
39 Capgras is a real but rare disorder caused by disconnect between areas of the temporal cortex, where facial features are recognised, and the limbic system, that attributes emotional responses and memory. See: Chad A. Noggle, Raymond S. Dean and Arthur M. Horton (eds), *The Encyclopaedia of Neuropsychological Disorders* (New York: Springer Publishing, 2012), p. 158; for a case study see: Ramachandran and Blakeslee, *Phantoms of the Brain: Probing the Mysteries of the Human Mind*, pp. 115–122.
40 Charles B. Harris, 'The Story of the Self: *The Echo Maker* and Neurological Realism', in *Intersections: Essays on Richard Powers*, ed. Stephen J. Burn and Peter Dempsey (Champaign, IL: Dalkey Archive, 2008), p. 238.
41 In addition, Powers' third novel, *The Gold Bug Variations* (1991), intertwines the discovery of the chemical structure of DNA with the stories of two love affairs set in the 1950s and 1980s. Powers writes about the cell as he would later write about consciousness in *The Echo Maker*, as a self-contained, self-operating and self-writing system, a mystery that scientists hope to solve, but that increasingly reveals the underlying fragmentation of all processes. His fifth novel, *Gain* (1998) links the

history of a chemical conglomerate, established in the early eighteenth century and a woman who develops ovarian cancers when living near the company's headquarters in contemporary America. Powers' latest novel, *Orfeo* (2014), also bridges the gap between art and science, telling the story of a musician who attempts to inscribe musical notation into genomes of bacteria as part of a 'DIY biology' movement who practice science in their back rooms.

42  Richard Powers, *Galatea 2.2* (London: Picador, 1995), p. 10.
43  Ibid.
44  Ibid., pp. 14, 34.
45  Cognitive neurologist Rachel Herz suggests that Proust's representations of autobiographical memory remain unparalleled and controversial science writer Jonah Lehrer writes that recent developments in cognitivism are actually 're-discoveries' of earlier observations made by the novelist and other artists. See: Kirsten Sheperd-Barr and Gordon M. Shepherd, 'Madeleines and Neuromodernism; Reassessing Mechanisms of Autobiographical Memory', *Auto/Biography Studies*, 13:1 (1998), pp. 39–60; Herz, 'A Naturalistic Analysis of Autobiographical Memories Triggered by Olfactory Visual and Auditory Stimuli', *Chemical Senses*, 29:217 (2004), pp. 217–224; Russell Epstein, 'Consciousness, Art, and the Brain: Lessons from Marcel Proust', *Consciousness and Cognition*, 13:2 (June 2004), pp. 213–240; Jonah Lehrer, *Proust was a Neuroscientist* (London: Canongate, 2012); Maryanne Wolf, *Proust and the Squid: The Story and Science of Reading the Brain* (New York: Harper Perennial, 2007).
46  Powers, *Galatea 2.2*, p. 9.
47  Powers, 'An Interview with Richard Powers', p. 175.
48  In 'Discourse in the Novel', Bakhtin argues that variation within language leads to internal differentiation and outlines the difficulties of constructing authorial voice when this differentiation can express 'authorial intentions but in a refracted way.' Bakhtin names this phenomena '*double-voiced discourse*' for its dual expression of the character's intent and the 'refracted' intention of the author. Bakhtin, trans. Caryl Emerson and Michael Holquist, *The Dialogic Imagination*, ed. Michael Holquist, (London: University of Texas Press, 1981), p. 324. Feminist critic Elaine Showalter refers to double-voiced discourse as a way of reading seemingly conventional texts for more subversive meanings in her 'Feminist Criticism in the Wilderness', in *The New Feminist Criticism*, ed. Elaine Showalter (London: Virago, 1986), p. 263. Similarly, Dorothy Hale compares Bakhtin's concept to W. E. B. Du Bois' theory of double consciousness; to Hale, double-voiced discourse is a defining characteristic of many Americans' literary and linguistic life and a self-conscious feature of an African American identity that 'possesses no positive con-

tent of its own.' Hale, 'Bakhtin in African American Literary Theory', *English Literary History*, 61:2 (1994), p. 447.
49 Powers, 'An Interview with Richard Powers', p. 175.
50 Colson Whitehead, 'Migratory Spirits', *The New York Times*, Sunday Book Review (22 October 2006), http://www.nytimes.com/2006/10/22/books/review/Whitehead.t.html?n=Top%2FFeatures%2FBooks%2FBook%20Reviews.
51 Luc Herman and Bart Vervaeck, 'Capturing Capgras: *The Echo Maker* by Richard Powers', *Style*, 43:3 (fall 2009), p. 419.
52 Dennett, *Consciousness Explained*, p. 108.
53 Marco Roth, 'Rise of the Neuronovel', *n+1*, 8: Recessional (fall 2009), http://nplusonemag.com/rise-neuronovel.
54 Susan Sontag, *Illness as Metaphor and AIDS and Its Metaphors* (London: Penguin, 2013), p. 3. Sontag specifically discusses cancer's place as the 'master illness' of American culture, although she revisits and extends this argument in *AIDS and Its Metaphors*, published in 1988. In its earlier version, Sontag briefly links cancer's supremacy to a fear of isolation and interiority in American culture and, quoting Wilhelm Reich's influential description of Freud's cancer, she describes how Freud's decision to live 'a very calm, quiet, decent family life' led Reich to conclude that the analyst had 'yielded to resignation' and withdrawn from public life. Sontag, *Illness as Metaphor*, p. 23.
55 Whitehead, 'Migratory Spirits', http://www.nytimes.com/2006/10/22/books/review/Whitehead.t.html?n=Top%2FFeatures%2FBooks%2FBook%20Reviews.
56 Ann Keniston, 'Traumatic Brain Injury in Post-9/11 Fiction', *Post 45* (24 October 2015), http://post45.research.yale.edu/2015/10/traumatic-brain-injury-in-post-911-fiction/#identifier_4_6391.
57 Patricia Waugh, 'Thinking in Literature', *The Legacies of Modernism: Historicizing Postwar and Contemporary Fiction*, ed. David James (Cambridge: Cambridge University Press, 2011), p. 76. Analysis of modernist narratives as representations of 'damaged' minds is a growing field. See: Sowon Park, 'The "Feeling of Knowing" in *Mrs Dalloway*: Neuroscience and Woolf', *Contradictory Woolf: Select Papers from the Twenty-First Annual International Conference on Virginia Woolf* (May 2012), pp. 108–114; Jean-Michel Rabaté, 'Modernism and Cognitive Disability', *A Handbook of Modernist Studies* (Oxford: John Wiley & Sons, 2013), pp. 379–398; Marco Bernini and Marco Caracciolo, *Letteratura e Scienze Cognitive* (Rome: Carocci Editore, 2013).
58 Virginia Woolf, *The Waves* (London: Wordsworth Editions, 2000), p. 90.
59 Ibid., p. 161.
60 Ibid., p. 4.
61 Ibid., p. 165.

62  Ibid., p. 166.
63  Tim J. Lustig, '"Two-way Traffic"?: Syndrome as Symbol in Richard Powers' *The Echo Maker*', in *Diseases and Disorders in Contemporary Fiction: the Syndrome Syndrome*, ed. T. J. Lustig and James Peacock (London: Routledge, 2013), pp. 130–143; Charles B. Harris, 'The Story of the Self: *The Echo Maker* and Neurological Realism', in *Intersections: Essays on Richard Powers*, ed. Stephen J. Burn and Peter Dempsey (Normal, IL: Dalkey Archive Press, 2008), pp. 244–245.
64  Lustig, 'Syndrome as Symbol', p. 139; Ann Keniston, 'Traumatic Brain Injury in Post-9/11 Fiction', http://post45.research.yale.edu/2015/10/traumatic-brain-injury-in-post-911-fiction/#identifier_4_6391.
65  Lustig, 'Syndrome as Symbol', p. 139.
66  Richard Powers, interviewed by Alec Michod, 'The Brain is the Ultimate Storytelling Machine and Consciousness is the Ultimate Story', *The Believer* (February 2007), http://www.believermag.com/issues/200702/?read=interview_powers.
67  The Platte is at the centre of the Central Flyway, a corridor for many types of migratory birds, including species of endangered birds such as the sandhill cranes. See: Gary L. Krapu, 'Sandhill Cranes and the Platte River', in *Gatherings of Angels: Migrating Birds and Their Ecology*, ed. Kenneth P. Able (Ithaca, NY: Cornell University Press, 1999), pp. 103–117.
68  Patrick O'Donnell, *The American Novel Now* (Oxford: Wiley Blackwell, 2010), p. 90.
69  Ibid.
70  Lynne Tillman, *American Genius; a comedy* (New York: Soft Skull Press, 2006), p. 288. All further references will appear in the text as *AGAC*.
71  Eric Dean Rasmussen, 'Tillman's Turbulent Thinking', *electronic book review*, 31:6 (September/October 2010), http://www.electronicbookreview.com/thread/fictionspresent/turbulent.
72  Tillman, *The Madame Realism Complex* (New York: Semiotext(e), 1992), p. 37.
73  Dennett, *Consciousness Explained*, pp. 152, 258.
74  V. S. Ramachandran, *The Tell-Tale Brain: Unlocking the Mystery of Human Nature* (New York: Random House, 2012), p. 291.
75  Lynne Tillman, *No Lease on Life* (New York: Houghton Mifflin Harcourt, 1998), p. 141.
76  Ibid., p. 11.
77  Kasia Boddy, 'Lynne Tillman and the Great American Novel', *electronic book review* (24 July 2011), http://www.electronicbookreview.com/thread/fictionspresent/american.
78  In an interview with Tillman, the poet Geoffrey O'Brien attempted a summary of what he thought *American Genius* was 'about', offering 'a

partial list' of 'dogs, cats, the Tarot, breakfast, religion, chairs, Kafka, Leslie Van Houten and the Manson Family, bleeding, many aspects of American history, and then there's a Zulu phrasebook that comes up periodically'. O'Brien, 'Lynne Tillman', BOMB magazine (Autumn 2006), http://bombsite.com/issues/97/articles/2856.

79  Marilynne Robinson, *Gilead* (New York: Virago, 2004), p. 217.
80  Peter Nicholls, 'Skin Deep: Lynne Tillman's *American Genius; a comedy*', *electronic book review*, fictions present (24 July 2011), http://www.electronicbookreview.com/thread/fictionspresent/skindeep.
81  Ibid.
82  Robinson, *Gilead*, p. 10.
83  Ramachandran and Blakeslee, *Phantoms in the Brain*, p. vii.
84  Ibid.
85  Rosenfield, *The Strange, The Familiar and the Forgotten*, p. 184.
86  Tillman's adoration of Stein is well documented. See: Tillman, 'Reconsidering the Genius of Gertrude Stein', *The New York Times* (27 January 2012), http://www.nytimes.com/2012/01/29/books/review/reconsidering-the-genius-of-gertrude-stein.html?_r=0; Tillman, interviewed by Lydia Davis, Eric Dean Rasmussen and Ron Shavers, 'Uncovered', *electronic book review* (26 March 2011), http://www.electronicbookreview.com/thread/fictionspresent/uncovered; Tillman, 'S is for Stein and Saunders', *What Would Lynne Tillman Do?* (Brooklyn, NY: Red Lemonade, 2014), pp. 278–289.
87  Stein's use of repetition in her writing allowed her to build on one central argument in what she called a 'continuous' narrative present. Composition, she argued, is a way of being continuously present, a 'natural' way of synthesising ideas and linking them together in the same way that the brain would process information. Much like Tillman, Stein wrote multi-clausal discursive sentences that began, ended, and began again. 'In that there was a constant and recurring and beginning', she writes, 'there was a marked direction in the direction of being in the present although naturally I had been accustomed to past present and future, and why, because of the composition forming around me was a prolonged present.' Stein, 'Composition as Explanation', in *A Stein Reader*, ed. Ulla E. Dydo (Evanston, IL: Northwestern University Press, 1993), p. 498.
88  Thomas Mann, *The Magic Mountain* (London: Vintage, 1996), p. 95.
89  Tillman, 'Lynne Tillman', http://bombsite.com/issues/97/articles/2856.
90  Stein, 'Portraits and Repetition', *Lectures in America* (Boston, MA: Beacon, 1957), p. 170.
91  Harding, *Tinkers*, p. 160.
92  Nicholls, 'Skin Deep', http://www.electronicbookreview.com/thread/fictionspresent/skindeep.

93　Robinson, *Gilead*, p. 157.
94　Amy M. King, 'Quietism and Narrative Stillness', *Common Knowledge*, 16:3 (fall 2010), p. 534.
95　Robinson, *Lila* (London: Virago, 2014), p. 220.
96　'Experience is never limited, and it is never complete; it is an immense sensibility, a kind of huge spider-web of the finest silken threads suspended in the chamber of consciousness, and catching every airborne particle in its tissue.' Henry James, 'The Art of Fiction', in his *Partial Portraits* (New York: Haskell House Publishers, 1953), p. 388.

# 5

# The novel of '(dis)quiet'

In August 2011, two strikingly similar debut novels, Teju Cole's *Open City* and Ben Lerner's *Leaving the Atocha Station*, appeared to great acclaim.[1] The narrator of *Open City* is Julius, a Nigerian-German psychiatrist who travels through the boroughs of New York City where he is completing the final year of a fellowship. The narrator of *Leaving the Atocha Station* is Adam Gordon, a white, middle-class poet born and raised in Topeka, Kansas, educated in New York and living in Madrid on a prestigious arts fellowship. Both protagonists are highly educated young professionals in their early thirties whose fictional lives borrow freely from their authors' experiences; both writers tell similar stories by representing the interior life of a solipsistic *flâneur* who walks around a city in order to reflect. In my formulation, both texts are therefore quiet novels not only because the protagonists value reflection but also because they are peripatetic and thus ruminate a philosophical identity that serves as a metaphor for the ways in which the quiet protagonist thinks and, as I argue here, the ways in which quiet prose is written.

This final chapter differs from those that precede it in one significant way: unlike many quiet texts, *Open City* and *Leaving the Atocha Station* are quiet despite their urban setting. On the one hand, both novels meet the criteria for my quiet aesthetic because Julius and Adam's narration fixates on consciousness, recalling, debating and expanding the ideas already 'memorized by [their] brains' so that very little happens in either text that is external to the protagonist's thought processes.[2] Similar to *Gilead*, *Tinkers*, *The Echo Maker* and *American Genius; a comedy*, internal processes drive all narrative action and both novels, as Alexander Hartwiger writes of *Open City*, 'eschew a well-developed plot in favor of contemplative walks'.[3] However, on the other hand, critics and reviewers have noted the loud tenor of Cole and Lerner's prose. Both authors write from the perspective of young, ostensibly sociable narrators who live in and travel to noisy global cities and unlike the protagonists of *Gilead*, *Tinkers* and *The Echo Maker*, Julius and Adam reference topical events and global politics. In this respect, one reviewer's aside seems telling: *Open City*, he writes, is 'a quiet novel that somehow manages to scream'.[4]

There is something aesthetically loud, I argue, about the setting and narrative content of both these quiet texts. In the city, the rattling of transport systems, the beeping of communication technologies and the clamorous sounds of a growing population encroach noisily on an individual's consciousness; this noise often threatens to distract the individual from the acts of reflection that quiet novels prioritise as a way of understanding the present. The presence and production of urban noise further complicates the act of reflection for Julius and Adam because crowded locations make it harder to hide from unwanted sounds, noisy people and, ultimately, from the kind of national event that the quiet of the rural or small town avoids. This chapter therefore returns to the idea that noise is both an actual and ideological phenomenon, which I last explored in Chapter 2. In a review of *Leaving the Atocha Station*, poet Adam Fitzgerald writes that Lerner's novel is 'a thought-bomb in its own (dis)quiet way' precisely because the author represents Adam's quiet and discomforting reactions to 'intensely political' (*LTAS* 44) moments like the second Iraq War and the 2004 bombing of Madrid's Atocha Station.[5] Similarly, Cole contextualises the contemporary New York of *Open City* with details of centuries of American imperialism, alluding to a wide array of philosophical but also political and sociological ideas that articulate and amplify 'forgotten chapter[s] in colonial history' through the lens of cultural theorists such as Walter Benjamin and Roland Barthes.[6] Against what historian Emily Thompson describes as 'the technological crescendo of the modern city', Julius and Adam cultivate, pursue and expand existing states of quiet, acting to 'assimilate [the city's] noise' (*LTAS* 7) into their subjective experience of the present. However, the constant bombardment of urban sound and sensation also threatens the solitude of these quiet characters, continually confronting and thereby testing the limits of a quiet aesthetic as Cole and Lerner accentuate the relative economic and social advantages that cocoon their quiet protagonists.[7]

This final chapter proceeds as follows. First, I examine historical and cultural notions of urban noise and, second, ask how Cole and Lerner integrate the din of the city into the body of their quiet texts. In this, I return to questions posed at the very beginning of this study to ask what kinds of information can be read as quiet and what exactly determines a novel's volume. The third and fourth sections of this chapter apply the terms of my quiet aesthetic to close readings of *Open City* and *Leaving the Atocha Station* with brief consideration of Cole's recently republished novella, *Every Day is for the Thief* (2007; 2014), and Lerner's second novel, *10:04* (2014). Building on the four quiet criteria prioritised throughout this book, I argue that all four texts privilege the depiction of quiet characters, locations and interior life so that, ultimately, very little happens in the body of the narrative that might outwardly be perceived as action.

A fifth and final section concludes by reflecting on the relationship between the principles of my quiet aesthetic, the novel form and the act of walking. Cole and Lerner seem ambivalent, at best, about the novel's role as a vehicle for social and political commentary and neither author self-identifies as a novelist. Both also write in what Daniel Katz characterises as an autofictional mode 'so venerable as to be a post-modern cliché'; one that 'pointedly blur[s] the lines between autobiography or memoir on the one hand and fiction on the other' as well as eliding traditional distinctions between fiction and non-fiction, the novel and criticism and, in Lerner's case, prose and poetry.[8] Keeping the quiet contingency of *American Genius* very much in mind, I argue that it is precisely this elision that confirms the quiet status of *Open City* and *Leaving the Atocha Station*. Both novels challenge long-standing cultural assumptions about the relationship between author and text, a novel's plot and its political 'purpose' and, as I contend throughout, the cultural status of quiet and noisy narratives. Both of the quiet novels discussed in this chapter also depict contemporary protagonists who hear but choose not to fully engage with the noise of the world and whose decision *not* to speak risks silencing other citizens who are already marginalised and disenfranchised. It is in this way that I conclude this study with a consideration of the limits of a quiet aesthetic, introducing contemporary debates about who has access to quiet spaces and who has the right *not* to speak without sacrificing their identity.

## Noise and the urban

The curious '(dis)quiet' of *Open City* and *Leaving the Atocha Station* returns us to cultural notions of noise, specifically to the association of noise with urban environments. The *OED* defines noise as a 'disturbance' and an 'unwanted' variety of sound; physicists frame it as any sound that is 'out of place'; communications theorist David Hendy describes historical attitudes to noise as 'usually something unwanted, inappropriate, interfering, distracting, irritating.'[9] What is most interesting about noise is its subjective nature. Any definition of noise as 'unwanted' must acknowledge that its classification will vary not only between listening subjects but also within a single subject. The participants of a lively conversation, for instance, will find its noise desirable but any nearby non-participants may find the same noise offensive. The extent to which the listener deems the conversation 'out of place' will also depend on a number of contextual factors including time (instance and duration), space (distance between listener and speaker), affect (the listener's mood), content (the speaker's tone and subject matter) and action (the listener's activity during the conversation).[10]

Indeed, sound studies defines the production of all sound as an intensely subjective and 'public event' that moves 'from a single source and immediately arrives at multiple destinations.'[11] Noise is therefore 'intensely relational' and as Brandon LaBelle suggests to make noise 'is to live in more than one head, beyond an individual mind' so that listening becomes 'a form of participation in the sharing of a sound event, however banal.'[12] Here LaBelle touches on an aspect of sound studies famously noted by Roland Barthes who observes in his essay 'Listening' (1985) that the process of hearing is 'a physiological phenomenon' while the process of listening is 'a psychological act' in which consciousness shifts attention to that noise and internalises it.[13] There is an intimacy, then, both to the subjective definition of noise and to the act of listening when it is understood both as the internalisation of an externally produced sound and as a psychological or consciousness-based event in which interior life is altered or disturbed.

Ideologically, and as noted throughout this book, noise is also widely perceived as a symptom of America's consumer society and critics configure the noise of consumerism as both a real and symbolic threat to the individual's state of mind. David Foster Wallace reflects this notion in his introduction to *The Best American Essays 2007* when he praises contributors who practice 'a kind of trenchant reflection that becomes both numbing and euphoric, a kind of Total Noise that's also the sound of our U.S. culture right now'.[14] Similarly, Don DeLillo's 1985 novel, *White Noise*, which I discussed briefly in Chapter 2, describes a rampant consumerism that is 'awash with noise' in America, in 'the jangle and skid of carts, the loudspeaker and coffee-making machines, the cries of children', and even in 'a dull and locatable roar' emitted by industry.[15] Many Marxist critics conceive of the city's volume as a symbol and symptom of late capitalism: Fredric Jameson argues that advertisements are particularly 'noisy commodities' that speak over and suppress the individual's capacity for independent thought.[16] Cultural critics often regard noise similarly; they argue that noise is not only externally and literally dissonant but also an ideological and figurative threat that encroaches on spaces of quiet and disrupts mental processes. So, while noise is commonly viewed as a source of aural discomfort, popular use of the noun rarely describes sound alone and many writers use the term synesthetically, as a description of an image or piece of writing that pulls the mind in multiple directions by disrupting, interrupting, and distracting the production of meaning.

There is a creative flipside to the dissonance of late capitalism, which elevates noise as both an object of study and aesthetic of narrative. As economist Jacques Attali argues, noise can also be commandeered to disrupt social processes: '[t]o make noise', he suggests, 'is to interrupt a transmission, to disconnect, to kill'.[17] If noise disrupts the individual's capacity for reflection, it also challenges continuity and presents an opportunity to interrupt the narrative trajectory of capitalism. Indeed, as I argue throughout this book, the dual nature of noise presents any author wishing to represent their contemporary moment with a dilemma. An excess of 'unwanted' sounds may be toxic and a symptom of the overstimulation common to late capitalism but it also holds the potential to upset capitalist narratives, for the author to be heard above the din of society and to 'interrupt the signal' of the establishment. The dichotomy introduced in my discussion of 11 September 2001 therefore remains important to the argument advanced here. Should the author represent society's noise, reproducing and extending the 'unwanted' sounds of the world and contributing their own voice to the din of the contemporary? Or, as I suggest of quiet novels, should authors distance themselves from the loudspeakers, industrial machines and transport systems that Wallace, DeLillo and many contemporary writers associate with modern life and otherwise represent the quiet spaces required for sustained reflection, reading and writing?

This dilemma is no more obvious than in literary representations of the city. As the apex of capitalism, the city has always been characterised as noisy. It is a 'reservoir of noise' to historian Hillel Schwartz and 'pure noise' to art historian Yves-Alain Bois who, much like Jacques Attali, suggests that urban environments produce the kind of sounds that exceed the 'transmission of the message'.[18] Literary critics have also analysed the reproduction of urban soundscapes in a variety of fictions. The 'social shared aspects' of the city's 'acoustic environment' form the basis of Kate Flint's reading of 'modernist noise' in Virginia Woolf while Niall Martin's 2015 study of Iain Sinclair characterises the novelist's London-based work as 'noisy' because it so regularly explores 'the tensions between order and disorder [...] that characterize the global city'.[19] Despite the regularity with which critics associate noise with the city, urban studies and sonic studies rarely overlap. Geographer Torsten Wissman argues that urban studies remains concerned with 'the visual element of the city' and that the field is constrained by what Karin Bijsterveld calls the 'visual regime of Western culture'.[20] Here, Bijsterveld states what many sound historians have long observed: that 'in the West's hierarchy of the senses, the eye dominates the ear' because, she adds, 'our culture is deadly afraid of silence and of the passiveness associated with the absence of sound.'[21]

To my mind, Bijsterveld's comments affirm the value of reading for quiet in urban environments while also addressing the fundamental subjectivity of noise. The sounds of the city have the potential to reaffirm our humanity, relationality to others and ongoing relevance to the contemporary world, comforting those who fear silence, the cessation of action and, by not all that dramatic an extension, the ultimate quiet of death. Yet city environments also host a clash of sounds that are more likely to be 'unwanted' or 'unnecessary' noise by their sheer proximity and frequency. The study of sound, as Schwartz suggests, is therefore riddled by 'contrary presumptions about the widening presence or progressive absence of noise' because the lived, sonic environment of the city is so rarely studied.[22] As a result, there is no tacit agreement about whether urban spaces are growing louder, if urbanisation promotes the regulation of noise or if, in fact, urban environments are a 'relentless pandemonium' of sound and sensation that shatter all likelihood of quiet and tranquil space.[23]

## The quiet *flâneur*

Although diagnoses of societal 'pandemonium' are nothing new, a general fear of and distress at urban noise is firmly rooted in the experience of modernity. In her essay on Woolf, Kate Flint suggests that there have always been complaints about noise but that the character of these complaints began to change at the beginning of the twentieth century when '[t]he human and animal cacophony of the streets gave way to a mechanic roar and hum, the product, above all, of the internal combustion engine on the ground and – more intermittently – the drone and throb of the aeroplane in the sky above.'[24] Likewise, in her study of twentieth-century technology and 'public problems' of noise in America and Europe, Karin Bijsterveld claims that noise complaints often link the unnecessary production of sound with manmade and markedly 'unnatural' objects, especially those made by 'new technologies' that seem to threaten the individual's peace of mind with their mechanised and persistent sounds.[25]

Put simply, industrial and technological noises appear to be louder and more threatening than the sounds common to preindustrial environments. The claustrophobic environment of the city makes this threat more obvious. In 'The Metropolis and Mental Life' (1903), sociologist Georg Simmel famously wrote about the modern city's constant war on interior life, which forces the individual to act as 'a mere cog in an enormous organisation of things' in an attempt to transform the individual's subjective experience into 'a purely objective life'.[26] Simmel argues that this constant stimulation makes the urban dweller less sensitive and increasingly 'blasé' to new experiences and, notably, sounds; a notion he demonstrates through comparison of the distracted 'metropolitan child' to 'the children of quieter and less changeable milieus.'[27] Simmel's pupil Walter Benjamin also tried to capture the ways in which the sensory experience of modern city life changed in the first half of the twentieth century. In 'Some Motifs in Baudelaire' (1939), Benjamin describes moving through the traffic of a city as 'a series of shocks and collisions' that stimulate 'nervous impulses' to flow through the individual 'like the energy from a battery'.[28]

Important to any discussion of Cole and Lerner's peripatetic narrators, Benjamin was interested in how the 'shocks and collisions' of the city impacted the *flâneur*, the quintessential modern spectator who is at once an investigator of the city and a sign of the alienation imposed on the individual by capitalism. The *flâneur* was already a figure of nostalgia for Benjamin, although the act of walking remained 'a protest against the tempo of the crowd' whose joy in collective experience was almost completely negated by society.[29] By the 1930s, Poe's short story 'The Man of the Crowd' (1840), in which the quiet detachment of the aimless eponymous 'Man' so troubles the story's anxious narrator, seemed antiquated to Benjamin as if any genuine experience of *flânerie* had been forced out of existence by the 'shocks and collisions' of a traffic system that denied, amongst other things, the ability to loaf. The modern city was therefore different from the crowded but creative metropolises envisioned by earlier authors like Charles Baudelaire and, in the American tradition, Walt Whitman. These authors consider the *flâneur* to be both a literary device and a role available to the modern artist who could observe the physiognomy of the crowd but remain unobserved in the city's anonymous public spaces. In 'The Painter of Modern Life' (1863), Baudelaire suggests that the ability 'to merge with the crowd' is a primary object of the artist who should be bored by the private, restrictive spaces of domestic life and otherwise 'set up house in the heart of the multitude' to live both as part and apart from the crowd.[30]

The changing city of the 1860s provided a sense of political urgency for many artists. As Marshall Berman argues, Baudelaire and Whitman celebrate the 'personal encounter in the street [...] as a political event' and position the modern city 'as a medium in which personal and political life flow together and become one.'[31] Whitman, in particular, proposed 'physical, mental, and spiritual immersion in the city' in order to face what Catherine Nesci describes as 'the dissonances and degradation of urban life in New York'.[32] If we then read for noise in Whitman, his poetry can be said to observe and document the voices and experiences of others, to provide a louder national frame through which to amplify his own distinctive voice. In 'Song of Myself' (1855), the poet is a man of boundless appetites who listens to and interprets the many and multiple 'sounds of the city' in an attempt to understand many facets of American life, letting 'sounds contribute toward' his own sense of identity by walking through the city streets and listening to others.[33]

The importance of Whitman will become clear in this chapter's discussion of Lerner whose second novel, 10:04, makes frequent reference to the poet and questions whether Whitman's 'loafing' makes leisure 'a condition of poetic receptivity'.[34] The *flâneur* has also been a major preoccupation for scholarship on both Cole and Lerner. In the first essay to link *Open City* and *Leaving the Atocha Station*, Albert Wu and Michelle Kuo question 'the transformative potential of the *flâneur*'s wandering gaze' while subsequent essays by Peter Vermeulen and Alexander Hartwiger argue that Cole's *flâneur*, in particular, points to the limits of a cosmopolitan ideal.[35] To my mind, discussion of these nineteenth-century literary *flâneurs* also confirms the contradictory and fundamentally subjective nature of the noise comprehended within cityscapes. While the urban production of noise often threatens the peace of the individual, for Whitman the city encourages the exploration of the subjective and provides the only soundscape large enough to glimpse the many and varied individuals of the American nation.[36] The *flâneur* of the nineteenth century conceived their leisurely pace as an act of rebellion, one that opposed the accelerating tempo of modernity without entirely divorcing themselves from it. Unlike many quiet protagonists, and important to this chapter's discussion of Julius and Adam, the *flâneur*'s 'rebellion' slows the experience of modernity without removing the individual from the crowd. So, while *flânerie* is undeniably a socially privileged activity, which is clearly limited by gender, race and class, it must still be considered a counter-hegemonic *attempt* to install reflection and, as this chapter demonstrates, quiet at the centre of the urban landscape.

Between Baudelaire and Whitman, Cole and Lerner, public perception of the noise and overstimulation of the city also shifted. No longer thought of in opposition to the tranquillity of rural environments, quiet became associated with the suburbs. A culture of domesticity shaped early suburbanisation, facilitated by the separation of work and home through transport innovations and middle class movement out of the cities; this movement was encouraged not only by the availability of space but also by perceptions of urban disorder and fears about immigration that were deeply connected to issues of class. In sonic terms, the suburban ideal conceived of an urban space that was the spatial expression of bourgeois values: 'a place of quiet, beauty, wealth, and Arcadian delights' to which not everyone would have access.[37] In 1945, geographers Chauncy D. Harris and Edward

L. Ullman outlined the relationship between urban noise and real estate value in their essay 'The Nature of Cities', noting how 'high-class districts are likely to be well-drained, high land and away from nuisances such as noise, odors, smoke, and railroad lines.'[38] Noise thus became an urban 'nuisance' that raised the value of quieter residential areas and, by the end of the 1960s, social scientists underscored the importance of silence and tranquillity as a remedy to the pace of modern life.[39] During the 1970s, US law further reclassified noise as an environmental problem: the Noise Control Act of 1972 initiated a federal programme of regulation to protect 'all Americans' from commercially produced sounds and the Quiet Communities Act of 1978 extended these provisions to investigate noise's implications on public health.[40] A generalised dislike of noise was therefore pathologised: a representative study of noise pollution in Los Angeles County in 1973 notes the many and varied outcomes of noise exposure including but not limited to tinnitus, mental distress, heart disease, gastric and circulatory disorders, neurosis and psychosis.[41] Most shockingly, as the same study claims, the body 'may be absorbing [noise's] effects unconsciously' and many experts suggested that the individual might not be aware of the 'nervous-emotional stress' that noise so quietly creates.[42]

It is particularly important to note how the fraught dichotomy of urban noise and suburban quiet complicates the politics of a quiet aesthetic. In this instance, we might recall the 'lives of quiet desperation' that Thoreau alludes to in *Walden* (1854), or Richard Yates' *Revolutionary Road* (1961), a novel that so harshly critiques the post-war American suburban ideal as an attempt to suppress difference.[43] Yates' protagonists, Frank and April Wheeler, cannot be 'made to fit' the oppressive shackles of suburban life; yet who, Yates writes, 'could be frightened in as wide and bright, as clean and quiet a house as this?'[44] For Yates, and for the anti-noise leagues that proliferated in America and Europe throughout the 1950s, quiet was a valued commodity that allowed its occupants to avoid the threatening noise of existence. The quiet of the post-war suburbs was conceived as a tranquil, tree-lined haven, located far enough from the metropolis that its residents could benefit from industrial 'progress' without suffering the damaging effects of its noise. As hostility to noise grew, the legislative measures designed to protect US citizens therefore did much to attack the use of leaf blowers and little to protect the factory workers at risk of tinnitus, or provide for lower income families who could not afford quiet learning environments for their children.[45] Although the noise of the city has always been conceived as a nuisance and, at least since the 1970s, a pollutant to the body, in the second half of the twentieth century the perceived volume of the city also increased the value of residential areas, thus coding quiet as a prerequisite for middle-class tranquillity.

The noise of the city also retained some vital advocates. Historian Nicolas Kenny suggests that tour brochures often emphasise 'the incessant noise, the brouhaha' of a city because 'the excessive smoke, noise, and dust' that workers are forced to endure contrarily assures visitors that they have entered a 'great metropolis'.[46] The idea that a city's noise might attract tourists suggests two things: first, that noise, like quiet, is only favoured when it is chosen and, second, that tourists can be attracted to and ultimately undisturbed by urban noise because they retain the ability to leave. Economic and social privilege therefore decides whether the individual enjoys or endures the noise of the urban; just as the *flâneur*, arguably a kind of tourist, moves in and out of the city streets with a freedom that few can afford. Turning to the novels with which this chapter is concerned, the protagonists of *Open City* and *Leaving the Atocha Station* consider the noise of the city to be an antidote to the artificial and often suppressive quiet that they associate with their suburban childhoods in Lagos and Topeka, respectively. Both, however, shy away from the noise of others and voice a deep-seated discomfort with the stories they hear from urban residents of different nationalities, races, classes and genders. The remainder of this chapter therefore analyses how Cole and Lerner negotiate a mode of urban interiority, considering the practical and ethical limitations of maintaining a quiet life and, even, a quiet aesthetic through the perspective of protagonists whose social and economic advantages grant them rare moments of peace and quiet within the noise of city soundscapes.

## *Open City*

Teju Cole's debut novel *Open City* addresses the tension not only between the city and its noise but also between the resident and the tourist, the citizen and the immigrant. Like many quiet fictions, the novel is spatially restricted but intellectually ambitious. It concerns Julius, a Nigerian-German immigrant who walks around New York and, briefly, Brussels to break the monotony of his long days as a resident in psychiatry. Narrative action proceeds quietly; that is to say, it proceeds internally. On his long walks around the city, Julius reflects on his childhood in Nigeria, the death of his father, estrangement from his mother and a recent failed relationship. He also meets a variety of strangers, many of them immigrants who narrate their personal histories to the often-silent doctor. These strangers include Saidu, a Liberian detainee imprisoned in a facility in Queens whom Julius visits with his ex-girlfriend; Farouq, a Moroccan émigré and former graduate student whose expulsion from a Belgian university leaves him manning an Internet café in Brussels; and an unnamed Haitian 'bootblack' at Penn Station who claims, somewhat implausibly, to remember the Haitian Revolution of 1791–1804.

In the terms defined by this study, Julius is a quiet narrator who encounters the noise of the city through his walks and hears about the loudness of experience through other people's stories. As a narrator, and in common with quiet protagonists like the Reverend Ames, Helen and Dr Weber, Julius often thinks about social and critical theory, art, music and philosophy. In the opening pages alone, Julius recalls how he spent the fall of 2006 flitting 'from book to book: Barthes' *Camera Lucida*, Peter Altenberg's *Telegrams of the Soul*, Tahar Ben Jelloun's *The Last Friend*, among others' (*OC* 5). The narrator of *Open City* is an introvert and a book lover who reads seriously and for long periods but notably leaves the content of his reading unchallenged. It is not until Julius meets Farouq in Brussels that he interrogates the content of Jelloun's work, when the latter describes Jelloun's fiction as 'mythmaking' (*OC* 103) and compromised by an orientalism that undermines its social project. During this exchange, Julius admits internally that he admires Jelloun but offers little spoken defence of the author, outwardly yielding to Farouq's idea that a more 'authentic fiction' (*OC* 104) might exist in Moroccan writers from less privileged backgrounds. This exchange indicates a wider pacifism that resurfaces to greater effect at the text's climax and hints, crucially, at the limits of a kind of 'solitary liberalism' that James Wood identifies in Julius.[47] Although his reading leaves him well informed, and despite his ability to socialise with the young and politically engaged, Julius is disinclined to speak out or share personal details about himself, hinting from the very beginning of *Open City* at some of the limitations of a life so internally and quietly lived.

As a quiet protagonist, Julius is particularly sensitive to the geographical, cultural and historical soundscape of New York City, a location that Peter Brooker calls 'the city of modernity' because of its 'unprecedented pace of change'.[48] Fictive representations of New York often replicate and extend the noise that the city epitomises: contemporary responses to '9/11', for instance, exemplify the noisy aesthetic of contemporary fiction not only because of their authors' reliance on the catastrophic 'event' as a temporal structure but also because New York is so regularly characterised as a loud location. In *Falling Man*, DeLillo describes New York as 'loud and blunt' in character, a cornucopia of sounds that compound the experience of trauma.[49] Similarly, in *The Zero*, Jess Walter depicts the constant 'hum of the city' that precedes the living memory of his protagonist, Remy, and endures long after 2001.[50] Such renderings suggest a particularity to the noise of New York, which makes its events seem louder than those that occur in other city spaces and, in this instance, conceived of '9/11' as a threat to the volume of America's loudest metropolis.

In *Open City*, Cole relates the sounds of the city to the palimpsestic qualities of New York, where the events of 11 September 2001 are neither pressing nor prioritised. Time has lessened the howling noise of 'Ground Zero' so that the site is no longer an open wound: the road leading up to the site is so 'quiet' and 'narrow' that Julius feels as if the 'entire world had fallen away' (*OC* 52). This means that even when Julius stands regarding the site, it is easy for him to put thoughts of the event aside: 'I saw to my right, about a block north of where I stood, a great empty space. I immediately thought of the obvious but, equally quickly, put the idea out of my mind.' Noting the 'great empty space' where the towers once stood, Cole draws a longer comparison to the spaces that the initial construction of the World Trade Center displaced and Julius describes the communities that were 'written, erased, rewritten' to make way for the towers in the 1970s. Julius' mind integrates the events of '9/11' into the city's network of traumatic experience so that it no longer stands out as a loud or noisy device that diverts all attention to its traumatic aftermath. Similar to the ways in which cognitive science shows consciousness to constantly write over itself, New York then appears to be a system that can amalgamate the events of its past and rewrite them into its present. The quiet of Cole's prose places the physical absence of the World Trade Center in a longer continuum of trauma and loss, writing and rewriting, city planning and demolition that evades the contingency and rupture of the event.

Through Julius' invocations of *flânerie*, Cole also maps the dynamic variations of a cityscape where sounds permeate even the quietest spaces. Julius' scholarly interests represent one way of quietening the protagonist's engagement with the city's soundscape; Julius' interest in music represents another, one that enhances his apprehension of the city's symphonic qualities. Watching the New York Marathon, for example, Julius describes the crescendo of the cheering crowd as '[t]he noise outside rose again, and ebbed' (*OC* 12) and soon after he remarks that record stores 'should be silent spaces' (*OC* 16) to allow the consumer to mentally conceive of the music he is about to buy. Julius here recalls Barthes' suggestion that listening is a 'psychological act', characterising his comprehension of music as a mental process that can only occur when the mind is clear. Yet the sounds of the city constantly threaten Julius' concentration by intermingling in his mind, even when he is alone. As he sits in his room, the 'disembodied voices' of the radio mingle with the book he is reading aloud and an old memory, of the sound of violins, is drawn into the narrative present filling his mind with music but protecting him from the 'incessant loudness' (*OC* 6) of the city. In this moment, it is clear why Julius prefers quiet spaces: they allow him to distinguish the source and proximity of each sound and enable a quiet and focused appreciation of the present through lengthy contemplation of the past. If sound studies locates the power of noise in its disruptive potential, as an 'inharmonious', 'dissonant' and 'disorderly' aggregate of sounds, it is also clear why urban environments are more difficult to represent through a quiet aesthetic.[51] Sound artist Salomé Voegelin describes the contemporary metropolis as a 'sonic monstrosity' that continually overrides the 'little sounds' of contemporary experience.[52] Similarly, living deep within the city, in Manhattan's Morningside Heights, Julius attempts to acknowledge the contribution of every note to a far larger and dissonant sound effect that conflicts with his inner wish for and cultivation of quiet.

A similar discord can be read in the critical reception of the novel. On publication, reviewers praised *Open City* for its expansive cultural references and diverse representation of contemporary city life, but literary critics have since emphasised Cole's self-conscious presentation of a 'bland' cosmopolitanism that they read in *Open City*'s invocation of a 'post-national space'.[53] I would argue that the failed cosmopolitanism many critics read in *Open City* is also inextricable from the quiet spaces that Julius occupies. That is, what Madhu Krishnan calls

# The novel of '(dis)quiet' 165

the 'bland diversity' of cosmopolitanism might equally describe the quiet havens of a city: the libraries, art galleries and museums that Julius and Adam frequent as a respite from the urban soundscape. *Open City* also draws attention to the ways in which quiet spaces exclude the dissonance of global cities and their displaced people. On an unplanned visit to the American Folk Art Museum, an exhibition of the 'artists of stillness' John Brewster and Johann Vermeer leads Julius to reflect on what he calls the 'silent transaction' (*OC* 38) that occurs between artist and subject.[54] Noting how deafness afflicted Brewster throughout his life, Julius believes the artist's enforced silence is a key element of his creativity. Deafness excluded Brewster from the experience of the crowd and, in Julius' formulation, shifted his attention to the minutiae of the everyday, imbuing his images 'with what that long silence had taught him: concentration, the suspension of time, an unobtrusive wit' (*OC* 39). Importantly, Brewster's paintings affect Julius aurally and, therefore, synesthetically: standing before them, his 'mind quiet' (*OC* 38), Julius recalls the 'total ... quietness' of the artist's life, notes the 'quiet' of Brewster's painted figures and the 'silent' gallery in which he stands. In this passage, he even likens the ability of quiet spaces to facilitate the 'suspension of time' to the calm he perceives in Brewster's paintings, celebrating both the gallery space and its featured artists as facilitators of mental stillness.

The narrative quiet of *Open City* is particularly significant in this moment because of its relationship to temporality which I discussed at length in Chapter 2. Standing before the paintings, Julius becomes so lost in thought that time appears to alter around him: 'I lost all track of time before these images, fell deep into their world, as if all the time between them and me had somehow vanished' (*OC* 40). The experience is disorientating for Julius and the reader sees the narrator retreat into himself as the distance between the moment of the painting's creation and Julius' present moment in 2006 seems to disappear. This temporal shift recalls Wai Chee Dimock's articulation of 'deep time' and her attempts to write a history of American literature that challenges the linear abstractions of the mechanical clock. Conceiving history through 'loops of relations', Dimock argues for an ontology of time that could work outside of a standard nation-based model and that is capable of writing history, as Helen also wishes in *American Genius*, at 'a slower tempo, which sometimes almost borders on the motionless.'[55] In *Open City*, Cole contemplates how art, too, might represent a slower and ultimately longer history of its present moment, or of our present experience of it. Standing in the gallery, away from the noise of the city, Julius feels that Brewster's enforced engagement with silence is enviable for the 'suspension of time' that it allows the artist. Freed from the noise of his present time, he then believes that Brewster can communicate something universal that depicts the individual's experience of time in broader patterns than linearity.

This 'suspension of time' is, however, temporary and Julius' connection to a sense of 'deep time' that runs beyond his present moment ends as soon as he leaves the gallery. Coming back to the noise of reality is uncomfortable for Cole's protagonist: he stumbles onto Sixth Avenue where the noise of the traffic and an unexpected downpour contrast so 'violently' (*OC* 39) with the quiet of the gallery that he is disorientated, 'shouting' at a pedestrian and unable to speak to the driver whose cab he darts into. The moment of reflection Julius experiences in the gallery is followed by two louder moments of confrontation: first with the pedestrian and second with the driver who takes offence at Julius' silence because of what he considers to be their shared racial identity ('I'm African just like you'). The cab ride is marked by a hostile silence and what Julius describes as the 'anger of a shattered repose', a period of sonic discord that is permeated and compounded by the noise of 'people arguing loudly' on the radio.

It is here, in the anger of Julius' 'shattered repose', that the novel's quiet aesthetic connects most directly with the failed or 'negative' cosmopolitanism identified by Krishnan, Wu and Kuo, and Hartwiger. For Peter Vermeulen, *Open City* also interrogates rather than celebrates 'a literary cosmopolitanism' so that 'even if the novel is thoroughly occupied with the question of how aesthetic form can contribute to the furthering of cosmopolitan understanding, it ends up as a catalogue of failed attempts to forge intercultural connections by artistic means'.[56] That is, while the novel constructs what Hartwiger describes as 'romanticized ideas of connectedness' through Julius' deep connection with art, the profound sense of disconnect between the states of quiet that Cole's protagonist favours and the lived dissonance of New York City undermines quiet's use as a mode of engagement with the contemporary world.[57] A week after his visit to the Folk Art Museum, a 'dark-skinned' man (*OC* 49) named Kenneth approaches Julius in a bar; he is a security guard from the Museum whom Julius doesn't recognise. Unperturbed by his apparent invisibility, the guard recounts the story of his immigration from Barbuda, a place that he claims no American has heard of.

The encounter annoys Julius, who promptly cuts him off: 'I thought of the cabdriver who had driven me home from the American Folk Art Museum – hey, I'm African just like you. Kenneth was making a similar claim' (*OC* 50–51). In this instance, the memory of his almost transcendent experience at the museum amplifies Julius' failure to connect. His 'quiet' experience in front of Vermeer's painting leads to three failed exchanges – with the pedestrian, the cabdriver and the security guard – all three of which ultimately fail because of Julius' hostility and his unwillingness to break from that moment of contemplation. Importantly, these encounters also highlight the marginalisation of black faces in quiet spaces as well as Julius' feelings of resentment at the idea of a global African 'brotherhood'.[58] The oscillation between quiet and noisy spaces hints at the racial and economic exclusivity of quiet and Julius' inability to connect with the sounds of others reveals the dominance of the Western gaze in the valorisation of reflection.

A similar self-consciousness about the production, interpretation and availability of literary texts runs throughout Cole's fiction. His novella, *Every Day is for the Thief*, foregrounds an unnamed protagonist's search for quiet and contemplative spaces when he returns to Lagos after several years' absence.[59] Cole's protagonist bears a striking resemblance to Julius in *Open City*: he recalls his time at military school, his estrangement from his European mother, the death of his father at a young age and his work as a psychiatrist in New York. Just as *Open City* focuses on the streets of New York City, so the protagonist's journey on foot in *Every Day is for the Thief* intersects the story he tells about Lagos' inhabitants, relating the appeal of the urban landscape to a need in the protagonist to comprehend the fullness or noisiness of society in a Whitmanesque contemplation of multiple voices and stories. Like Whitman, Cole writes about the crowds in the markets of Lagos as the 'essence of the city' and, through the movement of a *flâneur*, notes how the crowd breaks the pattern of solipsism that otherwise threatens to divorce his introverted protagonist from the wider world. Returning to Lagos during a period of economic transition, the city fascinates the narrator as the 'strange, familiar environment' of his childhood, 'alive with possibility and with danger' because, as a resident of America, he is out of step with the noise of his hometown.[60] 'I am daydreaming at the market', he says, 'making myself a target' (*EDTT* 52), noting how dangerous the city can be when the tourist is lost in contemplation.

In *Every Day is for the Thief*, the volume of the urban crowd is therefore shown to be culturally specific, dependent on the economic conditions under which citizens draw into or away from the collective. In Lagos, noise is everywhere; in the crowded city streets but equally in the suburban houses 'filled with din' (*EDTT* 55) by appliances, electricity generators and the noise of nearby neighbours. Quiet, then, is a rare commodity and Cole laments the link between the noisy lives of Lagos and the quiet required to produce art, noting a 'disconnect between the wealth of stories available and the rarity of creative refuge' (*EDTT* 58). The novella ends when the narrator returns to New York, where he 'alone wander[s] with no particular aim' (*EDTT* 125), foreshadowing Julius' aimless walks in *Open City*. Read together, both texts attend to a dichotomy that I return to in this chapter's final section: the idealisation of quiet as a condition for literary production and the pull of society's noise as a source of inspiration for both the tourist and the literary *flâneur*.

### *Leaving the Atocha Station*

In contrast to Cole's immigrant narrator, *Leaving the Atocha Station* charts the temporary emigration of Adam Gordon, an American poet living in Madrid on an arts fellowship. Adam claims to be writing 'a long and research-driven poem, whatever that might mean' (*LTAS* 94) about the Spanish Civil War. In reality, he does everything to avoid his 'research' and 'the Foundation' that funds him; reading Lorca, scanning *The New York Times* online, smoking weed and attending parties with local artists who often try to discuss politics with their reluctant American guest. While based in Madrid, Adam also travels, first to Granada and then to Barcelona and towards the end of the novel he witnesses the aftermath of the 11-M commuter-train bombings at Madrid's Atocha Station on 11 March 2004. The novel's title therefore references the 2004 bombings while paying more direct homage to John Ashbery, the 'only' poet Adam who describes as 'major' (*LTAS* 72). In an act of naming that Daniel Katz calls 'ontological duplication', Lerner draws on the famously disjunctive structure of Ashbery's 1962 poem to quietly reimagine contemporary Madrid in a prose style that aims for 'the feel of thinking in the absence of thoughts' (*LTAS* 91).[61] The Atocha Station bombings are only significant, that is, because of their noted lack of significance in Adam's quest for

Ashbery's 'mediacy' (*LTAS* 91). As Katz observes, 'in Lerner's reading it is Ashbery himself who most forcefully opens the way to a literature which does something other than refer to things, to be "about" them' and *Leaving the Atocha Station* enacts a quiet aesthetic that is 'about' nothing more concrete than the conceptual frameworks that concern Adam as a researcher and poet.[62]

In keeping with the aesthetic examined in this study, *Leaving the Atocha Station* privileges meditation, reflection and quiet as engines of fiction to diminish the role of event, contingency, trauma and crisis in the invocation of the narrative present. Yet despite his preference for quiet spaces and pastimes, the communicative potential of noise fascinates Adam. Everything about Madrid is a source of overstimulation for the poet: the lights are 'intensely bright' and its sounds are 'intensely loud' (*LTAS* 134). As a writer, Adam is particularly interested in the aesthetic qualities of noise and during a poetry reading he listens as the respectful quiet of the audience slowly develops into applause, noting that the volume of the clapping is only ever 'what I *experience* as unusually loud' (*LTAS* 51, emphasis my own). In this phrase, volume is an entirely subjective measurement and, like Julius' summation of solitude and the 'subtle shift of air pressure' (*OC* 27) that he believes marks hushed environments, the reception of noise reflects more about the listener than it does about its producer. Like Julius, too, Adam describes his interest in noise as a process of composition and when he overhears a fight at a friend's house, he takes notes:

> I became fascinated with this phenomenon of hearing loud voices at a distance, in trying to account for how I knew they were loud when I could barely hear them, something about their shape or shapeliness, or the way they filtered through the walls, and I reached for my notebook to write this down. (*LTAS* 57)

Adam attributes an aesthetic quality to the voices he overhears in which the timbre of the shouts is expressed by something other than volume alone. Fascinated by the difference between the sound as it is created and the effect it has on the listener, Adam notes how the wall acts as an intermediary filter and how he, the poet, is unable to express what exactly facilitates his ability to recognise the volume of the shouts. Of course, Adam's distance from the sound is also a key factor in his favourable experience of it. As I discussed in the opening sections of this chapter, overheard sound is often classed as noise when the sounds are new and disruptive; as Karin Bijsterveld suggests, it is 'the newness of particular sounds' that draws the attention and inspection of the neighbour-listener who may then define the sound as 'unwanted' and classify it as noise.[63] It is significant, then, that when Adam overhears the argument he is a visitor to the house, finding himself inspired and able to note how loud voices alter the distribution of ideas within a phrase, providing a different 'shape' to the linguistic production of meaning without finding that those same sounds disturb his creative process.

Indeed, physical and emotional distances are determining factors in Adam's ability to process the noise of the urban and maintain a quiet life. Although the noise of Madrid fascinates the poet, Lerner's novel embeds his fascination in a quiet prose that reflects on the difficulties of representing noise in the body of the text. In this way, the bombings at Madrid's Atocha Station are one of the novel's crucial narrative events precisely because they highlight two difficulties: first, of connecting the literary with the writer's political or historical moment and, second, of writing about noisy events in quiet fiction. Much like Julius' residency in *Open City*, Adam's fellowship is marked by a profound sense of disconnect from the people, places and events around him, which Lerner evokes through descriptions of Adam's dispassionate love affairs, doubts over his obviously fluent command of Spanish and claims that he holds only 'a vaguely anthropological interest' (*LTAS* 18) in the history of Spain that he has been paid to research. Even after the attacks, as Adam's friends rush to protest, faced with watching 'history in the making' (*LTAS* 129), the poet removes himself from the crowd and returns home alone. 'When history came alive', he later complains with self-satisfied self-loathing, 'I was sleeping in the Ritz' (*LTAS* 158).

Every muted experience of Adam's further questions whether a truly unmediated and 'authentic' experience of the present is possible and, as in *Open City*, Lerner's text self-consciously reflects on the political and ethical uses of literature. Cursorily structured around the five stages of his project, Adam spends the 'first phase' of *Leaving the Atocha Station* looking at paintings in the Prado art museum and comparing other people's '*profound experience*' (*LTAS* 8) of art to his notable lack of affect. To Günter Leypoldt, these passages are an attempt by both the author and his character 'to distinguish between primary and secondary reactions to literary artefacts'.[64] Adam attempts to not only distinguish between 'real' and 'fake' emotions but to gesture towards a third, more performative category in which the emotional reaction is proxy for 'something else' that the feeling subject neither knows nor recognises. In this instance, it might also be claimed that Adam's observations of supposedly '*profound*' experiences replace the novel's plot and in lieu of narrative action, the quiet engine of Lerner's fiction is Adam's meditation on the relationship between artificiality, performativity and the difficulty of linking art with the lived 'reality' of the present. Much unlike Julius, then, whose visit to the American Folk Art Museum affects and disorientates his sense of self, Adam is either unable or unwilling to believe in art's connectivity despite his noted success as a poet.

Here, it is necessary to draw further similarities between Adam and Lerner, whose recent work of criticism, *The Hatred of Poetry* (2016), typifies Adam's antipathy to his profession.[65] Lerner was already an established poet when Granta published *Leaving the Atocha Station* in 2011 to widespread critical acclaim. An unusual novel for distribution by a major publishing house, favourable reviews by Jonathan Franzen, Paul Auster, James Meek and the (unknowing) champion of quiet fictions, James Wood, predicated its critical popularity. In his recommendation, Franzen suggests that *Leaving the Atocha Station* is the kind of novel 'faulted' by non-Americans 'for its insularity and self-involvement'.[66] Wood, too, celebrates Lerner's fiction for its lofty ambitions rather than its facile premise. It is a novel, Wood claims, that attempts 'to capture something that most conventional novels, with their cumbersome caravans of plot and scene and "conflict," fail to do: the drift of thought, the unmomentous passage of undramatic life.'[67] *Leaving the Atocha Station* is quiet, then, by both Franzen's and Wood's approximations and yet praise for Lerner often centres on his portrayal of an anxious and fragile 'millennial' masculinity rather than on the quiet aesthetic of his prose. In the opening to *How Literature Saved My Life* (2013), David Shields claims to be 'obsessed with [Ben Lerner] as my doppelgänger of the next generation, my aesthetic spawn', describing their shared 'agony' over the gulf between 'language' and 'experience' and a 'detachment from our own emotions' that typifies life under and perhaps after postmodernism.[68] Similarly, in an essay on the 'death of silence' in Lerner's second novel, *10:04*, Tom Evans proclaims the author to be the natural inheritor to Franzen and, more surprisingly, James Joyce, lauding *10:04* as 'the most (quietly) revolutionary modernist novel I have read' and praising Lerner's skill in capturing the 'passive gaze' inherent to twenty-first-century American life.[69]

What could be described as a gendered and even narcissistic identification between these male reviewers, Ben Lerner and his semi-autobiographical characters might more charitably confirm the slippage between quiet protagonists, readers and writers.[70] The 'unmomentous passage of undramatic life' for which James Wood commends *Leaving the Atocha Station* is prevalent not only in our cultural sense of the everyday but specifically in the daily routine of the writer. Both Adam and Julius, not to mention Ames, Helen and Dr Weber, are quiet in the ways that their authors also tend to be. For instance, Adam often narrates the processes of reading and writing in which, ordinarily, nothing really happens: 'I smoked and listened to the rain on the roof and turned the pages and smelled the wet stone smell' (*LTAS* 4). Later in the novel, Adam also acknowledges that the quiet of the world he inhabits, hiding from the rain in his flat or reading Tolstoy by himself, is 'impossible to narrate' (*LTAS* 63). The self-consciousness of his admission suggests to readers that *Leaving the Atocha Station* is the result of Adam's contemplations, that Adam and Lerner are one and the same and that the book they are reading is being created within the text. In a review of Caleb Crain's similarly quiet debut novel *Necessary Errors* (2013), Wood contends that novels written about and by a 'young, bookish protagonist' typically lead the reader to assume that the novel they are reading is a product of the protagonist: 'In the bildungsroman, more often than not, it is understood that the *Bildung* is building to the *Roman*.'[71] Whether or not the (non-) events narrated in *Leaving the Atocha Station* led to the creation of the text we are reading, the quiet characters and environments presented in Lerner's and, to a lesser extent, Cole's fiction refer to the circularity of their creation. Like the character of Marcel in Proust's *À la recherche du temps perdu* (1913–1927), Lerner earns the reader's interest in a plotless narrative by 'admitting the artificiality of fiction, like the conjuror revealing the secret of his trick'.[72] The allusions to autobiography that structure *Leaving the Atocha Station* are therefore a facilitator of quiet; they admit the unreality of the text because the author refuses to distinguish between diary, memoir, essay and fiction. As a result, quiet is more tangible, more convincing and more available to the reader, first, as a mode of reading and, second, as a way of engaging with the noisy contemporary world that exists around and beyond the quiet habits of the reader, the author and their protagonist.

The similarities between the quiet protagonist and many critics therefore plays a role in the wider popularity of quiet texts. Lerner's second novel, *10:04*, experienced even greater acclaim than his first; the text follows an unnamed protagonist on his walks around New York City, where the likeness between Lerner and his protagonist is even more acute. The novel begins at a meal to celebrate the protagonist's advance for his second novel, makes frequent reference to the unexpected success of his 'unconventional but really well received' (*10:04* 155) first book, and notes a tendency amongst readers to ask: 'what parts of the novel were autobiographical' (*10:04* 66). In the terms defined by this study, the narrator of *10:04* is a quiet man who, like both Lerner and Adam, frequents quiet locations and, like Julius, listens to the stories of others as he walks around the city. Yet notably unlike both Julius and Adam, the protagonist of *10:04* shows interest and even warmth to the people he meets and, while retaining Adam's acute self-consciousness, he demonstrates a 'genuine' desire to become an 'artist' of 'collectivity', 'possibility' and 'futurity' (*10:04* 108). Part of this desire seems based in the character's readings of Walt Whitman, whose poetry Lerner often paraphrases to elaborate the relationship between his protagonist, New York City and the people he meets. During a residency in Marfa, Texas, for instance, the narrator claims to only read Whitman's 'bizarre memoir' (*10:04* 168), *Specimen Days* (1882). In keeping with the poet's desire 'to stand for everyone', he then abandons the novel he is contracted to write and endeavours to emulate Whitman whose 'labor', he says, 'could be hard to tell apart from leisure, from loafing' (*10:04* 172). Importantly, the fellowship in Marfa gives Lerner's protagonist the time in which to research, write and think and *10:04*, like *Leaving the Atocha Station*, suggests that quiet is a necessary environment for composition. In Marfa, artistically 'loafing' without direction, Lerner's protagonist proves to be a sensitive reader of sounds; one who pointedly links ambient noise or the lack thereof to literary production and interpretation. He spends long periods composed simply of 'silence and my Whitman' (*10:04* 180), noting his ability to 'read if it's quiet' but 'write against noise' (*10:04* 173). When *10:04*'s narrator then returns to New York he believes that 'everything ... sounds like Whitman' (*10:04* 239) and the distant din of the 'jackhammer' and 'airplane noise' (*10:04* 224) positively contribute to his experience of the present. Broadly speaking, that is, in both of Lerner's novels, quiet is a necessary condition for artistry but noise remains necessary to the artist's comprehension of the world.

This point extends to *Open City* as neither Adam, the narrator of *10:04*, nor Julius ever propose leaving the urban environment. Indeed, both voice a dislike of the countryside and move between cities when they travel. To the city dwellers of *Open City*, 'those people' (*OC* 171) in rural areas are primitive in their politics and while there are locations like parks and allotments where Julius and his friends can act out rural scenarios, Cole self-consciously defines them as an 'orchestrated fantasy of country life' (*OC* 194). Similarly, in *Leaving the Atocha Station* Adam suggests that all rural landscapes tend to blur into one and lose cultural specificity when he travels, even claiming that 'Spanish countryside looked a lot like Kansas' (*LTAS* 127). The ease with which these characters travel further betrays their lack of self-reflection. As Cole writes in *Every Day is for the Thief*, and as I discuss in this chapter's concluding section, the ability to travel between quiet and noisy spaces is not available to everyone. The particularity of the quiet environments that Cole and Lerner's protagonists frequent in the city prove immensely valuable to the artist but potentially alienating to those readers for whom fellowships, library memberships and even art galleries are distant or foreign objects. Neither Adam, Julius nor the unnamed narrator of *10:04* question their reading of the city's volume, which, as this chapter argues, is both highly subjective and culturally specific. Moreover, all three seem happy to equate any area outside the city with the apolitical and the backward, two accusations that, as this study argues, are commonly and historically associated with quiet.

## Walking and whiteness: the limits of a quiet aesthetic

Franzen's celebration of Lerner's 'self-involvement' finally returns us to the limits of a quiet aesthetic hinted at throughout this study. In ways that feel similar to Franzen's increasingly divisive literary output, female critics have widely debated the originality of Lerner's novels. Reviewing *Leaving the Atocha Station* for *NPR*, Maureen Corrigan both praised and dismissed the novel as a 'boy book' composed by 'ruminations [...] on the instability of words' that women are not socialised to write.[73] Memoirist Leslie Jamison similarly challenges the critical dominance of 'memoir-novels' by men and compares the rapturous reception of Lerner and Karl Ove Knausgård to that of women writers like Chris Kraus and Sheila Heti whose autofictional works occupy comparable 'space[s] of uncertainty' but receive less critical attention.[74]

Whether women are discouraged from writing 'plotless' narratives led by nothing more than their 'ruminations' on language, writers on both sides of this debate are invariably and always white. That is, although the principles of the quiet aesthetic outlined throughout this study are not racially exclusive, the dominance of white narratives in the most celebrated quiet fictions, by writers like Lerner, Marilynne Robinson and Paul Harding, does nothing to trouble the centrality of whiteness to America's cultural consciousness or, indeed, to cultural notions of interiority. If this does not mean that quiet is a white aesthetic, it does mean that quiet is often coded as white. Kevin Everod Quashie of course argues as much in *The Sovereignty of Quiet: Beyond Resistance in Black Culture* (2012) when he suggests that public expressiveness is the dominant framework for black culture and when blackness is commonly understood as loud, dramatic and public, the black subject is denied a quiet 'sense of inwardness'.[75] Quashie's study then identifies and reads 'the right to be nothing to anyone but self' in twentieth-century African American literature.[76] Yet despite Quashie's intervention, the critics and journalists who celebrate quiet fiction for its privileging of a universal quotidian speak to a very limited idea of conscious experience, one that values and has access to the time and space for reflection that is particular to and privileged within middle-class American life. Although quiet and its associations with interiority are not, therefore, an expression of whiteness, it is important to acknowledge the white middle-class context represented both in this study and in newspapers like *The New York Times*, whose reviewers regularly associate 'quiet novels' with white novelists without ever defining or questioning their use of the term.

Assuming that quiet is a globally valued or available commodity similarly denies the social and economic status of those in the West or 'Global North' who valorise and have access to quiet states for lengthy periods of self-contemplation.[77] Cole acknowledges this idea in *Every Day is for the Thief* when he notes a 'disconnect between the wealth of stories available [in Lagos] and the rarity of creative refuge' (*EDTT* 58) available to the Nigerian artist. Moreover, if a postcolonial critique of *Open City* is rooted in Julius' detachment from other immigrants, then the novel's quiet prose may also act as a form of silencing. Cole's narrative recalls the many and varied sounds of the city and its inhabitants but Julius, the novel's only narrator, rarely responds to the stories he hears. While navigating New York, mimicking the transitory patterns of the nineteenth-century *flâneur*, Julius silences the many voices he invites to speak, moving quickly away from their disclosures and failing to respond when the speakers, who are often immigrants, call on him to hear, act or offer support.

The act of walking is a similarly particularised notion that Julius and Adam take for granted. As Mpalive-Hangson Msiska notes, popular conception of the *flâneur* is by turns white, male, heterosexual and middle-class:

> Benjamin's much celebrated figure of the *flâneur* was essentially imagined as White within a universalist ideology in which the city as the embodiment of rationality and civilisation was seen as the radiating source of the civilising values, of which the Black subject, thought of diametrically opposed to European subjectivity, was merely a recipient in the far flung colonies rather than an active participant.[78]

For Msiska, the Black *flâneur*, who he renames the '*Blaneur* or *Afraneur*', is a figure of possibility who embodies 'a living tension between his racialized metropolitan identity and his universal claim to an identity beyond his racial collectivity – as a man of the city as a whole.' Others have written about the limitations of the *flâneur* as a literary device that it is 'driven by a scopophilia' and, like the appreciation of quiet, 'marked by gender, race and class'.[79] To sociologist Rob Shields, the *flâneur* 'mimics the actions of the explorer who not only maps but also describes, designates and claims territories'.[80] To journalist Doreen St. Félix, writing in response to the killings of Michael Brown, Tamir Rice and Sandra Bland by policemen in 2014 and 2015, the 'roving that permits white fancy, white whim, white walking in our modern American cities, when observed in us and our [African American] children, reads criminal'.[81] The *flâneur*'s 'rebellion', then, which is constituted by the luxury of walking, observing and 'loafing', is a deeply politicised position that Adam and Julius occupy but never interrogate.

The act of walking remains crucial to the argument extended in this chapter because of the ways in which it mimics the progression of quiet narratives, which are equivocal, plotless and notably out of step with the pace of contemporary life. This long philosophical tradition of walking dates back to antiquity.[82] Notably, Henry David Thoreau describes the act of 'sauntering' as a way of letting go of the past and fully inhabiting the present and many recent histories of walking have extended Thoreau's philosophy, merging memoir with psychogeography to contextualise personal stories with profiles of historical and literary figures.[83] In *Wanderlust* (2001), Rebecca Solnit suggests that 'the mind, like the feet, works at about three miles an hour' and that 'modern life is moving faster than the speed of thought, or thoughtfulness'.[84] Solnit's formulation is similar to the ways in which I argue the quiet novel also works: when embedded in fictions that move at 'the speed of thought', the strolls that Julius and Adam undertake slow the pace of the protagonist and the reader, returning the time and space for reflection in both experiences of the narrative present. Similarly, in *The Practice of Everyday Life* (1980), Michel de Certeau compares the rhythms of travelling on foot with the phrasing of a sentence, arguing that walking has a 'rhetoric' that is composed by 'a series of turns (*tours*) and detours that can be compared to "turns of phrase" or "stylistic figures".'[85] By instilling walking at the centre of both texts, and arguably as an engine of Cole's and Lerner's fiction, the prose of *Open City* and *Leaving the Atocha Station* becomes a patchwork of ideas that intersect the sensory experience of the narrator, setting a tempo that operates outside the city's mechanical and commercial drive.

Still, as this chapter has discussed in detail, the peripatetic trips of Julius and Adam are primarily similar because both walkers are unable to empathise with the people they meet and both feel their contemplations threatened by other walkers. As Michelle Kuo and Albert Wu suggest, the act of strolling gestures towards a larger 'political abstinence' which undercuts *Open City* and *Leaving the Atocha Station* when '[i]nstead of committing themselves to an ideological position, [both protagonists] wander'.[86] Julius claims to practise 'the art of listening' (*OC* 9) as he walks but Adam is more honest, admitting that he does not listen to the people around him and claiming to 'barely' (*LTAS* 11) speak Spanish when he is obviously fluent. This unwillingness to communicate is central to the limits of quiet that I argue both texts demonstrate. Adam is fatalistic about his capacity for empathy: 'I *was* a sinking feeling', he says, 'an unplayable adagio for strings' (*LTAS* 20), notably linking his failure to connect with others to a piece of therapeutic music that is inarticulate. By comparison, although Julius self-prescribes daily walks to overcome a 'feeling of genuine isolation' (*OC* 196), Cole is sceptical about the extent to which his quiet protagonist can escape this kind of solipsism. The act of walking is useful as an academic and philosophical exercise: it is a way of losing oneself in thought but, for these quiet protagonists, it is never conducive to a lasting or meaningful connection with others.

Moreover, Julius, unlike Adam, is made vulnerable by his contemplative walks and in one instance he is beaten and mugged. Lacking the awareness of Cole's unnamed narrator in *Every Day is for the Thief*, who realises that by 'daydreaming' in crowds he makes himself 'a target' (*EDTT* 52), Julius is lost in thought about the 'mutual respect' felt between everyone who identifies as 'young, black, male' (*OC* 186) when two young, black men beat him to the ground. Here, Julius' solipsism comes back to haunt him: after the mugging, he is unable to get the assistance or even the acknowledgment of strangers and he notes how a passer-by 'did not notice, or did not care to notice' (*OC* 188) his injuries. Julius' walks around New York therefore physically threaten his body and the incident points to further ambiguities in Cole's interrogation of a cosmopolitan ideal. Invoking Msiska's idea of the *Blaneur*, Julius freely practices *flânerie*, repeatedly rebuffs the connections attempted by his fellow pedestrians and is ultimately wounded by his belief that 'a quick solidarity' (*OC* 185) can be formed by the exchange of glances between black men.

To conclude, I want to also draw attention to another one of *Open City*'s major crises. In a novel replete with many competing voices and narratives, it is notable which characters are silenced. Cole first uses Julius' silence about his mother's estrangement to make visible the holes in the quiet life he has constructed for himself. At the beginning of the novel, Julius closes the window when he gets annoyed by the 'martial tone' (*OC* 22) of a Take Back the Night demonstration, criticising the women's shouts because 'the words did not resolve into meaning' for him. Julius means this literally: the noise of whistles and shouts that the march against sexual violence produces is unintelligible from where he sits in his apartment. Yet the phrase also has deeper connotations. The words of the protestors have no meaning to Julius and so he gives them no further thought but the significance of the episode is revealed towards the end of the novel when Moji, an old acquaintance from Nigeria, accuses Julius of raping her. Quietly, in a voice which Julius notes 'never increased in volume' (*OC* 244), Moji details how Julius 'forced himself on her' (*OC* 243) during a party in late 1989. Moji's voice, now 'strained' and 'shattered' (*OC* 244), recounts her experience after decades of silence, describing her brother's refusal to discuss 'these things' and balking at Julius' inability to remember the rape she accuses him of. This time it is Julius' turn to fall silent; revisiting the context of the assault and detailing the effect it has had on her life, Moji concludes by asking: 'But will you say something now? Will you say something?' (*OC* 245). She invites a direct response from Julius and waits for a reaction not only to his current moment of inaction but to the act of sexual violence he committed twenty years previously. Her plea, however, is met with nothing and her questions go unanswered. 'Other people had woken up', Julius tells the reader, 'I thought that [Moji] would begin to cry but, to my relief, she didn't.' In a novel so attuned to quiet, and from a protagonist who so often seeks quiet in which to hide from a noisy environment, this silence is profoundly disturbing. Cole invites the reader to fill the silence that Julius will not, suggesting that he is hiding a deeper, darker and perhaps a noisier history that we, as readers, have not been privy to.

Although Julius does not respond to Moji's allegation, or to her emotional appeal, Cole does not side with his protagonist. His position is reflected narratologically: in the sequence that leads to the revelation of Julius' crime, the narrative proceeds in a linear fashion through the day until Julius meets Moji for a party at her apartment. Throughout the novel, Moji is a peripheral character. Julius first encounters her in Union Square, unable to recall quite who she is or how he knows her but certain 'she expected me to remember her' (*OC* 282). From then on, Julius meets with Moji occasionally and, when he does, casually objectifies her, noting the pleasantly 'dark curve of her breast' (*OC* 359) and suggesting that 'she was not beautiful in the way I expected dark women to be' (*OC* 358). On the day of Moji's revelation, their third meeting in Cole's narrative and only twenty pages before the novel's end, Julius skips the detail of the party itself, moving from his arrival at the apartment to the point in the morning, around 2am, when most people begin to go home. The change in atmosphere is striking because it is described as a shift in the party's music that moves from loud to quiet: 'Someone replaced the electronic dance music that had been playing on the stereo with a recording of Sarah Vaughan with strings' (*OC* 240). This is the time of night that introverts like Julius (and, indeed, Woolf's Clarissa Dalloway), prefer; the late evening of a party as it begins to slow down and one finds 'old friends; quiet nooks and corners; and the loveliest views'.[87] After accompanying Moji onto the balcony to take in the view, the narrative skips again to sunrise, which Julius watches over the Hudson River from the vantage point of the George Washington Bridge. At this point, Moji's revelation is yet to be recounted and, passing a man who has fallen asleep in his car, Julius describes how 'The reflection of the sun turned half of the windshield into a bright metallic field' (*OC* 241) before describing the remainder of his walk home.

This detail is only important because a few pages later, after recalling Moji's accusation of assault, Julius describes the same sunrise for the second time. This time, he watches 'the just risen sun' (*OC* 246) coming up over the Hudson, from the quiet of the balcony where he and Moji are sitting. The similes are the same as in Cole's first description: he likens the rising sun to the sheen of 'aluminium roofing' (*OC* 246) and focuses on the otherworldliness of Manhattan's surrounding waters, the presence of which has fascinated Julius throughout the novel. Cole makes it clear, however, that the reader is not seeing the same scene twice, but observing the same sunrise at different times, described in reverse order. The disorientation that this effect provokes mimics the reconfiguring of Julius' self-image because, at least for the moment of Moji's revelation, he is forced to see himself through another's perspective. '[I]n someone else's version', he says, 'I am the villain' (*OC* 243). Even in this statement Julius cannot give Moji a name, referring to the accusation of assault as an amorphous and vague idea, so far outside his conception of himself that it is in 'someone else's version' of his story. Julius' failure to respond to Moji is the closest to absolute silence that the novel can reach. Internally, Julius deflects her words and, following his second account of the sunrise, he turns to think about Camus' journals, intellectualising the situation he finds himself in to avoid dealing with its emotional and moral repercussions. The narrative then skips forward several days when Julius returns to the journals to check a detail. However, he does not return to the thought or idea of rape or, indeed, give the act a name. The temporal inversion of Moji's allegation emphasises Julius' wider lack of empathy and reveals an absence of self-reflection that is shocking within so quiet a narrative of interiority.

Although critics have largely overlooked Julius' rape of Moji, Cole attributes great significance to the act, remarking in interviews that he 'can't imagine Julius' story without it' and even suggesting that '*Open City* is very much about rape, though I doubt this word "about".'[88] Cole, then, acknowledges that his novel, like all quiet texts, is 'about' very little; that there is no subject or plot development in *Open City*, at least in the traditional sense of these terms. In this chapter, I have argued that the novel is quiet when it provides a conceptual space

# The novel of '(dis)quiet'   181

in which to reflect upon the present, even when it takes place in the noisy environment of the city. Reflecting upon the relationship between literature and quietism, Douglas Mao also asks:

> Why does no one seem to praise quietness anymore, in our clamorous world? [...] Don't you wonder why, when the world seems ever shriller – why almost no one, at least in this country, seems to care about quietness?[89]

But if, as Mao suggests, we live in a culture that privileges drama, trauma and noise, is it possible to prioritise quiet without also retreating from the necessary noise of protest and dissent? This chapter has argued that there are benefits to conceiving of quiet from within a setting that is close to noise. The dynamic variation between noisy and quiet moments creates an aesthetic that is precarious but perhaps more compelling, and when set within the confines of the city, the quiet novel also introduces the possibility that quiet might hold a collective value located in public spaces.

However, the young, artistic protagonists who are drawn to the symphony of noise in the city test the limits of a quiet aesthetic because they display a troubling lack of empathy that keeps them too far from the noise of others. Amongst the cacophony of the urban, the call to action is easy to miss and, as both *Open City* and *Leaving the Atocha Station* show, Julius and Adam do not possess the emotional intelligence to comprehend the events that loudly, and even quietly, happen around them. Although the noise of an urban setting can, therefore, be represented by the subjective quiet of consciousness, this final chapter has demonstrated the dangers of quiet when it becomes a retreat and when quiet individuals are unwilling to apply the call to action found in the philosophical and political works they study to the narrative of their own lives. Indeed, this chapter stresses just how 'intensely relational' noise can be when the space for contemplation is shared, drawing out many, possibly contradictory ideas about the subjective experience of quiet and noise through a close reading of Cole's and Lerner's fiction.[90]

## Notes

1. *Open City* was nominated for the National Book Critics Circle Award and won the Hemingway Foundation/PEN Award in 2012; *Leaving the Atocha Station* won the 2011 Believer Book Award and was nominated for the *Los Angeles Times* Book Award.
2. Ben Lerner, *Leaving the Atocha Station* (London: Granta, 2011), p. 183. All further references will appear in the text as *LTAS*.
3. Andrew Hartwiger, 'The Postcolonial Flâneur: *Open City* and the Urban Palimpsest', *Postcolonial Text*, 11.1 (2016), http://postcolonial.org/index.php/pct/article/viewArticle/1970.
4. Joseph Peschel, 'Stoic Man Walking through *Open City*', *Boston Globe* (24 February 2011), http://www.boston.com/ae/books/articles/2011/02/24/first_time_novelist_teju_cole_presents_a_stoic_man_walking_through_open_city/.
5. Adam Fitzgerald, 'Ben Lerner', *BOMB* (September 2011), http://bombsite.com/issues/999/articles/6081.
6. Teju Cole, *Open City* (New York: Faber & Faber, 2011), p. 50. All further references will appear in text as *OC*.
7. Emily Thompson, *The Soundscape of Modernity: Architectural Acoustics and the Culture of Listening in America* (Cambridge, MA: MIT Press, 2002), p. 2.
8. Daniel Katz, '"I Did not Walk Here all the Way from Prose": Ben Lerner's Virtual Poetics', *Textual Practice*, 31.2 (2017), p. 316. Julius is living and studying in New York in 2006, living near Columbia University where Cole studied for a doctorate in art history; he experiences flashbacks to his childhood in Lagos where Cole also grew up. Similarly, Adam meanders through Madrid in 2004, the same year that Kansas-born Lerner took up a Fulbright Scholarship in the city.
9. 'noise, n.' *OED Online* (June 2016), Oxford: Oxford University Press, http://www.oed.com/view/Entry/127655?rskey=DZC9hD&result=1&isAdvanced=false; G. W. C. Kaye, quoted in Karin Bijsterveld, *Mechanical Sound: Technology, Culture, and Public Problems of Noise in the Twentieth Century* (Cambridge, MA: MIT Press, 2008), p. 240; David Hendy, *Noise: A Human History of Sound and Listening* (London: Profile Books, 2014), p. viii.
10. Bijsterveld suggests that complaints about noise are generally based on the volume or level of a sound, its frequency (high or low), how often the sound is made, whether it is steady or intermittent and, most subjectively, whether the noise is deemed to be 'necessary'. Bijsterveld, *Mechanical Sound*, p. 103.

11  Brandon LaBelle, *Background Noise: Perspectives on Sound Art* (London: Bloomsbury, 2006), p. xi.
12  Ibid.
13  Roland Barthes, 'Listening', in *The Responsibility of Forms*, ed. Richard Howard (Oakland: University of California Press, 1985), p. 245.
14  David Foster Wallace, 'Deciderization 2007 – A Special Report', in his *Both Flesh and Not* (London: Penguin, 2012), p. 110.
15  Don DeLillo, *White Noise* (New York: Viking Press, 1985), p. 27.
16  Fredric Jameson, 'Fear and Loathing in Globalization', *New Left Review*, p. 23 (September–October 2003), http://newleftreview.org/II/23/fredric-jameson-fear-and-loathing-in-globalization. According to Jameson, advertisements are also predatory, just like noise is often conceived to be and their role in society is constantly evolving until, as Marx always thought, they become 'to be living entities preying on the humans that coexist with them'.
17  Jacques Attali, *Noise: The Political Economy of Music*, trans. Brian Massumi (Minneapolis: University of Minnesota Press, 1977), p. 26.
18  Yves-Alain Bois, Rosalind Krauss, 'Zone', *Formless: A User's Guide* (New York: Zone Books, 1997), p. 230; Hillel Schwartz, *Making Noise: From Babel to the Big Bang and Beyond* (Cambridge, MA: MIT Press, 2013), p. 708.
19  Kate Flint, 'Sounds of the City: Virginia Woolf and Modernist Noise', in *Literature, Science, Psychoanalysis 1830–1970: Essays in Honour of Gillian Beer*, ed. Helen Small and Trudi Tate (Oxford: Oxford University Press, 2003), p. 192; Niall Martin, *Iain Sinclair: Noise, Neoliberalism and the Matter of London* (London: Bloomsbury, 2015), p. 8.
20  Bijsterveld, *Mechanical Sound*, p. 2.
21  Torsten Wissmann, *Geographies of Urban Sound* (Farnham: Ashgate Publishing, 2014), p. 1; Bijsterveld, *Mechanical Sound*, p. 2. Wissmann continues: 'Sound has long been neglected in urban studies. Traffic, music, language, and nature, as primary examples, help to create unique soundscapes essential to the place-based character of each city, and no consideration of these cityscapes should fail to include them.'
22  Schwartz, *Making Noise*, p. 21.
23  Ibid.
24  Flint, 'Sounds of the City: Virginia Woolf and Modern Noise', p. 181.
25  Bijsterveld, *Mechanical Sound*, p. 1.
26  Georg Simmel, 'The Metropolis and Mental Life', in *The City Cultures Reader*, ed. Malcolm Miles, Tim Hall and Iain Borden (London: Routledge, 2000), p. 18.
27  Ibid., p. 15.
28  Walter Benjamin, 'On Some Motifs in Baudelaire', *Selected Writings, 1938–1940*, Volume 4, ed. Howard Eiland and Michael W. Jennings,

trans. Edmund Jephcott (Cambridge, MA: Harvard University Press, 2003), p. 328.

29   Benjamin, 'Central Park.' *Selected Writings, 1938–1940*, p. 181. Although the *flâneur* is a recurring motif in cultural representations and discussions of the urban, it was first brought to the attention of scholars by Benjamin's analysis of Baudelaire. For more on the cultural history of the *flâneur* see: Dana Brand, *Spectator and the City in Nineteenth-Century American Literature* (Cambridge: Cambridge University Press, 1991); Keith Tester (ed.), *The Flâneur* (London: Routledge, 1994); David Harvey, *Paris, Capital of Modernity* (New York: Routledge, 2003).

30   Charles Baudelaire, 'The Painter of Modern Life', in *Baudelaire: Selected Writings on Art and Artists*, trans. P. E. Charvet (Cambridge: Cambridge University Press, 1981), p. 399.

31   Marshall Berman, *All that is Solid Melts into Air: The Experience of Modernity* (New York: Verso, 1983), p. 229.

32   Catherine Nesci, 'Memory, Desire, Lyric: The *Flâneur*', in *The Cambridge Companion to the City in Literature*, ed. Kevin R. McNamara (Cambridge, Cambridge University Press, 2014), p. 80. Although *flânerie* is a central narrative device in *Leaves of Grass* (1855), the extent to which Whitman's authorial persona can be described as a *flâneur* has been debated. See: Jason Frank, 'Promiscuous Citizenship', in *A Political Companion to Walt Whitman*, ed. John Evan Seery (Lexington: The University Press of Kentucky, 2011), p. 172; J. Thomas Chaffin Jr., 'Give Me Faces and Streets: Walt Whitman and the City', *Walt Whitman Review*, 23 (1977), pp. 109–120; Dana Brand, '"Intense Phantom Concourse": Whitman and the Urban Crowd', in *Spectator and the City in Nineteenth-Century American Literature*, pp. 156–185.

33   Walt Whitman, 'Song of Myself', in *Leaves of Grass* (Oxford: Oxford World Classics, 2008), p. 51. Whitman also invites the creation of noise: 'Sound out, voices of young men! loudly and musically call me by my nighest name!' Whitman, 'Crossing Brooklyn Ferry', in *Leaves of Grass*, p. 133.

34   Lerner, *10:04* (London: Granta, 2014), p. 168. All further references will appear in text as *10:04*.

35   Albert Wu and Michelle Kuo, 'Imperfect Strollers: Teju Cole, Ben Lerner, W. G. Sebald, and the Alienated Cosmopolitan', *Los Angeles Review of Books* (2 February 2013), http://lareviewofbooks.org/article/imperfect-strollers-teju-cole-ben-lerner-w-g-sebald-and-the-alienated-cosmopolitan; Peter Vermeulen, 'Flights of Memory: Teju Cole's *Open City* and the Limits of Aesthetic Cosmopolitanism', *Journal of Modern Literature*, 37:1 (fall 2013), pp. 40–57; Hartwiger, 'The Postcolonial Flâneur', http://postcolonial.org/index.php/pct/article/view Article/1970.

36   We might even consider Whitman's proclivity for noise and people to

be a performance of 'extroversion'. As noted in previous chapters, Carl Jung's definition of the introvert/extrovert binary delineates the extrovert as one who is gratified by activities outside of the self: by extension, the extrovert is largely at home in the city while the acoustic sensitivity of the introvert makes the constant stimulation of the urban a threat to their well-being.

37  Becky M. Nicolaides and Andrew Wiese, *The Suburb Reader* (New York: Routledge, 2006), p. 14.
38  Chauncy D. Harris and Edward L. Ullman, 'The Nature of Cities', *The Annals of the American Academy of Political and Social Science*, 242 (1945), p. 16.
39  Bijsterveld, *Mechanical Sound*, p. 182.
40  Noise Control Act of 1972, Public Law 92-574, (27 October 1972), https://www.gpo.gov/fdsys/pkg/PLAW-114publ38/html/PLAW-114publ38.htm.
41  Melville Campbell Branch, *Urban Air Traffic and City Planning: Case Study of Los Angeles County* (New York: Praeger Publishers, 1973), p. 29. Scholars have also compared 'acoustic pollution' with 'the excremental smell pollution in cities of former times.' See: Bijsterveld, *Mechanical Sound*, pp. 3–4; Klaus Dürrschmid, 'Food and the City', in *Senses and the City: An Interdisciplinary Approach to Urban Sensescapes*, ed. Mădălina Diaconu, Eva Heuberger, Ruth Mateus-Berr and Lukas Marcel Vosicky (Vienna: Lit Verlag, 2011), p. 191.
42  Branch, *Urban Air Traffic and City Planning*, p. 29. Similar studies proliferated in the 1970s due to a range of factors, including increased air travel. See: George Bugliarello, Ariel Alexandre, John Barnes and Charles Wakstein, *The Impact of Noise Pollution: A Socio-Technological Introduction* (Oxford: Perhamon Press, 1976), pp. 225–227.
43  Henry David Thoreau, *Walden* (Princeton: Princeton University Press, 2004), p. 8.
44  Richard Yates, *Revolutionary Road* (London: Vintage, 2010), p. 30.
45  Bijsterveld, *Mechanical Sound*, pp. 53–90; Colleen F. Moore, 'Noise: A Barrier to Children's Learning', in *Silent Scourge: Children, Pollution, and Why Scientists Disagree* (Oxford: Oxford University Press, 2009), pp. 140–174.
46  Nicolas Kenny, *The Feel of the City: Experiences of Urban Transformation* (Toronto: University of Toronto Press, 2014), pp. 99, 3.
47  James Wood, 'The Arrival of Enigmas', *The New Yorker* (28 February 2011)  http://www.newyorker.com/arts/critics/books/2011/02/28/110228crbo_books_wood.
48  Peter Brooker, *New York Fictions: Modernity, Postmodernism, The New Modern* (New York: Longman, 1996), p. 43.
49  Don DeLillo, *Falling Man* (New York: Picador, 2007), p. 69.
50  Jess Walter, *The Zero* (New York: Harper, 2006), p. 116.

51  Siegmund Levarie, 'Noise', *Critical Inquiry*, 4:1 (autumn 1977), p. 21.
52  Salomé Voegelin, *Listening to Noise and Silence: Towards a Philosophy of Sound Art* (New York: Continuum, 2010), p. 33.
53  Madhu Krishnan, 'Postcoloniality, Spatiality and Cosmopolitanism in the *Open City*', *Textual Practice*, 29:4 (2015), p. 677. Krishnan argues that Cole's invocation of cosmopolitanism, which many reviewers observe in Julius' *flânerie* and his interactions with passers-by as well as direct references to the work of Kwame Anthony Appiah, highlights the many ways in which cosmopolitanism acts as an alibi for fragmentation by reinforcing the 'bland diversity' through which the postcolonial destroys plurality. Other critics suggest that Julius' cosmopolitanism fails because of a lack of empathy, demonstrated by his inability to sustain interest in the stories of other people. See: Wu and Kuo, 'Imperfect Strollers', http://lareviewofbooks.org/article/imperfect-strollers-teju-cole-ben-lerner-w-g-sebald-and-the-alienated-cosmopolitan; Hartwiger, 'The Postcolonial *Flâneur*', http://postcolonial.org/index.php/pct/article/viewArticle/1970.
54  Marilynne Robinson also discusses Vermeer's 'Young Woman with a Water Jug' (1662) during an interview with *The Paris Review* and uses a discussion of the painting to qualify her personal definition of beauty. Robinson roots her love of Dutch painting, which was also the subject of Cole's PhD, in the ability of artists like Vermeer to uncover beauty outside of society's prescriptive notions, to show 'that beauty is a casual glimpse of something very ordinary'. Marilynne Robinson, quoted in Sarah Fay, 'The Art of Fiction #198', *The Paris Review*, 186 (fall 2008), http://www.theparisreview.org/interviews/5863/the-art-of-fiction-no-198-marilynne-robinson.
55  Wai Chee Dimock, *Through Other Continents: American Literature across Deep Time* (Princeton, NJ: Princeton University Press, 2006), p. 6. Deep time is a geological concept, developed in its modern philosophical sense during the eighteenth century and used by Dimock to encompass the 'complex tangle of relations' that make up American literature. Ibid., p. 3.
56  Vermeulen, 'Flights of Memory', p. 42.
57  Hartwiger, 'The Postcolonial *Flaneur*', http://postcolonial.org/index.php/pct/article/viewArticle/1970.
58  Although Julius twice refers to the cab driver as 'my brother' (*OC* 39), he is annoyed by other black immigrants and Americans who assume a shared sense of ancestry and experience through reference to their 'brotherhood' (*OC* 52, 164, 185).
59  Originally published by Cassava Republic, a Nigerian press, Cole subsequently revised, extended and rereleased the text for publication by Faber & Faber in March 2014.

60  Teju Cole, *Every Day is for the Thief* (New York: Faber & Faber, 2014), pp. 53, 35. All further references will appear in the text as *EDTT*.
61  Katz, 'Ben Lerner's Virtual Poetics', p. 6. Lerner revisits this notion in *10:04* when his unnamed protagonist expresses admiration for the 'palimpsestic plagiarism' (*10:04* 114) of Ronald Reagan's speech writers.
62  Katz, 'Ben Lerner's Virtual Poetics', p. 7.
63  Bijsterveld, *Mechanical Sound*, pp. 163, 162.
64  Günter Leypoldt, 'Shifting Meridians: US Authorship in World Literary Space', *American Literary History*, 27:4 (winter 2015), p. 783.
65  The volume is an extended version of Lerner's essay, 'Diary: on Disliking Poetry', published in *The London Review of Books*, 37:12 (8 June 2015), pp. 42–43. Lerner's first volume of poetry, *The Lichtenberg Figures* (2004), won the Hayden Carruth award for poetry the year that Lerner returned from Madrid and completed a second collection, *Angle of Yaw* (2006). As Daniel Katz observes, Lerner's fame for his fiction and the critical neglect of his poetry is perhaps a predictable consequence of the fiction itself: both *Leaving the Atocha Station* and its follow-up, *10:04*, are about the marginalisation of poetry as a genre. Katz, 'Ben Lerner's Virtual Poetics', p. 4.
66  Jonathan Franzen, 'Books of the Year 2011', *The Guardian* (25 November 2011), https://www.theguardian.com/books/2011/nov/25/books-of-the-year.
67  James Wood, 'Reality Testing', *The New Yorker* (31 October 2011), http://www.newyorker.com/magazine/2011/10/31/reality-testing.
68  David Shields, *How Literature Saved My Life* (New York: Vintage, 2013), p. 3.
69  Tom Evans, 'Ben Lerner, *10:04* and the Death of Silence', *The Quietus* (22 February 2015), http://thequietus.com/articles/17286-ben-lerner-10 04-silence-art-sontag.
70  As a study of quiet's philosophically active potentiality, this book has rarely touched on the relationship between gender and silence, which has been written about extensively particularly in relation to sexual violence. See, among many: Anna Clark, *Women's Silence, Men's Violence: Sexual Assault in England 1770–1845* (London: Pandora, 1987); Kennedy Fraser, *Ornament and Silence: Essay's on Women's Lives* (London: Vintage, 1998); Alice Crary, 'A Question of Silence: Feminist Theory and Women's Voices', *Philosophy* 76.297 (July 2001), pp. 371–395; Patti Duncan, *Tell This Silence: Asian American Women Writers and the Politics of Speech* (Iowa City: University of Iowa Press, 2004).
71  James Wood, 'Eastern Promises', *The New Yorker* (2 September 2013), http://www.newyorker.com/arts/critics/books/2013/09/02/130902crb o_books_wood?currentPage=all.
72  Gabrielle Townsend, *Proust's Imaginary Museum: Reproductions and*

*Reproduction in À la recherché du temps perdu* (Bern: Peter Lang, 2008), p. 214.
73 Maureen Corrigan, 'Life without Plot in *Leaving the Atocha Station*', Philadelphia: NPR (2011), ProQuest, http://search.proquest.com/docview/902740950?accountid=14693.
74 Leslie Jamison and Daniel Mendelsohn, 'Bookends', *New York Times Book Review* (28 December 2014), ProQuest, http://search.proquest.com/docview/1640813267?accountid=14693.
75 Kevin Everod Quashie, *The Sovereignty of Quiet: Beyond Resistance in Black Culture* (New Brunswick, NJ: Rutgers University Press, 2012), p. 3.
76 Ibid., p. 70.
77 Jacques Attali is just one of many writers who defines nineteenth- and twentieth-century attempts to regulate noise as a form of political oppression that targets an underclass. See: Ronda L. Sewald, 'Forced Listening: The Contested Use of Loudspeakers for Commercial and Political Messages in the Public Soundscape', in *Sound Clash: Listening to American Studies*, ed. Karen Keeling and Josh Kun (Baltimore, MD: Johns Hopkins University Press, 2012), p. 319, but also Mary Chapman's analysis of the 'noisy' tactics of the Progressive Woman Suffrage Union, Adam Mack's study of the 'sounds' of the 1894 Pullman Strike and Mark M. Smith's suggestion that middle-class black Americans adopted the sensorial refinements they deemed fitting of their class. Mary Chapman, *Making Noise, Making News: Suffrage Print Culture and U.S. Modernism* (Oxford: Oxford University Press, 2014), pp. 27–53; Adam Mack, *Sensing Chicago: Noisemakers, Strikebreakers, and Muckrakers* (Urbana: University of Illinois Press, 2015), pp. 51-70; Mark M. Smith, *How Race is Made: Slavery, Segregation, and the Senses* (Chapel Hill: University of North Carolina Press, 2006), pp. 93, 98.
78 Mpalive-Hangson Msiska, 'Sam Selvon's *The Lonely Londoners* and the Structure of Black Metropolitan Life', in *African Diaspora and the Metropolis: Reading the African, African American and Caribbean Experience*, ed. Fassil Demissie (London: Routledge, 2010), p. 9.
79 James Procter, *Dwelling Places: Postwar Black British Writing* (Manchester: Manchester University Press, 2003), p. 97.
80 Rob Shields, *Places on the Margin: Alternative Geographies of Modernity* (London: Routledge, 1991), p. 55.
81 Doreen St. Félix, 'The Perils of Black Mobility', *GOOD* 36 (29 March 2016), https://www.good.is/features/issue-36-flanerie.
82 See, for example: Robert Sharples, 'The Peripatetic School', in *From Aristotle to Augustine: Routledge History of Philosophy*, ed. David Furley (London: Routledge, 2003), pp. 147–187.
83 Henry David Thoreau, 'Walking', *The Atlantic* (1 June 1862), http://www.theatlantic.com/magazine/archive/1862/06/walking/304674/.

84 Rebecca Solnit, *Wanderlust: A History of Walking* (London: Penguin, 2001), p. 21. See also: Geoff Nicholson, *The Lost Art of Walking: The History, Science, Philosophy, and Literature of Pedestrianism* (New York: Riverhead Books, 2008); Matthew Beaumont and Geoffrey Dart (eds), *Restless Cities* (London: Verso, 2010); Merlin Coverley, *The Art of Wandering: The Writer as Walker* (Harpenden: Oldcastle Books, 2012); Will Self, 'Walking is Political', *The Guardian* (20 March 2012), http://www.theguardian.com/books/2012/mar/30/will-self-walking-cities-foot; Karen O'Rourke, *Walking and Mapping: Artists as Cartographers* (Cambridge, MA: MIT Press, 2013); Frédéric Gros, *A Philosophy of Walking* (London: Verso, 2014).
85 Michel de Certeau, *The Practice of Everyday Life*, trans. Steven Rendell (Berkeley: University of California Press, 1988), p. 100.
86 Kuo and Wu, 'Imperfect Strollers', http://lareviewofbooks.org/article/imperfect-strollers-teju-cole-ben-lerner-w-g-sebald-and-the-alienated-cosmopolitan.
87 Virginia Woolf, *Mrs Dalloway* (London: Wordsworth Editions, 2003), p. 139.
88 Cole, interviewed by Max Liu, 'Palimpsest City', *3:AM Magazine* (16 August 2011), http://www.3ammagazine.com/3am/palimpsest-city/; Cole, interviewed by Aaron Bady, 'Interview: Teju Cole', *Post-45* (19 January 2015), http://post45.research.yale.edu/2015/01/interview-teju-cole/.
89 Douglas Mao, 'The Lack of Repose', *Common Knowledge*, 15:3 (2009), p. 429.
90 LaBelle, *Background Noise*, p. xi.

# Conclusion

This book has argued that 'quiet' is a literary aesthetic, used frequently in contemporary American fiction to privilege reflection and contemplation as a way of engaging with the present. Tracing a long history of quiet in Anglo-American literature and focusing more specifically on American works published since 2000, I have argued that the contemporary American novel is quiet when its narrative is focalised through the mind of a quiet character and set in a quiet location where the protagonist has the time and space to reflect on their present moment. In many ways, New York City is a fitting location in which to end this study. In Chapter 2, I argued that narrative depictions of '9/11' fixate on three forms of noise: the literal noise of the World Trade Center collapse, the global resonance of American exceptionalism and the symbolic noise of the event as a temporal structure. My fifth and final chapter returned to the streets of New York in *Open City* (2011), a novel published a decade after the attacks, to examine how urban noise can coexist with a quiet aesthetic when a novel does not privilege the event as a narrative structure. In the conceptual leap between Chapters 2 and 5, between novels by Don DeLillo and Marilynne Robinson, Jonathan Franzen and Teju Cole, it is clear that if the quiet novel exists then it does so in conjunction with the loud. Indeed, what I hope that this study has proven are the ways in which a quiet aesthetic is expressive and illuminating beyond the confines of a quiet text and that all novels can be read for both their quiet and noisy qualities.

Finally, looking past the examination of fiction, the quiet novel can be understood in terms of a growing interest in quiet activities that are couched as an anomalous force within a system of late capitalism, particularly in wider cultural movements that challenge the ways in which the individual receives information and values. Groups promoting 'slow' activities, for example, date back to the movement for slow food that began in Italy in 1986 and led to the establishment of the World Institute of Slowness in 1999. Such organisations promote the awareness and practice of 'slow' processes, placing a high value on 'transparency', 'simplicity' and 'consciousness' in the protection of slow cities, living, travel, design and art.[1] This ethos extends to minor strands of publishing. As noted in my Introduction, editor Laura Stanfill established Forest Avenue Press in 2012 with the intention of publishing '[q]uiet books for a noisy world' and in 2011, the quarterly magazine *Delayed Gratification* launched what they describe as a movement for 'slow journalism', covering the news of the previous three months 'after the dust has settled'.[2] Although the terms are vague and the organisations marginal, the worldwide movement for slowness represents a political attempt to do something from scratch; to be involved in the process of production as well as consumption and to do so at a 'slower' rate than the accelerated speed of mass production. Members often advocate the farming and purchase of produce that is seasonal and local and promote activities that are not reliant on developing technologies. As Rebecca Solnit suggests, these movements constitute an attempt to measure productivity against something other than industrial and mechanical lines of production, an endeavour that is 'both laughably small and heroically ambitious' in its engagement with contemporary existence.[3]

The protagonists of quiet fictions also go against the grain of a consumerist America. As demonstrated in this book, capitalism marginalises introverted and quiet personality types; the protagonists of quiet texts therefore live in the shadows of American capitalism. It is striking, for instance, how many of these fictions represent 'slow' activities through protagonists who are interested in creating their own possessions; in particular, their own homes. In *American Genius*, the neglected history of chair design fascinates Helen because it 'records human sensitivity, or consciousness' through which she rediscovers the close relationship between the body and the designer.[4] The opening of *Tinkers* narrates how George built his house from scratch: he 'poured the foundation, raised the frame, joined the pipes, [ran] the wire, plastered the walls, and painted the rooms.'[5] George's desire to build a home is also echoed in his passion for building clocks; both activities are an attempt to carve out time in the present by returning autonomy and control to the hands of the individual.[6] In *The Echo Maker*, Mark Schluter considers the purchase of his 'catalog house' to be a declaration of independence after his parents die.[7] However, the 'Homestar', named after the company who designed it, is unrecognisable once he suffers the symptoms of Capgras and Karin points out that Mark's home is the ultimate simulacrum. While Mark believes that his prefab house is 'the only one in the world', Capgras' attendant delusions comically disabuse him of this notion.[8] The quiet novel is often concerned, then, with the traditional, well-worn motif of the home but rather than seeking new ways in which to represent domestic space, these authors narrate a cultural moment in which a return to 'old-fashioned' pursuits appear to liberate the individual from the restrictive possibilities of creative acts in an age of mechanical production. Moreover, these authors succeed in disassociating contemporary life from the noise of consumption. To quote again from Solnit, crafts, hobbies and houses are an attempt to return the 'rhythm' of a 'bygone time' to the present and, in doing so, they create 'room for you to do one thing at a time' rather than everything at once.[9]

The age group of the quiet protagonist speaks to similar concerns. Although I argue that the quiet novel is never simply nostalgic, the advanced age of protagonists like Reverend Ames and George Washington Crosby changes the function of narrative in the present as both inch closer to death. As Alice Bennett suggests, the prospect of an afterlife and 'all its iterations of alternative times and spaces' makes 'every ending provisional' for these dying protagonists.[10] Their age and faith in an afterlife therefore evades the will to conclude that structures noisier texts. In Ames' case, this evasion is made possible by his belief in heaven and the concept of eternity, a temporal structure that expands the limitations of the physical world and extends our idea of the protagonist's ongoing experience past the end of the novel and, potentially, Ames' death. Still, the quiet novel is not religious so much as Christian practices atune the individual to the reflective processes, moments of contemplation and prayer that constitute 'quiet' modes of living in the present. In *Tinkers*, George also comes from a long line of preachers and 'God' is frequently invoked in exhortations about the 'terrifying' state of the world.[11] Yet the world of *Tinkers* proves more transparent than *Gilead*'s and with fewer references to period detail and no indication of date, *Tinkers* depicts human presence as the faintest trace of existence. Temporality then defers to broader ecological cycles and, as in *The Echo Maker*, individuals are perceived as fading from their natural world even from the moment of their birth. The present moments of these quiet texts are therefore placed on a continuum, through the promise of eternal life and/or nature's quiet continuance, which promotes the acceptance of contingency as I argued in Chapter 4.

If the quiet protagonist is neither old nor religious, however, they must develop ways of distancing themselves from the noise of contemporary life. This noise, as Chapter 5 expounded, is both real and metaphorical: it is the noise of other people, their technologies and other non-human sounds but it is also the mental noise of topical event, mounting deadlines and the overstimulation that many link to online cultures. For Julius in *Open City*, religious spaces are therefore attractive because they offer the closest environment to 'total silence' that a city dweller can find.[12] But Julius also practices 'the suspension of time' through his interactions with art, an act that exemplifies the many ways in which an author's narration of quiet activities enables and elaborates the quiet of their prose.[13] Like Julius, Adam in *Leaving the Atocha Station* spends much of his time reading episodes which, by his own admission, are 'impossible to narrate'.[14] Similarly, in *American Genius; a comedy*, Helen describes long periods of time spent 'drawing, reading, listening to the radio', periods that are, by their nature, long, uneventful and quiet.[15]

It is in this way that all quiet novels are also ultimately about 'nothing'. From the beginning to the end of a quiet contemporary American novel, nothing really happens, very little changes, and each narrative follows the slow progression of everyday life or the ruminations of conscious thought rather than the hectic and noisy tenor often attributed to the twenty-first century. As an act of protest, quiet may be available to a privileged few but writing a quiet novel remains a refusal to accept consensus and popularised narratives that frame the twenty-first century as unavoidably noisy and traumatic. Quiet novels do not raise their voices to compete with those shouting around them and, as a result, critics often describe them as 'old-fashioned', 'unusual', 'slow' or even 'small' because of the movement of their prose. Yet without valorising quiet as a mode of expression, and while acknowledging the aesthetic limitations, describing a contemporary novel as quiet reveals new and resonant ways of both processing and paying attention to American existence. By slowing the rate at which the reader receives ideas, these novels narrate processes of incremental external change and continual interior evolution that undermine the centrality of the event or the development of a narrative arc to the movement of narrative fiction. By paying attention to the quieter aspects of everyday experience, the quiet novel also reveals how quiet can be a multi-faceted state of existence, one that is communicative and expressive in as many ways as noise but filled with the potential for radical discourse by its marginalisation as a mode of expression.

**Notes**

1. See: Lars Hallnäs and Johan Redström, 'Slow Technology: Designing for Reflection', *Journal of Personal and Ubiquitous Computing*, 5:3 (2001), pp. 201–212; Peter Popham, 'Carlo Petrini: The Slow Food Gourmet Who Started a Revolution', *The Independent* (10 December 2009), http://www.independent.co.uk/life-style/food-and-drink/features/carlo-petrini-the-slow-food-gourmet-who-started-a-revolution-1837223.html; Anna-Louise Taylor, 'Slow Food: What Is its Legacy?' *BBC Food* (29 October 2012), http://www.bbc.co.uk/food/0/19993496; Daniel Kahneman, *Thinking Fast and Slow* (New York: Farrar, Straus, and Giroux, 2012). Kahneman, in particular, outlines differences between 'fast' intuitive thinking and 'slow' rational thinking that chime with a quiet aesthetic, arguing that our minds are erroneously prejudiced towards quick decisions but can be re-taught to favour slow thinking and processes.
2. Rob Orchard, *Delayed Gratification*, http://www.slow-journalism.com.
3. Rebecca Solnit, 'In the Day of the Postman: Diary', *The London Review of Books*, 35:16 (29 August 2013), p. 32.
4. Lynne Tillman, *American Genius; a Comedy* (New York: Soft Skull Press, 2006), p. 40.
5. Paul Harding, *Tinkers* (London: Random House, 2011), pp. 1–2.
6. Building a house from scratch is also an important trope in Robinson's earlier novel, *Housekeeping*, and other contemporary quiet novels: Elizabeth Strout's *Olive Kitteridge: A Novel in Stories* and Denis Johnson's *Train Dreams*.
7. Richard Powers, *The Echo Maker* (London: Vintage, 2007), p. 13.
8. Ibid., p. 177.
9. Solnit, 'In the Day of the Postman: Diary', p. 32.
10. Alice Bennett, *Afterlife and Narrative in Contemporary Fictions* (London: Palgrave Macmillan, 2012), p. 198.
11. Harding, *Tinkers*, pp. 72, 73, 122, 130.
12. Teju Cole, *Open City* (New York: Faber & Faber, 2011), p. 131.

13 Ibid., p. 39.
14 Ben Lerner, *Leaving the Atocha Station* (London: Granta, 2011), p. 63.
15 Tillman, *American Genius*, pp. 34, 278.

# Bibliography

Abel, Elizabeth. *Virginia Woolf and the Fictions of Psychoanalysis*. Chicago: University of Chicago Press, 1989.
Acocella, Joan. 'Lonesome Road'. *The New Yorker*, 6 October 2014. http://www.newyorker.com/magazine/2014/10/06/lonesome-road. Accessed 10 January 2011.
'Ada Cambridge's New Novel'. *The New York Times*. Saturday Review of Books and Art, 25 June 1898. http://query.nytimes.com/mem/archive-free/pdf?res=F70A16F83C5C1173 8DDDAC0A94 DE405B8885F0D3. Accessed 15 June 2013.
Adorno, Theodor W. 'Cultural Criticism and Society'. *Prisms*, trans. Samuel Weber and Sherry Weber. New York: Doubleday, 1981, pp. 17–34.
——. 'After Auschwitz'. *Negative Dialectics*, trans. E. B. Ashton. New York: Continuum, 2005, pp. 361–364.
Akbar, Arifa. 'John Williams' Stoner Enjoys Renaissance'. *The Independent*, 4 June 2013. http://www.independent.co.uk/arts-entertainment/books/features/john-williams-stoner-enjoys-renaissance-8642782.html. Accessed 10 June 2013.
Alameddine, Rabih. *An Unnecessary Woman*. New York: Grove Press, 2011.
Alden, Henry Mills. 'Miss Tommy'. *Harper's New Monthly Magazine* 69.414 (November 1884).
Alexander, Jeffrey C. 'Toward a Theory of Cultural Trauma', in *Cultural Trauma and Collective Identity*, ed. Jeffrey C. Alexander. Berkeley: University of California Press, 2004, pp. 1–20.
Almond, Steve. 'Lost and Found'. *The Rumpus*, 26 January 2009. http://therumpus.net /2009/01/lost-and-found-by-steve-almond/. Accessed 13 June 2013.
Alter, Alexandra. 'The World is Ending'. *The New York Times*, 5 September 2014. http://www.nytimes.com/2014/09/06/books/station-eleven-joins-falls-crop-of-dystopian-novels.html. Accessed 10 October 2015.

# Bibliography

Altman, Janet. *Epistolarity: Approaches to Form.* Columbus: Ohio State University, 1982.
Amis, Martin. 'The Voice of the Lonely Crowd'. *The Guardian*, 1 June 2002. http://www.theguardian.com/books/2002/jun/01/philosophy.society. Accessed 24 October 2010.
*A Moment of Silence.* New York: Marvel Comics, 2001.
Anderson, Douglas. 'Re-Reading *The Silence of Bartleby*'. *American Literary History* 20:3 (fall 2008), pp. 479–486.
Anderson, Jon. *Understanding Cultural Geography: Places and Traces.* Abingdon: Routledge, 2010.
'An Iowan Troy'. *The Economist*, 13 January 2005. http://www.economist.com/node/3555878. Accessed 13 April 2012.
Antrim, Taylor. 'The Best Debut of 2011'. *The Daily Beast*, Books, 2 July 2011. http://www.thedailybeast.com/articles/2011/02/07/open-city-by-teju-cole-review.html. Accessed 21 January 2016.
Arensberg, Ann. 'Seven Seconds', in *Conversations with Don DeLillo*, ed. Thomas DePietro. Jackson: University of Mississippi Press, 2004, pp. 40–46.
Aristotle. *Metaphysics*, translated by Thomas Taylor. London: Davis, Wilks & Taylor, 1801.
Arnold, Andrew D. 'The Most Serious Comix Pt. 2'. *Time*, 5 February 2002. http://www.time.com/time/arts/article/0,8599,198966,00.html. Accessed 2 November 2011.
Atkins, Stephen. ed. *The 9/11 Encyclopaedia: Second Edition.* Santa Barbara, CA: ABC-CLIO, 2011.
Attali, Jacques. *Noise: The Political Economy of Music*, trans. Brian Massumi. Minneapolis: University of Minnesota Press, 1977.
Auster, Paul. *The Brooklyn Follies.* New York: Picador, 2005.
Bachner, Sally. *The Prestige of Violence.* Athens: University of Georgia Press, 2011.
Badiou, Alain. *L'Être et l'Événement.* Paris: Seuil, 1988.
Bady, Aaron. 'Interview: Teju Cole'. *Post-45*, 19 January 2015. http://post45.research.yale.edu/2015/01/interview-teju-cole/. Accessed 2 February 2015.
Baelo-Allué, Sonia. 'The Depiction of 9/11 in Literature: The Role of Images and Intermedial References'. *Radical History Review*, 111 (2011), pp. 184–193.
Bakhtin, Mikhail. *The Dialogic Imagination*, ed. Michael Holquist, trans. Caryl Emerson and Michael Holquist. London: University of Texas Press, 1981.
Barnes, Julian. *The Sense of an Ending.* London: Vintage, 2011.
Barron, John. '*Enon* by Paul Harding'. *Chicago Tribune*, Printers' Row Preview, 15 September 2013. http://articles.chicago tribune.com/2013-09-15/features/ct-prj-0915-enon-paul-harding-20130915_1_paul-harding-prin ters-row-journal-enon. Accessed 17 September 2013.

Barthes, Roland. *The Responsibility of Forms*, ed. Richard Howard. Oakland: University of California Press, 1985.
——. *The Rustle of Language*, trans. Richard Howard. Berkeley: University of California Press, 1986.
Baudelaire, Charles. 'The Painter of Modern Life'. *Baudelaire: Selected Writings on Art and Artists*, ed. and trans. P. E. Benjamin. Harmondsworth: Penguin, 1972, pp. 390–436.
——. 'L'Horloge', in *The Flowers of Evil*. Oxford: Oxford World Classics, 1993, p. 160.
Baudrillard, Jean. *The Spirit of Terrorism and Requiem for the Twin Towers*, trans. Chris Turner. London: Verso, 2002.
Beaumont, Matthew and Geoffrey Dart, eds. *Restless Cities*. London: Verso, 2010.
Beckett, Samuel. 'Proust in Pieces'. *The Spectator*, 23 June 1934, pp. 63–65.
Benaim, Alexander. 'Q&A'. By. *Intelligent Life*, The Blog. http://moreintelligentlife.com/blog/alexander-benaim/qa-paul-harding-author-pulitzer-prize-winner. Accessed 13 July 2014.
Benjamin, Walter. 'The Image of Proust', in *Illuminations: Essays and Reflections*, ed. Walter Benjamin and trans. Harry Zohn. New York: Random House, 1968, pp. 201–216.
——. *Selected Writings, 1938–1940*, vol. 4, ed. Howard Eiland and Michael W. Jennings, trans. Edmund Jephcott. Cambridge, MA: Harvard University Press, 2003.
Bennett, Alice. *Afterlife and Narrative in Contemporary Fictions*. London: Palgrave Macmillan, 2012.
Berger, Kevin. 'The Art of Fiction No. 175'. *The Paris Review*, 164 (winter 2002–3). http://www.theparisreview.org/interviews/298/the-art-of-fiction-no-175-richard-powers. Accessed 4 June 2013.
Bergson, Henri. 'Creative Evolution'. *Henry Bergson: Key Writings*, ed. Keith Ansell-Pearson and John Mullarkey. London: Continuum, 2002.
Berlant, Lauren. 'Intuitionists: History and the Affective Event'. *American Literary History* 20:4 (winter 2008), pp. 845–860.
——. *Cruel Optimism*. Durham, NC: Duke University Press, 2012.
Berman, Emmanuel, ed. *Essential Papers on Literature and Psychoanalysis*. New York: New York University Press, 1993.
Berman, Marshall. *All that is Solid Melts into Air: The Experience of Modernity*. New York: Simon and Schuster, 1982.
Bickman, Martin. *Walden: Volatile Truths*. New York: Twayne Publishers, 1992.
Bijsterveld, Karin. *Mechanical Sound: Technology, Culture, and Public Problems of Noise in the Twentieth Century*. Cambridge, MA: MIT Press, 2008.
Birkerts, Sven. *American Energies: Essays on Fiction*. London: Faber & Faber, 1992.

———. *The Gutenberg Elegies: The Fate of Reading in an Electronic Age*. London: Faber & Faber, 1994.

Birnbaum, Robert Ellis, 'Brett Easton Ellis'. *The Morning News*, 19 January 2006. http://www.themorningnews.org/article/bret-easton-ellis. Accessed 13 March 2016.

Block, Lawrence. *Small Town: A Novel of New York*. New York: Orion Paperbacks, 2003.

Boddy, Kasia. 'Review: *Home* by Marilynne Robinson'. *The Telegraph*, Culture, 28 September 2008. http://www.telegraph.co.uk/culture/books/fictionreviews/3561288/Review-Home-by-Marilynne-Robinson.html. Accessed 13 March 2016.

———. 'Lynne Tillman and the Great American Novel'. *electronic book review*, 24 July 2011. http://www.electronicbookreview.com/thread/fictionspresent/american. Accessed 3 December 2015.

Boehmer, Elleke and Stephen Morton, eds. *Terror and the Postcolonial*. Oxford: Blackwell, 2010.

Bois, Yves-Alain and Rosalind Krauss. *Formless: A User's Guide*. New York: Zone Books, 1997.

Bond, Lucy. 'Compromised Critique: A Meta-Critical Analysis of American Studies After 9/11'. *Journal of American Studies*, 45: special issue 4 (November 2011), pp. 733–756.

Bouchard, Larry D. 'Belief, Revelation, and Trust: Faith and the Mind's Margins in Ian McEwan's *Saturday* and Paul Harding's *Tinkers*'. *Christianity and Literature*, 63:4 (summer 2014), pp. 449–465.

Bouson, J. Brooks. *Quiet As It's Kept: Shame, Trauma, and Race in the Novels of Toni Morrison*. New York: State University of New York Press, 1999.

Boyd, Brian. *On the Origin of Stories: Evolution, Cognition, and Fiction*. Cambridge, MA: The Belknap Press of Harvard University Press, 2009.

Boxall, Peter. 'Late: Fictional Time in the Twenty-First Century'. *Contemporary Literature*, 53:4, Fiction Since 2000: Post-Millennial Commitments (winter 2012), pp. 681–712.

Brackett, Virginia and Victoria Gaydosik. 'The Warden', in *The Eighteenth and Nineteenth Century British Novel*, ed. Virginia Brackett and Victoria Gaydosik. New York: Facts on File, 2006, pp. 468–474.

Bradshaw, David. 'Woolf's London, London's Woolf', in *Virginia Woolf in Context*, ed. Jane Goldman and Bryony Randall. Cambridge: Cambridge University Press, 2012, pp. 229–242.

Branch, Melvin Campbell. *Urban Air Traffic and City Planning: Case Study of Los Angeles County*. New York: Praeger Publishers, 1973.

Brand, Dana. *Spectator and the City in Nineteenth-Century American Literature*. Cambridge: Cambridge University Press, 1991.

Brockes, Emma. 'Welcome to the Summer of Nothingness: How One Book Made it Hip to Be Bored'. *The Guardian*, 5 June 2014. http://www.the

guardian.com/commentisfree/emma-brockes-column/2014/jun/05/sum mer-karl-ove-knausgard-book-hip-to-be-bored. Accessed 25 June 2014.
Brooker, Peter. *New York Fictions: Modernity, Postmodernism, The New Modern*. New York: Longman, 1996.
Brooks, Geraldine. *March*. New York: Viking Press, 2005.
Brooks, Peter. *Reading for the Plot: Design and Intention in Narrative*. Cambridge, MA: Harvard University Press, 1984.
Brown, Jeffrey. 'Conversation: Pulitzer Prize Winner in Fiction, Paul Harding'. *PBS Newshour*, 16 April 2010. http://www.pbs.org/newshour/art/blog/2010/04/conversation-pulitzer-prize-winner-in-fiction-paul-hardi ng.html. Accessed 13 July 2014.
Buell, Lawrence. *Emerson*. Cambridge, MA: Harvard University Press, 2003.
Burn, Stephen J. *Jonathan Franzen at the End of Postmodernism*. London: Continuum, 2008.
———. 'An Interview with Richard Powers'. *Contemporary Literature*, 49:2 (summer 2008), pp. 163–179.
———. 'Reading the Multiple Drafts Novel'. *Modern Fiction Studies*, 58:3 (fall 2012), pp. 436–458.
Cage, John. '45' for a Speaker'. *Silence: Lectures and Writings*. Middletown, CT: Wesleyan University Press, 2001, pp. 146–193.
———. 'Lecture on Nothing'. *Silence: Lectures and Writings*. Middletown, CT: Wesleyan University Press, 2001, pp. 109–127.
Cain, Susan. *Quiet: The Power of Introverts in a World that Can't Stop Talking*. London: Penguin, 2012.
Campbell, Lisa. 'New Marilynne Robinson Novel for 2014'. *The Bookseller*, News, 20 September 2013. http://www.thebookseller.com/news/new-mar ilynne-robinson-novel-2014.html. Accessed 9 October 2013.
Cameron, Claire. 'A Forgotten Bestseller: The Saga of John Williams' *Stoner*'. *The Millions*, 6 June 2013. http://www.themillions .com/2013/06/a-for gotten-bestseller-the-saga-of-john-williamss-stoner.html. Accessed 10 June 2013.
Cannon, Michael. *Lachlan's War*. London: Penguin, 2006.
Caruth, Cathy. *Unclaimed Experience: Trauma, Narrative, and History*. Baltimore, MD: Johns Hopkins University Press, 1996.
Chapman, Mary. *Making Noise, Making News: Suffrage Print Culture and U.S. Modernism*. Oxford: Oxford University Press, 2014.
Charles, Ron. 'Robinson Confident of a Fourth Gilead Novel'. *The Washington Post*, 31 March 2015. http://www.washingtonpost.com/blogs/style-blog/wp/2015/03/31/marilynne-robinson-confident-about-a-fourth-gilead-novel/. Accessed 4 May 2016.
Chesser, Eustace. *Unquiet Minds: Leaves from a Psychologist's Casebook*. New York: Roy Publishers, 1952.
Churchwell, Sarah. 'A Man of Sorrows'. *The Guardian*, 4 October 2008.

http://www.theguardian.com/books/2008/oct/04/fiction. Accessed 10 October 2010.
———. 'Marilynne Robinson's Lila – A Great Achievement in US Fiction'. *The Guardian*, 7 November 2014. http://www.theguardian.com/books/2014/nov/07/marilynne-robinson-lila-great-achievement-contemporary-us-fiction-gilead. Accessed 8 November 2014.
Clayton, Jay. *The Pleasures of Babel: Contemporary American Literature and Theory*. Oxford: Oxford University Press, 1993.
Cole, Teju. *Open City*. London: Faber & Faber. 2011
———. 'By the Book'. *The New York Times*, Sunday Review, 9 March 2014, p. 8.
———. *Every Day is for the Thief*. New York: Faber & Faber, 2014.
Corrigan, Maureen. 'Could "'Submission" Be America's Sept. 11 Novel?' *NPR*, Books, 6 September 2011. http://wap.npr.org/news/Books/139942267. Accessed 11 November 2011.
———. 'Life without Plot in *Leaving the Atocha Station*'. NPR, 2011. ProQuest. http://search.proquest.com/docview/902740950?accountid=14693. Accessed 15 December 2016.
Costello, Matthew J. 'Spandex Agonistes: Superhero Comics Confront the War on Terror', in *Portraying 9/11: Essays on Representations in Comics, Literature, Film and Theatre*, ed. Véronique Bragard, Christophe Dony and Warren Rosenberg. Jefferson, NC: McFarland and Company Inc., Publishers, 2011, pp. 30–43.
Coughlan, Robert. 'How We Appear to Others'. *Life*, 23 December 1957, pp. 150–156.
Coverley, Merlin. *The Art of Wandering: The Writer as Walker*. Harpenden: Oldcastle Books, 2012.
Cowles, Gregory. '*Tinkers* by Paul Harding: The One that Got Away'. *The New York Times*, 12 April 2010. http://artsbeat.blogs.nytimes.com/2010/04/12/the-one-that-got-away/?_php=true&_type= blogs&_r=0. Accessed 12 December 2011.
Crain, Caleb. *Necessary Errors*. New York: Penguin, 2013.
Currie, Mark. *Postmodern Narrative Theory*. London: Palgrave Macmillan, 1998.
———. 'The Expansion of Tense'. *Narrative*, 17:3 (October 2009), pp. 353–367.
———. *About Time: Narrative Fiction and the Philosophy of Time*. Edinburgh: Edinburgh University Press, 2010.
Dainton, Barry. *Stream of Consciousness: Unity and Continuity in Conscious Experience*. Abingdon: Routledge, 2000.
Damasio, Antonio. *The Feeling of What Happens: Body, Emotion and the Making of Consciousness*. New York: Random House, 2000.
Dames, Nicholas. 'The Theory Generation'. *n+1*, 24 October 2012. http://nplusonemag.com/the-theory-generation. Accessed 30 October 2012.

Davis, Clark. '"Not Like Any Form of Activity": Waiting in Emerson, Melville, and Weil'. *Common Knowledge*, 15:1 (winter 2009), pp. 39–58.

Davis, Lydia, Eric Dean Rasmussen and Ron Shavers. 'Uncovered'. *electronic book review*, 26 March 2011. http://www.electronicbookreview.com/thread/fictionspresent/uncovered. Accessed 10 April 2012.

de Certeau, Michel. *The Practice of Everyday Life*, trans. Steven Rendell. Berkeley: University of California Press, 1988.

DeFalco, Amelia. 'In Praise of Idleness: Aging and the Morality of Inactivity'. *Cultural Critique*, 92 (winter 2012), pp. 84–113.

Degnan, Luke. 'Phoned-In #4'. *BOMB Magazine*, 19 March 2010. http://bombsite.com/issues/1000/articles/4500. Accessed 19 June 2013.

DeLillo, Don. *White Noise*. New York: Viking Press, 1985.

——. *Mao II*. New York: Random House, 1991.

——. 'In The Ruins of the Future'' *Harper's Magazine*, December 2001, pp. 33–40.

——. *Falling Man*. New York: Picador, 2007.

——. *Libra*. London: Penguin, 2011.

DeMille, Nelson. *Night Fall*. New York: Grand Central Publishing, 2004.

Dennett, Daniel. *Consciousness Explained*. London: Penguin, 1991.

Deresiewicz, William. 'Why Has "My Struggle"' Been Anointed a Literary Masterpiece?' *The Nation*, 2 June 2014. http://www.thenation.com/article/179853/why-has-my-struggle-been-anointed-literary-masterpiece. Accessed 5 August 2014.

DeRosa, Aaron. 'Analysing Literature after 9/11'. *Modern Fiction Studies*, 57:3 (fall 2011), pp. 607–618.

Derrida, Jacques. *Archive Fever: A Freudian Impression*, trans. Eric Prenowitz. Chicago: University of Chicago Press, 1995.

——. *Philosophy in a Time of Terror: Dialogues with Jürgen Habermas and Jacques Derrida*, trans. Giovanna Borradori. Chicago: University of Chicago Press, 2003.

——. 'A Certain Impossible Possibility of Saying the Event', trans. Gila Walker. *Critical Inquiry*, 33 (winter 2007), pp. 441–461.

Desai, Kiran and Susan Koshy. 'Postcolonial Studies after 9/11: A Response to Ali Behdad'. *American Literary History*, 20:1–2 (spring/summer 2008), pp. 300–303.

Dickstein, Morris. 'The Inner Lives of Men'. *The New York Times*, 17 June 2007. http://www.nytimes.com/2007/06/17/books/review/Dickstein-t.html?pagewanted=1&_r=2&. Accessed 5 October 2013.

Diekman, Stefanie. 'How Marvel Dealt with 9/11'. *The Guardian*, 24 April 2009. http://www.guardian.co.uk/culture/2004/apr/24/guesteditors3. Accessed 12 October 2010.

Dilgen, Regina. 'The Original Occupy Wall Street: Melville's "Bartleby, the Scrivener"'. *Radical Teacher*, 93 (spring 2012), pp. 54–55.

Dimock, Wai Chee. *Through other Continents: American Literature across Deep Time*. Princeton, NJ: Princeton University Press, 2006.
Doidge, Norman. *The Brain's Way of Healing: Remarkable Discoveries and Recoveries from the Frontiers of Neuroplasticity*. London: Penguin, 2015.
Donato, Claire. 'Acclaimed young poet Ben Lerner relocates to Pittsburgh'. *Pittsburgh City Paper*, 24 January 2008. http://www.pghcitypaper.com/pittsburgh/acclaimed-young-poet-ben-lerner-relocates-to-pittsburgh/Content?oid=1339655. Accessed 19 June 2013.
Dos Passos, John. *Manhattan Transfer*. New York: Houghton Mifflin Company, 2000.
Douglas, Alan Walwrath. *Displacing the Divine: The Minister in the Mirror of American Fiction*. New York: Columbia University Press, 2010.
Douglas, Christopher. 'Christian Multiculturalism and Unlearned History in Marilynne Robinson's *Gilead*'. *Novel: A Forum in Fiction*, 44:3 (2011), pp. 333–353.
Dunst, Alexander. 'After Trauma: Time and Affect in American Culture Beyond 9/11'. *parallax*, 18:2 (2012), pp. 56–71.
Duvall, John N. and Robert P. Marzec. 'Narrating 9/11'. *Modern Fiction Studies*, 57:3. (fall 2011), pp. 381–400.
Edwards, Zachary. *Primitae*. London: Provost and Co. 1869, p. 203.
Egan, Jennifer. *Look at Me*. New York: Random House, 2001.
——. *A Visit from the Goon Squad*. New York: Random House, 2010.
Egan, Maurice Francis. 'The Return of the Quiet Novel'. *The Bookman*, September 1921, p. 18.
Einstein, Albert. 'Civilisation and Science.' Published as 'Personal Liberty' in *The New York Herald Tribune*, 4 February 1934, pp. 12–14.
Emerson, Gloria. *Conversations with Graham Greene*. Edited by Henry J. Donaghy. Jackson: University Press of Mississippi, 1992.
Emerson, Ralph Waldo. 'Self Reliance'. *The Essential Writings of Ralph Waldo Emerson*, ed. Brooks Atkinson. New York: Random House, 2000, pp. 132–153.
——. 'The American Scholar'. *The Essential Writings of Ralph Waldo Emerson*, ed. Brooks Atkinson. New York: Random House, 2000, pp. 43–62.
Epstein, Russell. 'Consciousness, Art, and the Brain: Lessons from Marcel Proust'. *Consciousness and Cognition*, 13:2 (June 2004), 213–240.
Euripides. *The Bakkhai*. *The Essential Euripides*, trans. Robert Emmet Meagher. Amherst: University of Massachusetts Press, 1995.
Fay, Sarah. 'The Art of Fiction #198'. *The Paris Review*, 186 (fall 2008). http://www.theparisreview.org/interviews/5863/the-art-of-fiction-no-198-marilynne-robinson. Accessed 12 June 2015.
Fitzgerald, Adam. 'Ben Lerner'. *BOMB*, September 2011. http://bombsite.com/issues/999/articles/6081. Accessed 5 April 2017.
Fletcher, Chris. 'Leaving the Atocha Station'. *The Quarterly Conversation*, 5

December 2011. http://quarterlyconversation.com/leaving-the-atocha-station-by-ben-lerner. Accessed 5 April 2017.

Flint, Kate. 'Sounds of the City: Virginia Woolf and Modernist Noise', in *Literature, Science, Psychoanalysis 1830–1970: Essays in Honour of Gillian Beer*, ed. Helen Small and Trudi Tate. Oxford: Oxford University Press, 2003, pp. 181–194.

Fludernik, Monika. *An Introduction to Narratology*. Oxford: Routledge, 2009.

Franzen, Jonathan. 'Perchance to Dream: In the Ages of Images, A Reason to Write Novels'. *Harper's Magazine*, April 1996, pp. 35–54.

——. 'Why Bother?', in *How to Be Alone*. London: Harper Collins, 2002, pp. 55–97.

——. *The Corrections*. New York: Harper Perennial, 2007.

——. *Freedom*. London: Fourth Estate, 2010.

——. 'Books of the Year 2011'. *The Guardian*, 25 November 2011. https://www.theguardian.com/books/2011/nov/25/books-of-the-year. Accessed 5 April 2017.

Freele, Stefanie. 'The Makings of a Regional Press: In Conversation with Laura Stanfill'. *Late Night Library*, 20 November 2013. http://latenightlibrary.org/the_makings_of_a_regional_press_laura_stanfill/. Accessed 22 November 2013.

Freeman, John. 'Lynne Tillman: The Author who Inspired the Manhattan Avant-Garde'. *Belfast Telegraph*, 14 December 2007. http://www.belfasttelegraph.co.uk/lifestyle/books/lynne-tillman-the-author-who-inspired-the-manhattan-avantgarde-28070792.html. Accessed 9 April 2013.

Freud, Sigmund. *The Unconscious*, trans, Graham Frankland. London: Penguin, 2005.

Frost, Laura. 'Still Life: 9/11's Falling Bodies', in *Literature after 9/11*, ed. Ann Keniston and Jeanne Follansbee Quinn. London: Routledge, 2002, pp. 180–208.

Fujii, Hikaru. *Outside, America: The Temporal Turn in Contemporary American Fiction*. New York: Bloomsbury, 2013.

Furst, Lilian R. *Realism*. New York: Longman, 1992.

Galchen, Rivka. *Atmospheric Disturbances*. London: Harper Collins, 2008.

Genette, Gérard. *Narrative Discourse: An Essay in Method*, trans. Jane E. Lewin. Ithaca, NY: Cornell University Press, 1983.

Geppert, Hans Vilmar. '"A Cluster of Signs" Semiotic Micrologies in Nineteenth-Century Realism: Madame Bovary, Middlemarch, Effi Briest'. *The Germanic Review: Literature, Culture, Theory*, 73:3 (1998), pp. 239–250.

Gioia, Ted. 'The Rise of the Fragmented Novel: An Essay in 26 Fragments'. *Fractious Fiction*, 17 July 2013. http://fractiousfiction.com/rise_of_the_fragmented_novel. Accessed 15 July 2014.

Glejzer, Richard. 'Witnessing 9/11: Art Spiegelman and the Persistance of

Trauma', in *Literature after 9/11*, ed. Ann Keniston and Jeanne Follansbee Quinn. London: Routledge, 2002, pp. 99–122.

Glenn, Cheryl. *Unspoken: A Rhetoric of Silence*. Carbondale: Southern Illinois University Press, 2004.

Gonzalez, Jeffrey. 'Ontologies of Interdependence, the Sacred, and Health Care: Marilynne Robinson's *Gilead* and *Home*'. *Critique: Studies in Contemporary Fiction*, 55:4 (2014), pp. 373–388.

Gray, Richard. 'Open Doors, Closed Minds: American Prose Writing at a Time of Crisis'. *American Literary History*, 21.1 (spring 2009), pp. 128–142.

———. *After the Fall*. Oxford: Wiley Blackwell, 2011.

Green, Jeremy. *Late Postmodernism: American Fiction at the Millennium*. New York: Palgrave Macmillan, 2005.

Greene, Graham. *The Quiet American*. London: Vintage, 2004.

Greif, Mark. '"The Death of the Novel" and Its Afterlives: Toward a History of the "Big, Ambitious Novel"'. *boundary 2*, 36:2 (2009), pp. 11–30.

Gros, Frédéric. *A Philosophy of Walking*. London: Verso, 2014.

Gunn, James. *Paratexts: Introductions to Science Fiction and Fantasy*. Plymouth: Scarecrow Press, 2013.

Habash, Gabe. '*Stoner* finds overseas success'. *Publisher's Weekly*, 20 April 2013. http://www.publishersweekly.com/pw/by-topic/international/international-book-news/article/56913-stoner-finds-overseas-success.html. Accessed 15 June 2014.

Haddon, Mark. *The Curious Incident of the Dog in the Night-time*. London: Vintage, 2004.

Hadley, Tessa. 'An Attic Full of Sermons'. *London Review of Books*, 27:8 (21 April 2005), p. 19.

Hale, Dorothy. 'Bakhtin in African American Literary Theory'. *English Literary History*, 61:2 (1994), pp. 445–471.

Hallnäs, Lars and Johan Redström. 'Slow Technology: Designing for Reflection'. *Journal of Personal and Ubiquitous Computing*, 5:3 (2001), pp. 201–212.

Hamid, Mohsin. *The Reluctant Fundamentalist*. New York: Hamish Hamilton, 2007.

Hammond, Claudia. *Time Warped: Unlocking the Mysteries of Time Perception*. London: Harper Perennial, 2012.

Harding, Paul. *Enon*. London: Random House, 2013.

———. 'Second Coming'. *Boston Globe*. 25 August 2013. http://www.bostonglobe.com/magazine/2013/08/24/author-paul-harding-his-follow-tinkers/WCY3CQ7ucDjM7IPEpRPvYN/story.html. Accessed 14 July 2014.

———. *Tinkers*. London: Random House, 2011.

Harris, Charles B. 'The Story of the Self: *The Echo Maker* and Neurological Realism', in *Intersections: Essays on Richard Powers*, ed. Stephen J. Burn and Peter Dempsey. Champaign, IL: Dalkey Archive, 2008, pp. 230–259.

Harris, Chauncy B. and Edward L Ullman. 'The Nature of Cities'. *The Annals of the American Academy of Political and Social Science*, 242 (1945), pp. 7–17.
Hart, Jeffrey. *The Living Moment: Modernism in a Broken World.* Evanston, IL: Northwestern University Press, 2012.
Hartwiger, Andrew. 'The Postcolonial Flâneur: *Open City* and the Urban Palimpsest'. *Postcolonial Text*, 11:1 (2016). http://postcolonial.org/index.php/pct/article/viewArticle/1970. Accessed 1 April 2017.
Harvey, David. *Paris, Capital of Modernity.* New York: Routledge, 2003.
Hassan, Ihab. *The Postmodern Turn: Essays in Postmodern Theory and Culture.* Columbus: Ohio State University Press, 1987.
Hassan, Robert. 'Globalization and the "Temporal Turn": Recent Trends and Issue in Time Studies'. *The Korean Journal of Policy Studies*, 25:2 (2010), pp. 83–92.
Hawthorne, Nathaniel. *The Scarlet Letter.* New York: Penguin, 1983.
———. *The Blithedale Romance.* New York: Tark Classic Fiction, 2008.
Heidegger, Martin. *Being and Time*, trans. Max Verlag. Albany: State University of New York Press, 2001.
Hendy, David. *Noise: A Human History of Sound and Listening.* London: Profile Books, 2014.
Herman, Luc and Bart Vervaeck. 'Capturing Capgras: *The Echo Maker* by Richard Powers'. *Style*, 43:3 (fall 2009), pp. 407–428.
*Heroes: The World's Greatest Super Hero Creators Honor The World's Greatest Heroes.* New York: Marvel, 2001.
Herz, Rachel. 'A Naturalistic Analysis of Autobiographical Memories Triggered by Olfactory Visual and Auditory Stimuli'. *Chemical Senses*, 29:217 (2004), pp. 217–224.
Heti, Sheila. *How Should a Person Be?* London: Random House, 2013.
Hitchens, Peter. 'Some Reflections on the Novels of Marilynne Robinson'. *Daily Mail*, 8 January 2015. http://hitchensblog.mailonsunday.co.uk/2015/01/some-reflections-on-the-novels-of-marilynne-robinson.html. Accessed 22 February 2015.
Hoby, Hermione. 'Norway's Proust and a Life Laid Bare'. *The Observer.* 1 March 2013, p. 36.
Huelsenbeck, Richard. 'First German Dadaist Manifesto', in *Art in Theory 1900–1990: An Anthology of Changing Ideas*, ed. Charles Harrison and Paul Wood. Oxford: Blackwell, 1992, pp. 253–255.
Hughes, Robert. *The Shock of the New.* London: Faber & Faber, 1991.
Hume, Kathryn. *Aggressive Fictions: Reading the Contemporary American Novel.* Ithaca, NY: Cornell University Press, 2011.
Hungerford, Amy. *Postmodern Belief: American Literature and Religion since 1960.* Princeton, NJ: Princeton University Press, 2010.
'In Other Days'. *The Spectator*, Fiction, 16 June 1915, p. 22.

James, David. 'Introduction: Mapping Modernist Continuities', in *The Legacies of Modernism: Historicizing Postwar and Contemporary Fiction*, ed. David James. Cambridge: Cambridge University Press, 2011, pp. 1–20.
———. 'A Renaissance for the Crystalline Novel?' *Contemporary Literature* 53:4 (winter 2012), pp. 845–874.
James, Henry. *Partial Portraits*. New York: Haskell House Publishers, 1953.
James, William. 'The Stream of Consciousness', in *Writings: 1878–1899*. New York: Library of Congress, 1992, pp. 388–408.
Jameson, Fredric. 'Magical Narrative: Romance as Genre'. *New Literary History*, 7:1, Critical Challenges: The Bellagio Symposium (autumn 1975), pp. 135–163.
———. *The Political Unconscious: Narrative as a Socially Symbolic Act*. Ithaca, NY: Cornell University Press, 1981.
———. 'Fear and Loathing in Globalization.' *New Left Review*, 23 (September–October 2003). http://newleftreview.org/II/23/fredric-jameson-fear-and-loathing-in-globalization. Accessed 24 June 2014.
Jamison, Leslie and Daniel Mendelsohn. 'Bookends'. *New York Times Book Review*, 28 December 2014. ProQuest. http://search.proquest.com/docview/1640813267?accountid=14693. Accessed 5 May 2016.
Johnson, Charles Frederick. *Outline History of English and American Literature*. New York: American Book Company, 1900.
Johnson, Denis. *Train Dreams*. London: Granta, 2012.
Joyce, James. *Ulysses*. Oxford: Oxford University Press, 2008.
Jung, Carl Gustav. *Psychological Types*, trans. H. G. Baynes. Princeton, NJ: Princeton University Press, 1990.
Junod, Tom. 'The Falling Man'. *Esquire*, September 2003, pp. 177–199.
———. 'The Submission'. *Esquire*. Fiction. 2 December 2011. http://www.esquire.com/fiction/best-books-2011-1211-2. Accessed 5 December 2011.
Kahneman, Daniel. *Thinking Fast and Slow*. New York: Farrar, Straus, and Giroux, 2012.
Kakutani, Michiko. 'Books of the Times; A Hero with 9/11 Peripheral Vision'. *The New York Times*, Books, 18 March 2005. http://query.nytimes.com/gst/fullpage.html?res=9E01E0DD103CF93BA25750C0A9639C8B63. Accessed 17 March 2011.
Kaplan, E. Ann. *Trauma Culture: The Politics of Terror and Loss in Media and Literature*. Piscataway, NJ: Rutgers University Press, 2005.
Katz, Daniel. '"I Did not Walk Here all the Way from Prose": Ben Lerner's Virtual Poetics'. *Textual Practice*, 31.2 (March 2016), pp. 1–23.
Keeling, Kara and Josh Kun, eds. *Sound Clash: Listening to American Studies*. Baltimore, MD: Johns Hopkins University Press, 2012.
Keen, Suzanne. *Empathy and the Novel*. New York: Oxford University Press USA, 2010.

Keizer, Garret. *The Unwanted Sound of Everything We Want: A Book about Noise*. New York: Public Affairs, 2010.
Keniston, Ann. '"Not Needed, Except as Meaning": Belatedness in Post-9/11 American Poetry'. *Contemporary Literature*, 52:4 (winter 2011), pp. 658–683.
Kennedy, Seán. 'Beckett Reviewing MacGreevy: A Reconsideration'. *Irish University Review*, 35:2 (winter 2005), pp. 273–287.
——. 'Traumatic Brain Injury in Post-9/11 Fiction'. *Post 45*, 24 October 2015. http://post45.research.yale.edu/2015/10/traumatic-brain-injury-in-post-911-fiction/#identifier_4_6391. Accessed 4 January 2016.
Kenny, Nicolas. *The Feel of the City: Experiences of Urban Transformation*. Toronto: University of Toronto Press, 2014.
Kern, Stephen. *The Culture of Time and Space: 1880–1918*. Cambridge, MA: Harvard University Press, 1983.
Kiberd, Declan. *Ulysses and Us: The Art of Everyday Living*. London: Faber & Faber, 2010.
Kimball, Roger. 'The Great American Novel: Will there ever Be another?' *The Weekly Standard*, 17:23, 27 February 2012. http://www.weeklystandard.com/articles/great-american-novel_630022.html. Accessed 28 May 2014.
King, Amy M. 'Stillness: Alternative Temporalities in Nineteenth-Century Narrative'. *English Language Notes*, 46:1 (spring/summer 2008), pp. 95–103.
——. 'Quietism and Narrative Stillness'. *Common Knowledge*, 16:3 (fall 2010), pp. 532–551.
Knapp, Kathy. *American Unexceptionalism: The Everyman and the Suburban Novel after 9/11*. Iowa City: Iowa University Press, 2014.
Kohn, Robert E. 'Secrecy and Radiance in Marilynne Robinson's *Gilead* and *Home*'. *The Explicator*, 72:1 (2014), pp. 6–11.
Kosman, L. A. 'Charmides' First Definition: Sophrosyne as Quietness', in *Essays in Ancient Greek Philosophy II*, ed. John Peter Anton and Anthony Preus. New York: State University of New York Press, 1983.
Krapu, Gary L. 'Sandhill Cranes and the Platte River', in *Gatherings of Angels: Migrating Birds and Their Ecology*, ed. Kenneth P. Able. Ithaca, NY: Cornell University Press, 1999, pp. 103–117.
Krishnan, Madhu. 'Postcoloniality, Spatiality and Cosmopolitanism in the *Open City*'. *Textual Practice*, 29:4 (2015), pp. 675–696.
Kumar, Amitava. 'Pitch Forward'. *Guernica*, 15 March 2013. http://www.guernicamag.com/interviews/pitch-forward. Accessed 10 February 2016.
Kuo, Michelle and Albert Wu. 'Imperfect Strollers: Teju Cole, Ben Lerner, W. G. Sebald, and the Alienated Cosmopolitan'. *Los Angeles Review of Books*, 2 February 2013. http://lareviewofbooks.org/essay/imperfect-strollers-teju-cole-ben-lerner-w-g-sebald-and-the-alienated-cosmopolitan. Accessed 10 February 2016.
LaBelle, Brandon. *Background Noise: Perspectives on Sound Art*. London: Bloomsbury, 2006.

Ladd, Andrew. 'Blurbese: "Quiet".' *Ploughshares*, 27 July 2012. http://blog.pshares.org/index.php/blurbese-quiet/. Accessed 6 June 2013.
Lawrence, D. H. *Women in Love*. London: Penguin Classics, 2007.
———. E-mail communication with the author, 12 September 2013.
Lehrer, Jonah. *Proust Was a Neuroscientist*. London: Canongate, 2012.
Leise, Christopher. '"That Little Incandescence": Reading the Fragmentary and John Calvin in Marilynne Robinson's *Gilead*'. *Studies in the Novel*, 41:3 (fall 2009), pp. 348–367.
Leitch, Vincent B. 'Poststructuralist Cultural Critique', in *Cultural Criticism, Literary Theory, Poststructuralism in Literature: an Introduction to Fiction, Poetry, and Drama*. New York: Columbia University Press, 1992, pp. 3–15.
———. *Theory Matters*. London: Routledge, 2003.
Lerner, Ben. *The Lichtenberg Figures*. Port Townsend, WA: Copper Canyon Press, 2004.
———. *Angle of Yaw*. Port Townsend, WA: Copper Canyon Press, 2006.
———. *Mean Free Path*. Port Townsend, WA: Copper Canyon Press, 2010.
———. *Leaving the Atocha Station*. London: Granta, 2011.
———. *10:04*. London: Granta, 2014.
———. 'Diary: On Disliking Poetry'. *The London Review of Books*, 37:12 (8 June 2015), pp. 42–43.
———. *The Hatred of Poetry*. New York: Farrar, Straus & Giroux, 2016.
———. 'Once you start writing, the language has its own ideas...'. *booktrust*, (n.d.) http://www.booktrust.org.uk/books/adults/interviews/183. Accessed 10 February 2016.
Lethem, Jonathan. *Motherless Brooklyn*. New York: Faber & Faber, 2004.
Levarie, Siegmund. 'Noise'. *Critical Inquiry*, 4:1 (autumn 1977), pp. 21–31.
Lewis, Wyndham, ed. *Blast: Review of the Great English Vortex*, 1, 20 June 1913.
———. 'Rebel Art in Modern Life'. *Daily News*, 7 April 1914, p. 14.
Leypoldt, Günter. 'Shifting Meridians: US Authorship in World Literary Space'. *American Literary History*, 27:4 (winter 2015), pp. 769–787.
Limon, John. *Writing After War: American War Fiction from Realism to Postmodernism*. Oxford: Oxford University Press, 1994.
Lin, Tao. *Taipei*. London: Canongate Books, 2013.
Liu, Max. 'Palimpsest City'. *3:AM Magazine*, 16 August 2011. http://www.3ammagazine.com/3am/palimpsest-city/. Accessed 17 April 2013.
Lodge, David. *Thinks...* London: Vintage, 2001.
———. *Consciousness and the Novel: Connected Essays*. Cambridge, MA: Harvard University Press, 2002.
Lukas, David. 'A Multiplicity of Voices: On the Polyphonic Novel'. *The Millions*, 15 February 2013. http://www.themillions.com/2013/02/a-multiplicity-of-voices-on-the-polyphonic-novel.html. Accessed 20 March 2013.
Lurie, Susan. 'Spectacular Bodies and Political Knowledge: 9/11 Cultures and

the Problem of Dissent'. *American Literary History*, 25:1 (Special Issue: The Second Book Project, Spring 2013), pp. 176–189.

Lustig, T. J. '"Two-way Traffic"?: Syndrome as Symbol in Richard Powers' *The Echo Maker*', in *Diseases and Disorders in Contemporary Fiction: the Syndrome Syndrome*, ed. T. J. Lustig and James Peacock.London: Routledge, 2013, pp. 130–143.

Macarthur, David. 'Pragmatism, Metaphysical Quietism and the Problem of Normativity'. *Philosophical Topics*, 36 (2009), pp. 1–30.

Macarthur, David and Huw Price. 'Pragmatism, Quasi-Realism, and the Global Challenge', in *New Pragmatists*, ed. Cheryl Minsk. New York: Oxford University Press, 2007, pp. 91–120.

McCall, Dan. *The Silence of Bartleby*. New York: Cornell University Press, 1989.

McEwan, Ian. 'Beyond Belief'. *The Guardian*, G2, 12 September 2001, p. 2.

———. *Saturday*. London: Vintage, 2005.

McFarland, Kevin. 'Paul Harding: *Enon*'. *The AV Club*, 16 September 2013. http://www.avclub.com/review/paul-harding-ienoni-102847. Accessed 24 September 2015.

McGahern, John. *That They May Face the Rising Sun*. London: Faber & Faber, 2002.

McGregor, Jon. *If Nobody Speaks of Remarkable Things*. London: Bloomsbury, 2002.

McGurl, Mark. *The Program Era: Postwar Fiction and the Rise of Creative Writing*. Cambridge, MA: Harvard University Press, 2009.

McHale, Brian. *Pöstmödernist Fictiön*. London: Routledge, 1987.

McIlvanney, Liam and Ray Ryan, eds. *The Good of the Novel*. London: Continuum, 2002.

McInerney, Jay. *The Good Life*. London: Bloomsbury, 2006.

Mack, Adam. *Sensing Chicago: Noisemakers, Strikebreakers, and Muckrakers*. Urbana: University of Illinois Press, 2015.

Majumdar, Saikat. *Prose of the World: Modernism and the Banality of Empire*. New York: Columbia University Press, 2015.

Malone, Tess and Marisa Weiher. 'John Williams' Obscure *Stoner* Gets a Successful Second Chance'. *Vox*, 1 August 2013. http://www.voxmagazine.com/stories/2013/08/01/how-john-williams-obscure-stoner-went-jesse-hall-w/. Accessed 5 November 2013.

Mandel, Emily St. John.'On The Pleasures and Solitudes of Quiet Books'. *The Millions*, 27 August 2013. http://www.themillions.com/2013/08/on-the-pleasures-and-solitudes-of-quiet-books.html. Accessed 30 August 2013.

———. E-mail communication with the author, 1 September 2013.

Mao, Douglas. 'The Lack of Repose'. *Common Knowledge*, 15:3 (2009), pp. 412–437.

Martin, Niall. *Iain Sinclair: Noise, Neoliberalism and the Matter of London*. London: Bloomsbury, 2015.

May, Jon and Nigel Thrift, eds. *Timespace: Geographies of Temporality*. London: Routledge, 2001.
Meek, Allen. *Trauma and Media: Theories, Histories, and Images*. New York: Routledge, 2010.
Meister, Jan and Wilhelm Schernus, eds. *Time: From Concept to Narrative Construct*. Berlin: De Gruyter, 2011.
Melville, Herman. 'Bartleby, The Scrivener: A Story of Wall Street', in *Billy Budd and Other Stories*. Ware: Wordsworth Classics, 1998, pp. 1–38.
Mellor, Felicity. 'Shhhh? Scientists Need to Talk about not Talking'. *The Guardian*, Political science blog, 15 January 2014. http://www.theguardian.com/science/political-science/2014/jan/15/shhhh-scientists-need-to-talk-about-not-talking. Accessed 5 June 2014.
Messud, Claire. *The Emperor's Children*. New York: Knopf, 2006.
——. *The Woman Upstairs*. London: Picador, 2013.
Michaels, Walter Benn. *Gold Standard and the Logic of Naturalism*. Berkeley: University of California Press, 1987.
Michod, Alex. 'The Brain is the Ultimate Storytelling Machine and Consciousness is the Ultimate Story'. *The Believer*, February 2007. http://www.believermag.com/issues/200702/?read=interview_powers. Accessed 5 June 2013.
Miller, J. Hillis. 'Time and Literature'. *Daedalus*, 132:2 (On Time, Spring 2003), pp. 86–97.
Mishra, Pankja. 'The End of Innocence'. *The Guardian*, Guardian Review, 19 May 2007, p. 4.
Mitchell, W. J. T. '911: Criticism and Crisis'. *Critical Inquiry*, 28:2 (winter 2002), pp. 567–572.
Monteith, Sharon. 'Civil Rights Fictions', in *The Cambridge Companion to the Literature of the American South*, ed. Sharon Monteith. Cambridge: Cambridge University Press, 2013, pp. 1–10.
——. 'Revisiting the 1960s in Contemporary Fiction: "Where Do We Go from Here?"' in *Gender in the Civil Rights Movement*, ed. Sharon Monteith and Peter Ling. New York: Garland Publishing, 1999, pp. 215–238.
Moore, Colleen F. 'Noise: A Barrier to Children's Learning'. *Silent Scourge: Children, Pollution, and Why Scientists Disagree*. Oxford: Oxford University Press, 2009, pp. 140–174.
Morley, Catherine. 'Plotting Against America: 9/11 and the Spectacle of Terror in Contemporary American Fiction'. *Gramma*, 16 (2008), pp. 293–312.
Morrison, Toni. *The Bluest Eye*. London: Vintage, 1999.
——. *Love*. London: Chatto & Windus, 2003.
——. 'The Dead of September', in *Trauma at Home: After 9/11*, ed. Judith Greenberg. Lincoln: University of Nebraska Press, 2003, pp. 1–2.
——. *Beloved*. London: Vintage, 2007.
Msiska, Mpalive-Hangson. 'Sam Selvon's *The Lonely Londoners* and the

structure of Black Metropolitan Life', in *African Diaspora and the Metropolis: Reading the African, African American and Caribbean Experience*, ed. Fassil Demissie. London: Routledge, 2010, pp. 5–27.

Muntean, Laszlo. 'Naming the Unnameable: (De)constructing 9/11's "Falling Man"', in *Performing Memory in Art and Popular Culture*, ed. Liedeke Plate and Anneke Smelik. New York: Routledge, 2013, pp. 105–122.

Munzer, Stephen R. 'Self-Abandonment and Self-Denial: Quietism, Calvinism, and the Prospect of Hell'. *The Journal of Religious Ethics*, 33:4 (December 2005), pp. 747–781.

Nancy, Jean-Luc. *Listening*, trans. Charlotte Mandell. New York: Fordham University Press, 2007.

Neary, Lynn. 'Marilynne Robinson, at "Home" in the Heartland'. *NPR*, 20 September 2008. http://www.npr.org/templates/story/story.php?storyId =94799720. Accessed 17 August 2012.

Neria, Yuval, R. Marshall and E. Susser, eds. *9/11: Mental Health in the Wake of Terrorist Attacks*. Cambridge: Cambridge University Press, 2007.

Nesci, Catherine. 'Memory, Desire, Lyric: The *Flâneur*', in *The Cambridge Companion to the City in Literature*, ed. Kevin R. McNamara. Cambridge, Cambridge University Press, 2014, pp. 69–84.

Nicholls, Peter. 'Skin Deep: Lynne Tillman's *American Genius; a comedy*'. *electronic book review*, fictions present, 24 July 2011. http://www.electronic bookreview.com/ thread/fictionspresent/skindeep. Accessed 26 May 2012.

Nicholson, Geoff. *The Lost Art of Walking: The History, Science, Philosophy, and Literature of Pedestrianism*. New York: Riverhead Books, 2008.

Nicolaides, Becky M. and Andrew Wiese. *The Suburb Reader*. New York: Routledge, 2006.

Nin, Anaïs. *Linotte: The Early Diaries, Volume 1: 1927–1931*, trans. Jean L. Sherman. New York: Harcourt Brace & Company, 1978.

Nixon, Mark. 'Psychoanalysis, Quietism and Literary Waste', in *Samuel Beckett's German Diaries 1936–1937*. New York: Continuum Books, 2011, pp. 37–59.

Noggle, Chad A., Raymond S. Dean and Arthur M. Horton, eds. *The Encyclopaedia of Neuropsychological Disorders*. New York: Springer Publishing, 2012.

Noise Control Act of 1972. Public Law 92-574. 27 October 1972. https://www.gpo.gov/fdsys/pkg/PLAW-114publ38/html/PLAW-114publ38.htm. Accessed 12 December 2016.

Nowell, Danny. 'A Constant Current: Water and Loss in Marilynne Robinson's "Connie Bronson"'. *Tin House*, 5 November 2012. http://www.tinhouse.com/blog/19706/a-constant-current-water-and-loss-in-marilynne-robinsons-connie-bronson.html. Accessed 21 November 2015.

Nussbaum, Martha. 'The Professor of Parody'. *The New Republic*, 22 February

1999. http://www.tnr.com/archive/0299/022299/nussbaum022299.html. Accessed 12 June 2013.
O'Brien, Geoffrey. 'Lynne Tillman'. *BOMB Magazine*, autumn 2006. http://bombsite.com/issues/97/articles/2856. Accessed 10 April 2012.
O'Donnell, Patrick. *The American Novel Now*. Oxford: Wiley Blackwell, 2010.
Orchard, Rob. *Delayed Gratification*. http://www.slow-journalism.com. Accessed 10 January 2017.
Orecklin, Michele. 'On Her Time'. *Time Magazine*, Books, 22 November 2004. http://www.time.com/time/magazine/article/0,9171,995700,00.html. Accessed 27 April 2014.
O'Rourke, Karen. *Walking and Mapping: Artists as Cartographers*. Cambridge, MA: MIT Press, 2013.
O'Rourke, Meghan. 'A Moralist of the Midwest'. *The New York Times*, Magazine, 24 October 2004. http://www.nytimes.com/2004/10/24/magazine/24ROBINSON.html?_r=0. Accessed 27 April 2014.
Palmer, Alan. *Fictional Minds: Frontiers of Narrative*. Omaha: University of Nebraska Press, 2004.
Parini, Jay. 'Tinkers'. *The Guardian*, Guardian Review, Culture, 25 September 2010, p. 10.
Pease, Donald. '9/11: When Was "American Studies after the New Americanists"?', *boundary 2*, 33:3 (2006), pp. 73–101.
Peripatetic, A. 'The Piccadilly Papers: The Confessions of Novelists'. *London Society* XIII. London: William Clowes and Sons, February 1868, p. 155.
Perl, Jeffrey M. 'Introduction: More Trouble than They Are Worth'. *Common Knowledge*, 15:1 (winter 2009), pp. 1–6.
———. 'Introduction: *Meza Voce* Quietism?' *Common Knowledge*, 16:1 (winter 2010), pp. 22–30.
Peschel, Joseph. 'Stoic Man Walking through *Open City*'. *Boston Globe*, Book Review, 24 February 2011. http://www.boston.com/ae/books/articles/2011/02/24/first_time_novelist_teju_cole_presents_a_stoic_man_walking_through_open_city/. Accessed 10 February 2015.
Petit, Susan. 'Names in Marilynne Robinson's *Gilead* and *Home*'. *Names*, 58:3 (September 2010), pp. 139–149.
———. 'Field of Deferred Dreams: Baseball and Historical Amnesia in Marilynne Robinson's Gilead and Home'. *MELUS*, 37:4 (2012), pp. 119–137.
Pettit, Philip. 'Existentialism, Quietism, and Philosophy', in *The Future of Philosophy*, ed. Brian Leiter. Oxford: Oxford University Press, 2006, pp. 304–328.
Poe, Edgar Allan. 'The Man of the Crowd'. *The Collected Works of Edgar Allan Poe*. Chatham: Wordsworth Editions, 2004, pp. 207–213.
———. 'The Murder in the Rue Morgue'. *The Collected Works of Edgar Allan Poe*. Chatham: Wordsworth Editions, 2004, pp. 2–25.
Popham, Peter. 'Carlo Petrini: The Slow Food Gourmet Who Started a

Revolution'. *The Independent*, 10 December 2009. http://www.independent.co.uk/life-style/food-and-drink/features/carlo-petrini-the-slow-food-gourmet-who-started-a-revolution-1837223.html. Accessed 5 August 2014.

Powers, Richard. *The Gold Bug Variations*. New York: Harper Collins, 1991.

———. *Galatea 2.2*. London: Picador, 1995.

———. *The Echo Maker*. London: Vintage, 2007.

———. *Orfeo*. New York: W. W. Norton & Company, 2014.

Prendergast, Christopher. 'Introduction', in *Eugenie Grandet*. Oxford: Oxford University Press, 1990, pp. 2–10.

Preziosi, Dominic. 'Quiet Novel Goes Global'. *Commonweal*, 13 June 2013. http://www.commonwealmagazine.org/blog/quiet-novel-goes-global. Accessed 5 October 2013.

Prochnik, George. *In Pursuit of Silence: Listening for Meaning in a World of Noise*. New York: Random House, 2010.

Proctor, James. *Dwelling Places: Postwar Black British Writing*. Manchester: Manchester University Press, 2003.

Prodger, Michael. 'The Submission'. *The Financial Times*, 25 August 2011. http://www.ft.com/cms/s/2/5cdbf726-ca57-11e0-a0dc-00144feabdc0.html#axzz2AK00UMV1. Accessed 10 December 2011.

Proust, Marcel. *Swann's Way*, trans. Lydia Davis. London: Penguin, 2003.

Quashie, Kevin Everod. *The Sovereignty of Quiet: Beyond Resistance in Black Culture*. New Brunswick, NJ: Rutgers University Press, 2012.

Rahim, Sameer. 'Lila by Marilynne Robinson'. *The Telegraph*, 12 October 2014. http://www.telegraph.co.uk/culture/books/bookreviews/11151458/lila-by-marilynne-robinson.html. Accessed 17 June 2015.

Ramachandran, V. S. and Sandra Blakeslee. *Phantoms of the Brain: Probing the Mysteries of the Human Mind*. New York: Harper, 1998.

Ramachandran, V. S. *The Tell-Tale Brain: Unlocking the Mystery of Human Nature*. New York: Random House, 2012.

Randall, Martin. *9/11 and the Literature of Terror*. Edinburgh: Edinburgh University Press, 2011.

Rasmussen, Eric Dean. 'Tillman's Turbulent Thinking'. *electronic book review*, 31:6 (September/October 2010). http://www.electronicbookreview.com/thread/fictions present/turbulent. Accessed 18 April 2012.

Ray, Robert. 'Distance', in *Walden x 40: Essays on Thoreau*. Bloomington: University of Indiana Press, 2012, pp. 36–38.

Remnick, David, ed. 'Talk of the Town'. *The New Yorker*, 24 September 2001. http://www.newyorker.com/archive/2001/09/24/010924ta_talk_wtc. Accessed 24 October 2011.

———. 'Into the Clear: Philip Roth' in *Reporting: Writings from* The New Yorker. London: Picador, 2007, pp. 101–124.

Renker, Elizabeth. 'What Is American Literature?' *American Literary History*, 23:12 (2012), 1–10.

Ricœur, Paul. 'Narrative Time'. *Critical Inquiry*, 7:1 (On Narrative, autumn 1980), pp. 169–190.
——. *Time and Narrative: Volume 1*, trans. Kathleen McLaughlin and David Pellauer. Chicago: University of Chicago Press, 1984.
Rich, Motoko. 'Mr. Cinderella: From Rejection Notes to the Pulitzer'. *The New York Times*, 18 April 2010. http://www.nytimes.com/2010/04/19/books/19harding.html?pagewanted=all. Accessed 21 April 2012.
Richardson, Alan. 'Brains, Minds, and Texts: A Review of Mark Turner's *The Literary Mind*'. *Review*, 20 (1998), pp. 39–48.
——. *The Neural Sublime: Cognitive Theories and Romantic Texts*. Baltimore, MD: Johns Hopkins University Press, 2010.
Richardson, Alan and Francis F. Steen. 'Literature and the Cognitive Revolution: An Introduction'. *Poetics Today*, 23:1 (spring 2002), pp. 1–8.
Robinson, Marilynne. 'Writers and the Nostalgic Fallacy'. *The New York Times*, Book Review, 13 October 1985, pp. 34–36.
——. 'Connie Bronson'. *The Paris Review*, 100 (summer–fall 1998). http://www.theparisreview.org/fiction/2766/connie-bronson-marilynne-robinson. Accessed 12 June 2015.
——. *The Death of Adam: Essays on Modern Thought*. New York: Picador, 1999.
——. *Gilead*. London: Virago, 2004.
——. *Housekeeping*. London: Faber & Faber, 2005.
——. 'Onward Christian Liberals'. *American Scholar*, 75:2 (spring 2006), pp. 42–51.
——. *Home*. London: Virago, 2008.
——. *Absence of Mind*. New Haven, CT: Yale University Press, 2010.
——. *When I Was a Child I Read Books*. London: Virago, 2013.
——. *The Givenness of Things*. London: Virago, 2015.
Robson, Simon. *Catch*. London: Jonathan Cape, 2010.
Rolls, Edmund T. and Gustavo Deco. *The Noisy Brain: Stochastic Dynamics as a Principle of Brain Function*. Oxford: Oxford University Press, 2010.
Rorty, Richard. 'Naturalism and Quietism', in *Philosophy as Cultural Politics*. Vol. 4 of *Philosophical Papers*. Cambridge: Cambridge University Press, 2005, pp. 147–159.
Rosenfield, Israel. *The Strange, Familiar and Forgotten: An Anatomy of Consciousness*. New York: Knopf Doubleday Publishing, 1992.
Ross, Christine. *The Past is the Present; It's the Future Too: The Temporal Turn in Contemporary Art*. New York: Continuum, 2012.
Roth, Marco. 'Rise of the Neuronovel'. *n+1* 8 (recessional, fall 2009). http://nplusonemag.com/rise-neuronovel. Accessed 30 January 2013.
Roth, Philip. *Everyman*. London: Random House, 2006.
Rothberg, Michael. 'A Failure of Imagination: Diagnosing the Post-9/11 Novel'. *American Literary Studies*, 21:1 (spring 2009), pp. 152–158.

Roy, Arundhati. 'Come September', in *War Talk*. Cambridge, MA: South End Press, 2003, pp. 75–84.

Rushdie, Salman. 'Outside the Whale'. *Granta* XI: Greetings from Prague (spring 1984), pp. 123–129.

Rushkoff, Douglas. *Present Shock; When Everything Happens Now*. New York: Penguin, 2013.

Russell, Bertrand. *The Conquest of Happiness*. Oxford: Routledge Classics, 2006.

Ryan, Katy. 'Horizons of Grace: Marilynne Robinson and Simone Weil'. *Philosophy and Literature*, 29:2 (October 2005), pp. 349–364.

St. Félix, Doreen. 'The Peril of Black Mobility'. *GOOD*, 36, 29 March 2016. https://www.good.is/features/issue-36-flanerie. Accessed 1 April 2016.

Safran Foer, Jonathan. *Extremely Loud and Incredibly Close*. London: Penguin, 2005.

Said, Edward. *The World, the Text, and the Critic*. Cambridge, MA: Harvard University Press, 1983.

Sargant, William. *The Unquiet Mind: The Autobiography of a Physician in Psychological Medicine*. Boston: Little Brown, 1967.

Sayeau, Michael. *Against the Event: The Everyday and the Evolution of the Modernist Narrative*. Oxford: Oxford University Press, 2013.

Scanlen, Margaret. 'Migrating from Terror: the Postcolonial Novel after September 11'. *Journal of Postcolonial Writing*, 46:3–4 (2010), pp. 266–278.

Schmidt, Michael. *The Novel: A Biography*. Cambridge, MA: Harvard University Press, 2014.

Schuster, Joseph M. 'Post-40 Bloomers: The Risky Fiction of Paul Harding'. *The Millions*, 9 September 2013. http://www.themillions.com/2013/09/post-40-bloomers-the-risky-fiction-of-paul-harding.html. Accessed 2 March 2014.

Schwartz, Hillel. *Making Noise: From Babel to the Big Bang and Beyond*. Cambridge, MA: MIT Press, 2013.

Scofield, Martin. 'Introduction', in *The Cambridge Introduction to the American Short Story*. Cambridge: Cambridge University Press, 2002.

Searle, John. *Consciousness and Language*. Cambridge: Cambridge University Press, 2002.

Seethaler, Robert. *A Whole Life*, trans. Charlotte Collins. London: Picador, 2015.

Seidler, Victor Jeleniewski. *Remembering 9/11: Terror, Trauma and Social Theory*. New York: Palgrave Macmillan, 2013.

Seltzer, Mark. *Serial Killers: Death and Life in America's Wound Culture*. New York: Routledge, 1998.

Sharpe, Matthew. 'Best of the Millennium: #19: American Genius, A Comedy, by Lynne Tillman'. *The Millions*, 21 September 2009. http://

www.themillions.com/2009/09/19-american-genius-a-comedy-by-lynne-tillman.html. Accessed 12 May 2013.

Sharples, Robert. 'The Peripatetic School', in *From Aristotle to Augustine: Routledge History of Philosophy*, ed. David Furley. London: Routledge, 2003, pp. 147–187.

Sheperd-Barr, Kirsten and Gordon M. Shepherd. 'Madeleines and Neuromodernism; Reassessing Mechanisms of Autobiographical Memory'. *Auto/Biography Studies*, 13:1 (1998), pp. 39–60.

Shields, David. *Reality Hunger: A Manifesto*. New York: Hamish Hamilton, 2010.

———. *How Literature Saved My Life*. New York: Vintage, 2013.

Shields, Rob. *Places on the Margin: Alternative Geographies of Modernity*. London: Routledge, 1991.

Showalter, Elaine. 'Feminist Criticism in the Wilderness', in *The New Feminist Critique*, ed. Elaine Showalter. London: Virago, 1986.

Shtyeyngart, Gary. *Super Sad True Love Story*. New York: Granta, 2010.

Simmel, Georg. 'The Metropolis and Mental Life', in *The City Cultures Reader*, ed. Malcolm Miles, Tim Hall and Iain Borden. London: Routledge, 2000, pp. 12–19.

Simpson, David. *9/11: The Culture of Commemoration*. Chicago: University of Chicago Press, 2006.

Smelser, Neil J. 'Epilogue: September 11, 2001 as Cultural Trauma', in *Cultural Trauma and Collective Identity*, ed. Jeffrey C. Alexander. Berkeley: University of California Press, 2004, pp. 264–282.

Smith, Ali. 'The Damaged Heart of America'. *The Guardian*, 16 April 2005, p. 26.

Smith, Mark M. *How Race is Made: Slavery, Segregation, and the Senses*. Chapel Hill: University of North Carolina Press, 2006.

Smith, Zadie. 'This Is How it Feels to Be Me'. *The Guardian*, Books, 13 October 2001. http://www.theguardian.com/books/2001/oct/13/fiction.afghanistan. Accessed 2 November 2011.

———. 'Two Paths for the Novel'. *New York Review of Books*, 20 November 2008. http://www.nybooks.com/articles/archives/2008/nov/20/two-paths-for-the-novel/?pagination=false. Accessed 24 October 2011.

Soja, Edward. *Postmodern Geographies: The Reassertion of Space in Critical Social Theory*. London: Verso, 1989.

Solnit, Rebecca. *Wanderlust: A History of Walking*. London: Penguin, 2001.

———. 'Introduction: Prisons and Paradises', in *Storming the Gates of Paradise: Landscapes for Politics*. Los Angeles: University of California Press, 2007, pp. 1–14.

———. 'In the Day of the Postman: Diary'. *The London Review of Books*, 35:16 (29 August 2013), p. 32.

———. *The Faraway Nearby*. New York: Penguin, 2013.

Sontag, Susan. 'The Aesthetics of Silence', in *Styles of Radical Will*. New York: Picador, 2002, pp. 3–34.
——. *Illness as Metaphor and AIDS and Its Metaphors*. London: Penguin, 2013.
Sotirova, Violeta. *Consciousness in Modernist Fiction: A Stylistic Study*. London: Palgrave Macmillan, 2013.
Spahr, Clemens. 'Prolonged Suspension: Don DeLillo, Ian McEwan, and the Literary Imagination after 9/11'. *Novel*, 45:2 (2012), pp. 221–237.
Stanfill, Laura. E-mail communication with the author, 2 September 2013.
Stein, Gertrude. 'Portraits and Repetition', in *Lectures in America*. Boston: Beacon, 1957, pp. 165–208.
——. 'Composition as Explanation', in *A Stein Reader*, ed. Ulla E. Dydo. Evanston, IL: Northwestern University Press, 1993, pp. 493–503.
Straczynski, J. Michael. *Amazing Spider-Man*, 2:36. New York: Marvel, 2001.
Strout, Elizabeth. *Olive Kitteridge: A Novel in Stories*. New York: Random House, 2008.
Sturken, Marita. *Tourists of History: Memory, Kitsch, and Consumerism from Oklahoma City to Ground Zero*. Durham, NC: Duke University Press, 2006.
Sykes, Rachel. 'A Failure of Imagination? Problems in "Post-9/11" Fiction', in *Recovering 9/11 in New York*, ed. Robert Fanuzzi and Michael Wolfe. Cambridge: Cambridge Scholars Press, 2014, pp. 248–263.
Tabbi, Joseph. *Cognitive Fictions*. Minneapolis: University of Minnesota, 2002.
Taylor, Anna-Louise. 'Slow Food: What is its Legacy?' *BBC Food*, 29 October 2012. http://www.bbc.co.uk/food/0/19993496. Accessed 5 August 2014.
Teicher, Craig Morgan. 'Fault Lines'. *Boston Review*, Poetry, 1 September 2007. http://www.bostonreview.net/craig-morgan-teicher-fault-lines. Accessed 16 April 2013.
Tester, Keith, ed. *The Flâneur*. London: Routledge, 1994.
'The Wailing of One World Trade Center'. *Tribeca Citizen*, Community News, 29 November 2013. http://tribecacitizen.com/2013/11/29/the-wailing-of-one-world-trade-center/. Accessed 5 December 2013.
Thelwell, Michael. 'Modernist Fallacies and the Responsibility of the Black Writer'. *Duties, Pleasures, and Conflicts: Essays in Struggle*. Amherst: University of Massachusetts Press, 1987, pp. 218–234.
Thompson, Emily. *The Soundscape of Modernity: Architectural Acoustics and the Culture of Listening in America*. Cambridge, MA: Massachusetts Institute of Technology Press, 2002.
Thoreau, Henry David. 'Walking'. *The Atlantic*, 1 June 1862. http://www.theatlantic.com/magazine/archive/1862/06/walking/304674/. Accessed 19 August 2013.
——. *Walden*. Princeton, NJ: Princeton University Press, 2004.
Thurston, Anne. 'Marilynne Robinson and the Fate of Faith'. *Studies: An Irish Quarterly Review*, 99:396 (winter 2010), pp. 449–454.

Tillman, Lynne. *The Madame Realism Complex*. New York: Semiotext(e), 1992.
——. *No Lease on Life*. New York: Houghton Mifflin Harcourt, 1998.
——. *American Genius; a Comedy*. New York: Soft Skull Press, 2006.
——. 'Of Its Time'. *Frieze*, p. 151 (November–December 2012). http://www.frieze.com/issue/article/of-its-time. Accessed 15 February 2013.
——. 'Reconsidering Gertrude Stein'. *The New York Times*, Sunday Book Review, 27 January 2012. http://www.nytimes.com/2012/01/29/books/review/reconsidering-the-genius-of-gertrude-stein.html?_r=0. Accessed 10 April 2012.
——. *What Would Lynne Tillman Do?* Brooklyn, NY: Red Lemonade, 2014.
'Tinkers'. *The New Yorker*, Books Briefly Noted, 12 January 2009. http://www.newyorker.com/arts/reviews/brieflynoted/2009/01/12/090112crbn_brieflynoted2. Accessed 21 May 2012.
Toohey, Peter. 'The Cultural Logic of Historical Periodization', in *Handbook of Historical Sociology*, ed. Gerard Delanty and Egin F. Isin. London: SAGE Publications, 2003, pp. 208–220.
Townsend, Gabrielle. *Proust's Imaginary Museum: Reproductions and Reproduction in À la recherche du temps perdu*. Bern: Peter Lang, 2008.
Tournes, Anne-Laure Fortin. '*Saturday* by Ian McEwan or the Resurgence of 9/11 in Allegorical Form'. *L'Atelier*, 1: Accueil (2009). http://ojs.u-paris10.fr/index.php/latelier/article/view/25/78. Accessed 21 December 2010.
Trilling, Lionel. *The Liberal Imagination*. New York: Doubleday, 1953.
Trotter, David. *Paranoid Modernism: Literary Experiment, Psychosis, and the Professionalization of English Society*. Oxford: Oxford University Press, 2001.
Updike, John. *Terrorist*. London: Penguin, 2006.
Vermeulen, Peter. 'Flights of Memory: Teju Cole's *Open City* and the Limits of Aesthetic Cosmopolitanism'. *Journal of Modern Literature*, 37:1 (fall 2013), pp. 40–57.
Versluys, Kristiaan. *Out of the Blue: September 11 and the Novel*. New York: Columbia University Press, 2009.
Virvidakis, Stelios. 'Varieties of Quietism'. *Philosophical Inquiry*, 20:1–2 (2006), pp. 157–175.
Voegelin, Salomé. *Listening to Noise and Silence: Towards a Philosophy of Sound Art*. New York: Continuum, 2010.
Voss, Anne E. 'Portrait of Marilynne Robinson'. *The Iowa Review*, 22:1 (winter 1992), pp. 21–28.
Waldman, Amy. *The Submission*. London: Random House, 2011.
Walkowitz, Rebecca L. 'Virginia Woolf's Evasion: Critical Cosmopolitanism and British Modernism', in *Bad Modernisms*, ed. Douglas Mao and Rebecca L. Walkowitz. Durham, NC: Duke University Press, 2006, pp. 119–144.
Wallace, David Foster. 'The View from Mrs Thompson's', in *Consider the Lobster and Other Essays*. London: Abacus, 2005, pp. 128–140.

———. 'Deciderization 2007 – A Special Report', in *Both Flesh and Not*. London: Penguin, 2012, pp. 101–120.
Walter, Jess. *The Zero*. New York: Harper, 2006.
Ward, Joseph Anthony. *American Silences: The Realism of James Agee, Walker Evans, and Edward Hopper*. New York: Transaction Publishers, 2010.
Waugh, Patricia. 'Thinking in Literature', in *The Legacies of Modernism: Historicizing Postwar and Contemporary Fiction*, ed. David James. Cambridge: Cambridge University Press, 2011, pp. 75–96.
Westfeldt, Amy. 'Freedom Tower Has a New Preferred Name'. *Associated Press*, 26 March 2009. http://www.wtc.com/news/freedom-tower-has-a-new-preferred-name. Accessed 5 December 2013.
Whitehead, Colson. 'Migratory Spirits'. *The New York Times*, 22 October 2006. http://www.nytimes.com/2006/10/22/books/review/Whitehead.t.html?pagewanted=all&_r=0. Accessed 25 July 2012.
Whitman, Walt. *Leaves of Grass*. Oxford: Oxford World Classics, 2008.
Williams, John. *Stoner*. London: Vintage Classics, 2012.
Winter, Jessica. 'American Ingenious'. *Slate*, Books, 12 October 2006. http://www.slate.com/articles/news_and_politics/book_blitz/2006/10/american_ ingenious. html. Accessed 25 July 2012.
Wissman, Torsten. *Geographies of Urban Sound*. Farnham: Ashgate Publishing, 2014.
Wolfe, Tom. 'Stalking the Billion-footed Beast: A Literary Manifesto for the New Social Novel'. *Harper's Magazine*, November 1989, pp. 45–56.
———. *The Bonfire of the Vanities*. London: Vintage, 2010.
Wood, David. *The Deconstruction of Time*. Evanston, IL: Northwestern University Press, 2001.
Wood, James. 'Human, All Too Inhuman'. *The New Republic*, 24 July 2000. http://www.newrepublic.com/article/books-and-arts/human-all-too-inhuman. Accessed 2 November 2011.
———. 'Tell Me How Does It Feel?' *The Guardian*, 6 October 2001. http://www.guardian.co.uk/books/2001/oct/06/fiction. Accessed 2 November 2011.
———. '"Gilead": Acts of Devotion'. *The New York Times*, 28 November 2004. http://www.nytimes.com/2004/11/28/books/review/28COVERWOOD.html. Accessed 10 December 2011.
———. 'Hysterical Realism', in *The Irresponsible Self: On Laughter and the Novel*. New York: Picador, 2005, pp. 167–183.
———. 'Eastern Promises'. *The New Yorker*, Books, 2 September 2013. http://www.newyorker.com/arts/critics/books/2013/09/02/130902crbo_books_wood?currentPage=all. Accessed 10 October 2013.
———. '*Lowboy*'. *The New Yorker*, 30 March 2009. http://www.newyorker.com/arts/critics/books/2009/03/30/090330crbo_books_wood. Accessed 10 April 2012.

——. 'The Arrival of Enigmas'. *The New Yorker*, 28 February 2011. http://www.newyorker.com/arts/critics/books/2011/02/28/110228crbo_books_wood. Accessed 10 April 2012.

——. 'Reality Testing'. *The New Yorker*, 31 October 2011. http://www.newyorker.com/magazine/2011/10/31/reality-testing. Accessed 10 April 2012.

——. 'Youth in Revolt'. *The New Yorker*, 8 April 2013. http://www.newyorker.com/arts/critics/books/2013/04/08/130408crbo_books_wood?currentPage=all. Accessed 23 July 2015.

Woolf, Virginia. *Between the Acts*. New York: Harcourt, 1969.

——. 'A Sketch of the Past', in *Moments of Being*, ed. Jeanne Schulkind. New York: Harcourt Brace & Company, 1985, pp. 61–138.

——. *A Room of One's Own*. New York: Harvest Books, 1989.

——. *To the Lighthouse*. Oxford: Wordsworth Classics, 1994.

——. *Orlando*. Oxford: Oxford World Classics, 1998.

——. *The Waves*. London: Wordsworth Editions, 2000.

——. *Mrs Dalloway*. London: Wordsworth Editions, 2003.

——. 'Modern Fiction', in *Selected Essays*, ed. David Bradshaw. Oxford: Oxford University Press, 2008.

Wray, John. *Lowboy*. New York: Canongate, 2009.

Yates, Richard. *Revolutionary Road*. London: Vintage, 2010.

Žižek, Slavoj. *Welcome to the Desert of the Real!: Five Essays on September 11 and Related Dates*. London: Verso, 2002.

Zunshine, Lisa. *Why We Read Fiction: Theory of Mind and the Novel*. Columbus: Ohio State University Press, 2006.

——. 'Introduction: What Is Cognitive Cultural Studies', in *Introduction to Cognitive Cultural Studies*, ed. Lisa Zunshine. Baltimore, MD: Johns Hopkins University Press, 2010.

# Index

11 September 2001 7, 36, 48–79, 129–30, 155
'9/11' 7, 34, 48–9, 62–3, 127, 163, 190

action 5, 8, 14, 15, 17, 18, 21, 22, 28
 narrative and 6, 15–16, 33, 34–5
Adorno, Theodor 61–2
Alameddine, Rabih
 *Unnecessary Woman, An* 3
Alden, Henry Mills 4, 15–16, 17
American
 capitalism 20, 27, 30, 57, 154–5, 190–2
 civil rights 86–7
 Civil War 85, 105
 exceptionalism 49, 63, 68
 government 18
 military 8, 19
Amis, Martin 50, 60
Aristotle 15
Ashbery, John 168–9
Attali, Jacques
 *Noise* 57, 155
attention 2, 4, 8–9, 16, 21
Austen, Jane 27, 117
Auster, Paul 171
 *Brooklyn Follies, The* 51

Babbage, Charles 24
Bakhtin, Mikhail 58, 124

Barthes, Roland 152, 154, 162, 164
Baudelaire, Charles 101, 157–8
Beckett, Samuel 32, 34, 56
Benjamin, Walter 152, 157–8, 176
Bergson, Henri 102–3
Berlant, Lauren 49
Berman, Marshall 25, 56, 158
Bhaba, Homi K. 62–3, 68
Bijsterveld, Karin 24, 156, 157, 170
Boyd, Brian 120–1
Brooks, Geraldine
 *March* 3, 4
Butler, Judith 30

Cage, John
 'Lecture on Nothing' 61
Cain, Susan
 *Quiet* 20
class 24, 25, 52, 159–61
cognitive fiction 4, 8, 116–50
Cole, Teju 8
 *Every Day is for the Thief* 153, 167–8, 174, 175
 *Open City* 3, 151–3, 161–8, 174–82, 190, 193
Crain, Caleb
 *Unnecessary Errors* 4, 172
Currie, Mark 30, 93

Damasio, Antonio 117, 121
death 7, 18, 27, 61, 192

DeLillo, Don 49, 53, 54, 56, 57, 59, 119
   *Falling Man* 51, 52, 63–7, 163
   'In the Ruins of the Future' 65–6
   *White Noise* 57, 155
Dennett, Daniel 117, 126
   *Consciousness Explained* 120, 133
Derrida, Jacques 49, 65, 68, 97–9
   *Dire l'évènement, est-ce possible?* 62–3
Dos Passos, John
   *Manhattan Transfer* 27

Egan, Jennifer
   *Look at Me* 121
   *Visit from the Goon Squad, A* 66
Einstein, Albert 24
Ellis, Brett Easton 80–1
Emerson, Ralph Waldo 22, 28
   'American Scholar, The' 21
   'Self Reliance' 21–2
Euripides 15, 25
event 8, 22, 28–9, 54–5, 61–3
eventlessness 4, 9, 30, 33–5, 81, 91
extroverts *see* introverts

*flâneur* 151, 157–61, 167–8, 176–8
Foer, Jonathan Safran 49
   *Extremely Loud and Incredibly Close* 51, 52, 53, 59–60
Foucault, Michel 31
Franzen, Jonathan 50, 57, 59, 171, 174
   *Corrections, The* 57, 121
   *Freedom* 51
Freud, Sigmund 29

Galchen, Rivka
   *Atmospheric Disturbances* 4, 118, 121–2
Gennette, Gérard 35
Greene, Graham
   *Quiet American, The* 17
Greif, Mark 58–9

Haddon, Mark
   *Curious Incident of the Dog in the Night-time, The* 121
Hamid, Mohsin
   *Reluctant Fundamentalist, The* 51, 52, 54
Harding, Paul 8, 119
   *Enon* 3, 5, 111
   *Tinkers* 3–6, 80, 89–108, 124–5, 136, 140, 151, 191, 192–3
Hawthorne, Nathaniel 2, 20, 27
   *Blithedale Romance, The* 20
   *Scarlet Letter, The* 2, 20
Heti, Sheila 174
   *How Should a Person Be?* 4

Internet 7, 53, 57, 124, 162, 124
introverts 8, 20–1, 23, 29–30, 32, 82, 131–2, 179

Jameson, Frederic 51, 155
Jelloun, Ben 162
Johnson, Denis
   *Train Dreams* 3, 4, 107
Joyce, James 128, 171
   *Ulysses* 26–7
Jung, Carl
   *Psychological Types* 29–30

Kakutani, Michiko 52
Kalfus, Ken
   *Disorder Peculiar to the Country, A* 51, 52
Keniston, Ann 53, 61, 127
King, Amy M. 34, 141
Knausgård, Karl Ove 174
   *My Struggle* 4, 5

Lerner, Ben 8, 119
   *10:04* 153, 159, 171–2, 173–4
   *Leaving the Atocha Station* 3, 151–3, 161, 168–78, 181, 193
Lethem, Jonathan
   *Motherless Brooklyn* 4, 117, 122
literary prizes
   National Book Award 36, 83

# Index

PEN/Hemingway Award 83, 182
Pulitzer Prize 4, 5, 66, 80, 89
Lodge, David 116, 117
loud *see* noise

McEwan, Ian 50
  *Saturday* 51, 52
McInerney, Jay
  *Good Life, The* 51, 52
Mandel, Emily St. John 5
Mann, Thomas 139
Melville, Herman
  'Bartleby' 2, 21, 22
Messud, Claire
  *Emperor's Children, The* 51, 52
  *Woman Upstairs, The* 3
MFA culture 36
  Iowa Writers' Workshop 5, 80, 82, 89–90
Miller, J. Hillis 81, 98, 108
modernity 24–31, 157–9
  literary modernism
    dadaism 26
    futurism 25–6
    temporality 99–103
    the modernist novel 29, 30–4, 117 128–9
    vorticism 25–6
Morrison, Toni 37
  *Bluest Eye, The* 37
  'Dead of September, The' 60–1
Munro, Alice
  *Dear Life* 3
music 19, 24, 164

New York City 6, 19, 27, 48–9, 51–2, 59–61, 63–7, 134, 151–2, 161–8, 173–4, 190
*New York Times, The* 9, 16, 36, 50, 52, 83
Nin, Anaïs 37
noise 14–19
  America and 17–18
  the city and 8, 18, 20, 27, 154–89
  fiction and 48–79, 152–89
  pollution 24, 159–61

old-fashioned 7, 19, 27, 36
O'Neill, Joseph
  *Netherland* 51, 53, 55

periodicals
  *Blast* 25
  *Bookman, The* 28
  *Harper's* 2, 15–16, 19, 83
  *Life* 18
  *London Society* 2, 15
  *Spectator, The* 28
Plato 15
Poe, Edgar Allan 20, 27
  'Man of the Crowd, The' 20
postmodernism 35, 36, 55, 56–9, 61, 68, 90, 119, 171
Powers, Richard 8
  *Echo Maker, The* 3, 4, 117, 118, 122–32, 138–41, 151, 192, 193
  *Galatea 2.2* 123–4
Proust, Marcel 2, 35, 100–1, 124
  *A la recherche du temps perdu* 32–4, 172
psychoanalysis 29, 117–18, 120–1
Pynchon, Thomas 56, 59

Quashie, Kevin Everod 87
  *Sovereignty of Quiet, The* 7, 34, 175
quiet 14
  aesthetic 1–2, 7, 22, 30, 31, 32, 36, 49, 68–9, 81, 82, 86, 151, 190–1
  locations 3, 7, 8, 23, 32, 104, 106–7
  protagonists 3, 7, 8
  religious 14, 84–6, 192
quietism 14, 26, 27, 30–1, 32, 34, 36, 181

Ramachandran, V. S. 117, 133, 138
realism 32, 36, 55, 56, 124, 133
reflection 3, 9, 15, 20, 22, 23, 25, 27–9, 33, 37, 56, 61, 68, 80, 85
Ricœur, Paul 98–9

Robinson, Marilynne 1, 8, 119
  *Death of Adam, The* 83
  *Gilead* 1, 3, 4, 6, 16, 80–108,
    124–5, 135, 136, 140–1, 151,
    192
  *Home* 1, 3, 81, 83–4, 86–7,
    104–5
  *Housekeeping* 82–3, 84, 99
  *Lila* 1, 3, 81, 83–4, 87–9, 104, 141
  *Mother Country* 83
Rosenfield Israel 117
  *Strange, Familiar and Forgotten,
    The* 120, 138
Roth, Philip 57
  *Everyman* 51
Roy, Arundhati
  'Come September' 67–8
Russell, Bertrand
  *Conquest of Happiness, The* 28

Seethaler, Robert
  *Whole Life, A* 3
Shields, David 30, 171
Shtyengart, Gary
  *Super Sad True Love Story* 66
silence 1, 35, 36, 37, 46, 60–1
Simmel, Georg 157
Simpson, David 68–9
slowness 3, 5, 15, 16, 17, 191
Smith, Zadie 55, 56
Solnit, Rebecca 1–2, 177, 191, 192
Sontag, Susan 50, 127
Stanfill, Laura 6, 191
Stein, Gertrude 139
Strout, Elizabeth
  *Olive Kitteridge* 3, 4, 107

television 50, 53, 78, 104, 129, 130,
    140
temporality 93–9
terrorism 8, 49, 53, 61

Thoreau, Henry David 22, 23, 24,
    28, 82
  *Walden* 23–4, 106, 160
Tillman, Lynne 8
  *American Genius; a comedy* 3, 117,
    118, 132–42, 151, 191, 193
  *Madame Realism Complex, The* 133
  *No Lease on Life* 133–4

Updike, John 49, 50
  *Terrorist* 51, 52, 53

Versluys, Kristiaan 53–4

Waldman, Amy 49
  *Submission, The* 66–7
Wallace, David Foster 56, 59, 155
Walter, Jess 49
  *Zero, The* 51, 52, 60, 127, 163
Whitehead, Colson 125, 127
Whitman, Walt 158–9, 167, 173
Williams, John
  *Augustus* 36
  *Stoner* 2, 4, 35–6, 89
Wolfe, Tom
  'Stalking the Billion-footed Beast'
    56–7
Wood, James 56, 57, 89, 119, 162,
    171–2
Woolf, Virginia 9, 31–2, 156–7
  *Between the Acts* 29
  'Modern Fiction' 32
  *Mrs Dalloway* 2, 32, 179
  *Orlando* 101
  *Room of One's Own, A* 24, 58
  *To the Lighthouse* 31
  *Waves, The* 128
Wray, John
  *Lowboy* 4, 117, 122

Yates, Richard 160

EU authorised representative for GPSR:
Easy Access System Europe, Mustamäe tee 50,
10621 Tallinn, Estonia
gpsr.requests@easproject.com

www.ingramcontent.com/pod-product-compliance
Lightning Source LLC
Chambersburg PA
CBHW070237240426
43673CB00044B/1832